Hans Dieter Schaal

Landscape as Inspiration

Hans Dieter Schaal

Landscape as Inspiration

With pictures and texts by the author

Academy Editions   Ernst & Sohn

© 1994 the Academy Group Ltd., London,
and Ernst & Sohn Verlag für Architektur und
technische Wissenschaften GmbH, Berlin

ISBN 1 85490 303 9

Both publishing companies are members of the
VCH Publishing Group.

Published in Great Britain in 1994 by Academy
Editions
An imprint of the Academy Group Ltd.,
42 Leinster Gardens, London W2 3AN

Translated from German by Michael Robinson,
London

Typesetting: Ditta Ahmadi, Berlin
Reproductions: Reprowerkstatt Rink, Berlin
Printing: Druckerei Oskar Zach, Berlin
Binding: Heinz Stein, Berlin

Design: Sophie Bleifuß
Production: Fred Willer

Contents

Inspiration on Landscape
by Hans Dieter Schaal
A Design Source Book

The twentieth century opened with a revolution in man's attitude to the world about him. It sprang spontaneously from all branches of culture and from all countries across a Europe which stretches from Russia to Spain. The discoveries of Einstein in outer space corresponded with those of Jung into the inner subconscious. The arts themselves exploded into a new dimension. No longer was the inquiring mind satisfied with appearance, it needed to reach the truth. Thus the artist set out to combine the invisible with the visible, the abstract with the figurative. Foremost among the artists was Paul Klee, who dug deep into the subconscious to pull out goods that puzzle, delight and unaccountably exhilarate. Now at the end of the century we meet here another traveller in the subconscious, one far more sophisticated and specifically concentrating upon architecture, landscape and the cosmos generally. Let there be no mistake. These intriguing drawings and the accompanying statements of the obvious which is not so obvious, are dreams and not reality. How otherwise can we comprehend »the wind that blows through the architecture as though it were not there«, or look through trees that are not? Reader, explore these pages and you will first be puzzled, then delighted, and finally maybe, unaccountably inspired.

Geoffrey Jellicoe
November 1993

Inspiration on Landscape
by Hans Dieter Schaal
A Design Source Book

The literature of landscape is prolific and diverse, yet it is an amazing fact that there is no single publication currently available that offers a comprehensive survey of the range of elements and their component parts which today we recognise as constituting the environment which we on earth are constantly adapting and changing to suit man's needs. And perhaps equally necessary, no compendium exists which views all these realities both in their physical and their inspirational aspects.
Hans Dieter Schaal's work has opened up new avenues for landscape architect and student alike. It should be understood that it is not prescriptive in its message (there are numerous technical works already) but wholly inspirational. Viewed as a manual, either reader will find that the extensive range of Schaal's survey will enable new solutions to be derived to design questions in the field of the environment. Through Schaal's viewfinder, so to speak, a genuine articulation of those elements which compose or influence landscape is facilitated. A twentieth century sensibility on such matters is all that is required. For with Schaal such notions as the purely picturesque are displaced by a vision that is based on the wide range of twentieth century perception both in philosophy and art. The book is intended primarily for landscape designers. But architects themselves will surely find its signals ring true. Schaal's research has related primarily to the European landscape, but its findings can be universally applied.

Michael Spens
November 1993

Preface

*This book is not introducing a new theory of
landscape architecture. It is attempting to
describe and examine the phenomena of the
earth's surface that we include in the concept of
›landscape‹ and to redefine the relationship between man and landscape with various reflections and drafts.*

*This relationship is absurd and schizophrenic,
as we stand both inside and outside nature
simultaneously. We are part of nature from birth,
and thus inside it, and nevertheless look at it from
the outside, as an alien outside world.*

*»This double position leads to a lack of clarity.
The biologist Jean Dausset writes: ›Nature does
not speak, it is man who speaks.‹ It would be
equally tenable to say that man gives nature a
voice.« (H. Reeves) We are at one and the same
time inhabitants, observers, users, spokesmen,
admirers, consumers and destroyers of nature.
Nature is visible and invisible at the same time.
The visible outer skin is available to the eye, the
forces of nature work largely invisibly. Life and
death occur in silence, reservedly. The heart
beats, the lungs breathe, thoughts come and go,
blood circulates, the digestive system works
away – everything is part of nature.*

*A crack runs through the middle of the ego, a
crack dividing inside from outside, subject from
object, ego from nature, consciousness from the
world.*

*The landscape architecture and gardens sug-
gested in this book show this crack, show the
wound. All structures and compositions made up
of meadows, hills, grottoes, arbours, groves,
houses and staged situations are links in the
empty space between object and subject, between nature and ego, between outer and inner
space. Processes of confrontation, interconnection, superimposition, intensification and encirclement are triggered. Windows and doors
acquire the function of ways through, paths and
squares become areas of encounter and greater
closeness for man and nature.*

Phänomenologie der Landschaft
Ort des Geschehens: Raumschiff Erde

Phenomenology of landscape
Scene of the action: Spaceship Earth

*»5 thousand million years ago the sun and its
planets, of which the earth is one, came into being from a spinning cloud of interstellar gases
and dust, and became components of our galaxy.« (Ronald Fraser)*
*This galaxy floats in the ›infinity‹ of the universe
like a tiny cloud of mist. And yet the diameter of
this ›cloud‹ is estimated to be 100,000 light years.
The earth revolves around the sun as one of its
planets in a rhythm of years. Day and night are
produced by the rotation of the globe around its
own axis. The seasons come into being because
of the angle of the earth's axis in relation to its
orbit and the different distances and radiation
angles of the sun and its light associated with this.*

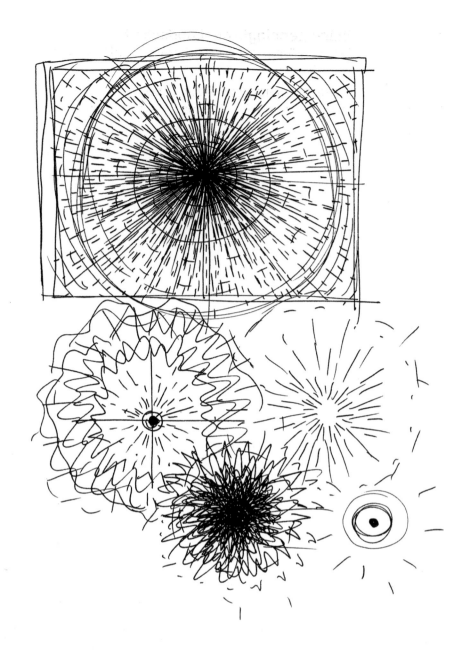

Vier Kräfte bilden die architektonische Struktur des Weltalls und der Welt: die Gravitation, die elektromagnetische Kraft, die schwache und die starke Kernkraft. Die Sonne ist das Energiezentrum unseres Planetensystems.

Four forces make up the architectonic structure of the universe and the world: gravity, electromagnetic forces, weak and strong nuclear fields. The sun is the centre of energy for our planetary system.

»Ohne Sonne fände nichts statt auf der Erde. Mit ihrem Licht, ihrer Wärme und ihrer Kraft sorgt sie dafür, daß Pflanzen, Tiere und Menschen blühen, wachsen und gedeihen können. Ohne ihr Licht gäbe es keine Farben. Sie liefert die Energie, die alles am Leben hält. Jeden Tag unvorstellbare 4 270 Billionen Kilowattstunden. Es würde 480 Jahre dauern, bis die Welt die Elektrizität aus einem Tag Sonnenenergerie verbraucht hätte, oder anders ausgedrückt: Alle drei Minuten schickt die Sonne den Weltstrombedarf eines Jahres zur Erde. Diese ungeheure Energiemenge prallt nun nicht direkt auf die Erdoberfläche, sondern durchquert die Atmosphäre. Dabei bleiben rund 35 % ›auf der Strecke‹. Die restliche Energie erreicht den Erdboden, der davon sofort wieder einen Teil an die Atmosphäre abgibt. Täte er das nicht, würde sich die Erdoberfläche pro Tag um 245 °C aufheizen, die Atmosphäre dagegen um 0,8 °C kälter werden« (Dieter Walch)

»Without the sun nothing would happen on this earth. Its light, its warmth and its power enable plants, animals and human beings to blossom, grow and flourish. Without its light there would be no colours. It provides the energy that keeps everything alive. An unimaginable 4 270 billion kilowatt hours every day. It would take 480 years for the world to use up the electricity produced by one day of solar energy. Or put in another way: the sun sends the world's energy requirements for a whole year to the earth every three minutes. This enormous quantity of energy does not immediately strike the earth's surface, but first passes through the atmosphere. In the course of this about 35 % »falls by the wayside«. The rest of the energy reaches the surface, which immediately passes another part to the atmosphere. If it did not do that the surface of the Earth would heat up by 245 °C per day, whereas the atmosphere would become colder by 0.8 °C.« (Dieter Walch)

Phänomenologie der Landschaft
Erdoberfläche, Landschaftsraum und Luftraum

Phenomenology of landscape
Earth's surface, landscape space and air space

Phänomenologie der Landschaft
Erdoberfläche, Landschaftsraum und Luftraum

Die überall gleichmäßig gekrümmte Oberfläche der Erde mit ihren rund 510 Millionen Quadratkilometern Landschaft wird zu 30 % von Festland und zu 70 % von Wasserflächen bedeckt.
Der geologische Aufbau der Erdkugel ist schalenförmig. Der vegetationsfähige Boden bedeckt die Festländer nur hauchdünn.
The surface of the earth is uniformly curved and has 510 million square kilometres of landscape, of which 30 % is dry land and 70 % water.
The geological composition of the globe is stratified. Soil that can produce vegetation forms only a wafer-thin covering of the dry land.

Die gesamte Kugel ist von einer Luftschicht umhüllt, der Atmosphäre. Sie besteht zu 1/5 aus Sauerstoff und zu 4/5 aus Stickstoff. Die Atmosphäre gliedert sich durch ihre Temperatur in klar unterscheidbare Stockwerke. Oberhalb 1000 km Höhe, in der Exosphäre, wird der Einfluß der Erdschwere so gering, daß Luftteilchen ungehindert in den Weltraum abströmen können.
Im untersten Stockwerk, der Troposphäre, spielt sich das Wetter ab. Am Wetterverlauf erkennt man, daß die Luftmassen der Atmosphäre in ständiger Bewegung sind. Bedingt durch Erwärmung steigen sie in die Höhe, durch Abkühlung fallen sie wieder in die Tiefe.
Zur Erde in ihrer Gesamtheit gehören Raum und Zeit, gehören die organische und die anorganische Natur, die Atome, Moleküle, die Zellen, Evolution, Leben und Tod, Körper und Geist, Ordnung und Chaos, Tiere, Pflanzen, Menschen, Physik, Chemie, Technik, Kultur, Kunst, Architektur usw.
The whole globe is surrounded by a layer of air, the atmosphere. It consists of one fifth oxygen and four fifths nitrogen. The atmosphere forms clearly discernible storeys because of its temperature. Above 1000 km, in the exosphere, the influence of gravity is so slight that air particles can stream into the atmosphere unimpeded.
The lowest storey, the troposphere, is where weather occurs. It can be seen from changing weather conditions that air masses of the atmosphere are constantly on the move. When heated they rise, and when they cool down they move downwards again.
Space and time are part of earth as a whole, and so are organic and inorganic nature, atoms, molecules, cells, evolution, life and death, body and spirit, order and chaos, animals, plants, human beings, physics, chemistry, technology, culture, art, architecture etc.

Die Landschaft ist die äußere Erscheinungsform der Erde. Für den Betrachter lebt sie aus ihrer Weite. In der Horizontlinie berühren sich Himmel und Erde.
Landscape is the outward form of the earth's appearance. For the observer it lives by its expanse. Sky and earth touch on the line of the horizon.

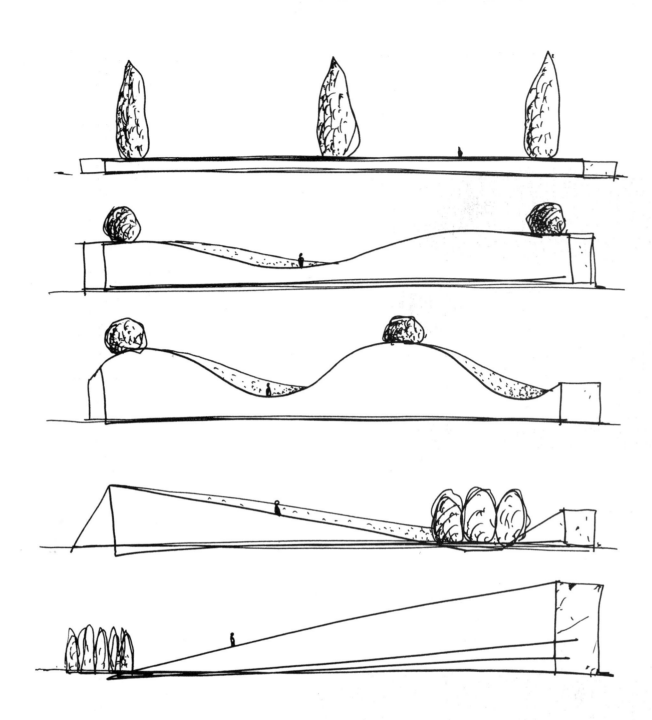

Zeichnet man das Diagramm der Landschafts-physiognomie, ergibt sich dieses Bild: Um die Waagrechte der Ebene (in Wirklichkeit gekrümmt) bewegt sich eine Wellenschwingung nach unten zu den Mulden und Tälern bis zum Meeresgrund, nach oben zu den Hügeln, Bergen und Gebirgen. Setzt man, wie es bei technisch-naturwissen-schaftlichen Diagrammen üblich ist, die Waag-rechte mit Ruhe gleich, so ergeben sich bei den Ausschlägen der Schwingungen Emotionen: die Sprache der Natur, ihre Erregung, ihre Ruhe?

If a diagram of the physiognomy of the landscape is drawn, this image is produced: an undulation moves around the horizontal plane (curved in re-ality) downwards to the dips and valleys, down to the bed of the sea and upwards to the mounds, hills and mountain ranges. If the horizontal is equated with rest – as is customary in technical and scientific diagrams – emotion will be pro-duced by the swing of the curves: the language of nature, its excitement, its repose?

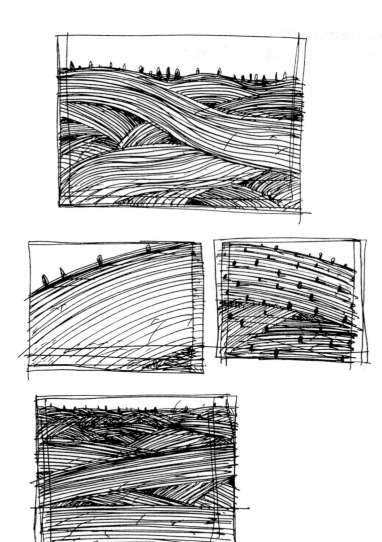

Blick auf die Landschaft, auf ihre Bewegungen, auf ihre Kräfte, ihre Linien und Punkte, auf ihre Licht- und Schattenzonen, ihre Wölbungen und Vertiefungen.

View of the landscape, its movements, its forces, its lines and points, its areas of light and shade, its upward and downward curves.

Der Zustand der Welt ist auch der Zustand der Landschaft. Herrscht direkte Sonneneinstrahlung, etwa an einem Hochsommertag, dann ist die Landschaft in grelles Sonnenlicht getaucht, herrscht die Dunkelheit der Nacht, dann ist die Landschaft schwarz und verkohlt wie ein verbranntes Bild.
Der eigentliche Raum, der Luftraum, ist unsichtbar. Man kann ihn zwar einatmen, aber man sieht ihn nicht in seiner Zusammensetzung, in seiner Anwesenheit. Nur die bewegte Luft (der Wind) ist in ihren Auswirkungen zu spüren und zu sehen.

Landscape is the epitome of exterior space. The condition of the world is also the condition of the landscape. If the sun is shining directly, on a high summer's day for example, then the landscape is bathed in harsh sunlight; under the darkness of night the landscape is black and charred like a burnt picture.
Actual space, the air space, is invisible. It is possible to breathe it in, but it cannot be seen in its composition, in its presence. Only moving air (the wind) can be felt and seen in its effects.

Phänomenologie der Landschaft
Boden und Vegetation – Jahreszeiten und Tageszeiten

Phenomenology of landscape
Soil and vegetation – seasons and times of day

»Unter Boden versteht man die oberste Erd-schicht, die den Pflanzen als Standort und zur Ernährung dient. Er besteht aus einem Gemisch von mineralischen und organischen Bestandteilen, in deren Hohlräumen Luft und Wasser in wechselnden Mengenverhältnissen enthalten sind. Die mineralischen Bestandteile sind un-organischer Herkunft und unverbrennlich im Gegensatz zu den organischen, verbrennlichen, d.h. von lebenden Wesen stammenden Bestand-teilen, dem Humus. Der Boden ist aber keines-wegs eine tote Masse, ein Gemenge der eben angegebenen Bestandteile, sondern ständig erfüllt vom Leben und Treiben verschiedenartiger Bodentiere und unzähliger Mikroorganismen (Algen, Pilze, Bakterien), durch deren Tätigkeit die Voraussetzung für das Pflanzenwachstum geschaffen wird. Allein in 1 g sehr fruchtbaren Ackerbodens können mehrere hundert Millionen, doch auch bis zu 5 Milliarden von Mikroorganis-men enthalten sein. Das gilt aber nicht für un-tätige Böden oder gar für Ödland; dafür können diese Zahlen wiederum für sehr fruchtbare Böden und Komposterben noch weit überschritten wer-den«. (Schlipf)

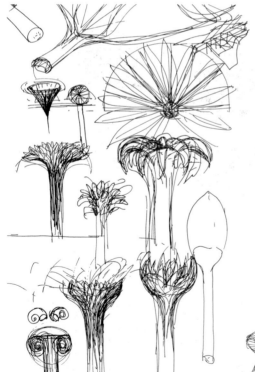
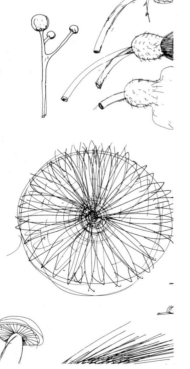

Dieser Boden ist die Grundlage der Vegetation. Wasser, Nährstoffe, Wärme (Sonne) und Luft bil-den die weiteren Voraussetzungen für das Wachstum der Pflanze. Aus Samen, Seitentrie-ben oder Knollen wachsen Gräser, Blumen, Büsche und Bäume, entfalten sich, blühen, samen aus, wachsen weiter oder sterben ab und tragen zur Fruchtbarkeit des Humus bei.

This soil is the basis for vegetation. Water, nutri-ents, warmth (sun) and air are further prerequi-sites for plant growth. Grasses, flowers, bushes and trees grow from seeds, side shoots or tu-bers, then develop, flower, seed, carry on grow-ing or die off and contribute to the fertility of the humus.

»By soil we understand the upper layer of soil, which provides plants with their site and their food. It consists of a mixture of mineral and organic components whose cavities contain air and water in varying proportions. The mineral components are inorganic in origin and incombustible in contrast with the organic and combustible ones, i.e. the components originating in living matter, the humus. But soil is by no means a dead mass, a mixture of the components that have just been listed, but consistently inhabited by the life and activities of various creatures that live in the soil and countless micro-organisms (algae, plants, bacteria), whose activities create the conditions for plant growth. A single gram of fertile arable land can contain several hundred million, but also up to five thousand million. But this is not true of inactive soil or even of uncultivated land; but in the case of very fertile soils and composts these figures can be considerably exceeded.« (Schlipf)

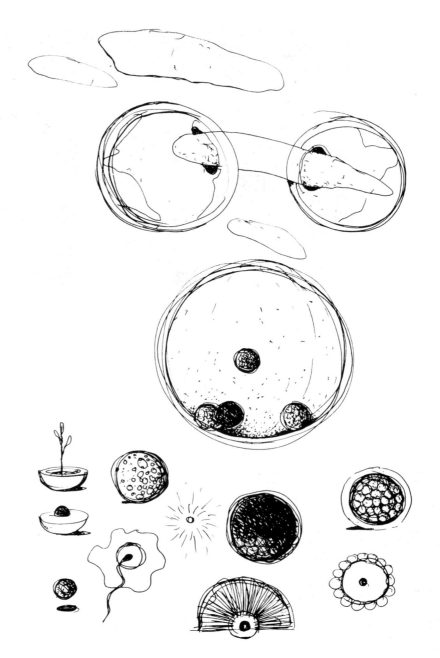

Grundbaustein allen Lebens ist die Zelle: Ei, Samen, Befruchtung. Die Idee der Geschlechtlichkeit: zwei Prinzipien zusammen ergeben einen neuen Körper, ein neues Wesen. »Fortpflanzung ist eine Notwendigkeit des Lebens, denn das Leben ist eine expansive Kraft, die danach drängt, in jeden Winkel der materiellen Welt zu gelangen, von den Tiefen des Ozeans bis zu den höchsten Schichten der Atmosphäre, von den Wüsten bis zu den Gebirgen, von der Arktis bis zum Äquator. Fortpflanzung ist die Basis der Evolution – sie stellt die Kontinuität des Lebens von seinen Anfängen vor mehr als drei Milliarden Jahren bis zum heutigen Tag her. Fortpflanzungsfähigkeit ist ein Kennzeichen aller Lebewesen, der einfachsten, etwa Viren, ebenso wie der höchstentwickelten.« (Renato Dulbecco)

The basic building block of all life is the cell: egg, seed, fertilization. The idea of sexuality: two principles together produce a new body, a new being. »Reproduction is a necessity of life, as life is an expansive force that follows the urge to penetrate into every corner of the material world, from the ocean depths to the highest layers of the atmosphere, from the deserts to the mountains, from the Arctic to the equator. Reproduction is the basis of evolution – it establishes continuity of life from its beginnings over three thousand million years ago to the present day. The ability to reproduce is a characteristic of all living beings, from the simplest, like viruses for example, to the most highly developed.« (Renato Dulbecco)

Die Pflanze ist ein lebendiges, organisches System. Unter der Erde die Wurzeln, über der Erde der Stiel, der Stamm, die Äste und die Blätter. Adern als Tunnelsystem, in dem die Nährflüssigkeit bis zur äußersten Blattspitze gesogen wird. Im Jahresrhythmus erfolgen die Entfaltung und das Abstoßen der Blätter und Blüten.

A plant is a living, organic system. Below the ground are the roots, above the ground the stem, the trunk, the branches and the leaves. Veins as a system of tunnels sucking nutritious fluids to every part right to the most extreme leaf-tip. Leaves and flowers open and are shed in an annual cycle.

Mit der Blüte bekennt die Pflanze Farbe. Die Sprache der Blütenformen und Blütenfarben scheint in ihrer Vielfalt unendlich. Klein, groß, dick, dünn, bunt, rund, bewaffnet, lasziv, bescheiden, ordinär, arrogant, gebeugt, sonnenförmig, mondartig, aggressiv, vielblättrig, einfach, spitzig, lippig, weiß, blau, rosa, gelb, violett. Empfangsgesten und Reklameplattformen für die umworbenen Insekten zwecks Befruchtung. Die Funktion der Blüten ist die Erzeugung von Samen.

Flowers allow plants to stake their claims to colour. The language of blossom forms and blossom colours seems endless in its diversity. Small, large, thick, thin, bright, round, armed, lascivious, modest, vulgar, arrogant, curved, sun-shaped, moon-like, aggressive, many-leafed, simple, pointed, lip-shaped, white, blue, pink, yellow, purple. Reception gestures and advertising platforms for the much sought-after insects, for fertilization purposes. The blossoms‹ function is to produce seeds.

Blüte: ein Spiegelbild der Sonne?

Blossom: a reflection of the sun?

Samen: »Wie unendlich wertvoll Saatgut – der zur Aussaat bestimmte Samen – sein kann, läßt sich durch Zahlen leicht belegen: 1 Kilo Kohlsamen bringt bei durchschnittlicher Ernte 1200 Zentner Weißkohl – im vielleicht vierhundertfachen Wert – hervor; 1 Kilo Blaukrautsamen ergibt rund 200 000 Köpfe; vom Mohrrübensamen gehen 1/2 Million Körner auf ein Kilo. Ob Samen keimfähig ist oder nicht, spielt eine wichtige Rolle. Wenn Wind, Wetter und Boden nicht so ungleichmäßige Auswirkungen hätten und es unter den Vögeln nicht so viele Körnerfresser gäbe – von Insekten ganz abgesehen, müßten die Vermehrungsmöglichkeiten des Samens als fast unvorstellbar bezeichnet werden. Geht man theoretisch davon aus, daß jedes Samenkorn aufginge, Blumen und wieder Samen erzeugte, und daß dies sechsmal hintereinander geschähe, so erhielte man weit über 4 000 000 000 000 000 000 000 000 (24 Nullen!) Samenkörner. Mit dieser Menge kann man die ganze Erdoberfläche bedecken. So verschwenderisch könnte die Natur sein … wenn sie sich nicht gewissermaßen gegen sich selbst schützte! Die Zahl der Samen bestimmter Pflanzen ist sehr verschieden, manche bringen alle 20 Jahre einen Samen hervor, die meisten haben 1 bis 100 Samen, die Schwarzpappel bringt es auf 28 Millionen Samen im Jahr. Manche Samen sind feiner als Mehl – bei einigen Orchideen wiegen 300 000 Samen ein Gramm. Das größte Samen»korn« stammt von einer Fächerpalme; die Seychellen-Nuß wiegt bis zu 50 Pfund.« (Peter Omm)

Seeds: »How infinitely important seeds intended for sowing are can easily be proved in figures: 1 kilo of cabbage seeds produces 1200 hundredweight of white cabbage in an average crop – perhaps 400 times as much; 1 kilo of red cabbage seed produces about 200,000 heads; a kilo of carrot seed contains about half a million grains. Whether seed is capable of germinating or not is an important factor. If wind, weather and soil did not have such uneven effects and there were not so many birds that ate seeds – to say nothing of insects – seed's possibilities of increase could be said to be almost inconceivable. If one works on the assumption that every grain of seed were to germinate and produce flowers and more seeds, and that this happened six times in succession, then 4,000,000,000,000, 000,000,000,000 (24 noughts!) seeds would be produced. This quantity would cover the entire surface of the earth. That is how extravagant nature could be – if she did not to an extent protect herself against herself! The number of seeds produced by certain plants differs a great deal, some produce one seed every twenty years, most have 1 to 100 seeds, the black poplar manages 28 million seeds per year. Some seeds are finer than flour – in the case of some orchids 300,000 seeds weigh one gram. The largest seed ›grain‹ comes from a fan palm; the Seychelles nut weighs up to 50 pounds.« (Peter Omm)

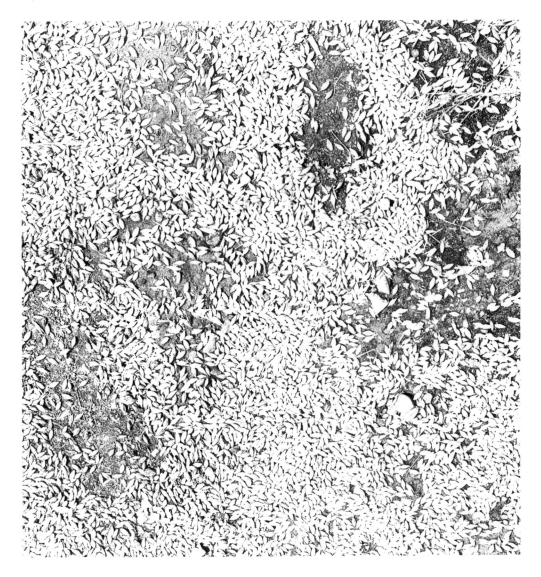

Für die Menschen sind Pflanzen und Früchte neben dem Fleisch der Tiere die wichtigste Nahrungsgrundlage.

For human beings plants and fruit are the most important basis for nutrition, along with the flesh of animals.

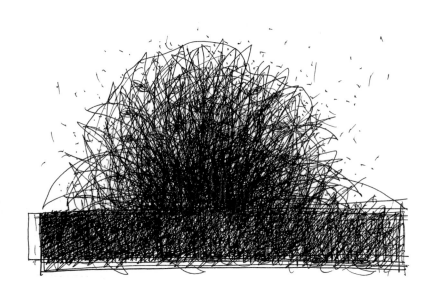

Der Baum ist ein organisch-architektonisches System, das aus einem Fundament, den Wurzeln, einer Säule, dem Stamm und aus dem Raumgeflecht der Äste besteht. Hinzu kommen bei Laubbäumen im Sommer die Blätter, die die kahle Winterkonstruktion umhüllen.
Die Sprache der Baumformen könnte ein kunstgeschichtlicher Entwurf sein. Es gibt schlichte und rundliche Bäume, niedrige, gedrungene, aber auch bizarr expressionistische und große barocke Baumkuppeln. Es gibt schmale schlanke Bäume (Zypressen, Pappeln). Es gibt steil nach oben strebende und hängende Bäume. Blätterdächer, Baumkuppeln, Walddome, Haine.

The tree is an organic-architectonic system consisting of a foundation, the roots, a column, the trunk and a spatial network of branches. In the case of deciduous trees leaves are an additional summer feature, covering the bare winter structure.
The language of tree shapes could be an art-historical draft. There are plain and plump trees, low, squat trees but also bizarrely expressionist and large baroque tree domes. There are narrow, slender trees (cypresses, poplars). There are trees that strive steeply upwards and trailing trees. Leaf roofs, tree domes, forest cathedrals, groves.

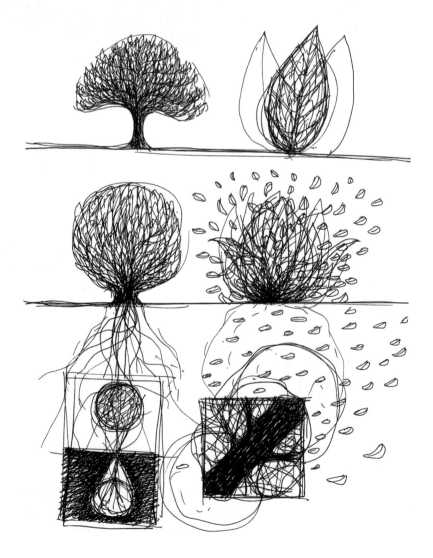

Der Baum unterscheidet sich vor allem durch das Holz von den krautigen Pflanzen. Holz ist das weitaus häufigste Naturprodukt.

Trees differentiate themselves from herbaceous plants through the wood. Wood is by far the most common natural product.

Ein Baum hat sich auf eine Stelle der Erde eingelassen, sich festgebissen.
Hier bleibt er, wächst, ist allem ausgeliefert, dem Wind und dem Schnee, der Sonne, nistenden Vögeln, nagenden Rehen, schnitzenden und sägenden Menschen. Er ist geduldig und biegsam.

A tree has become involved with a spot on the earth, it has fixed itself there firmly.
Here it will stay and grow, it is exposed to everything, wind, sun and snow, nesting birds, gnawing roe-deer, carving and sawing men. It is patient and pliant.

Wie sehr die Blätter der Bäume Antennen gleichen, empfangenden Antennen, Solarzellen-Antennen, stellt die neueste Forschung immer mehr fest. Sonnenenergie, Licht vor allem, wird hier wie mit einem Netz eingefangen und zu Sauerstoff verarbeitet (Photosynthese).
Aller Sauerstoff der Erde wurde und wird von den Pflanzen und Bäumen produziert.

The most recent research is increasingly establishing how much the leaves of trees are like aerials, receiving aerials, solar-cell aerials. Solar energy, light above all, is captured here as if by a net and converted into oxygen (photosynthesis). All the earth's oxygen was and will be produced by plants and trees.

In den Jahreszeiten des Werdens und Vergehens, im Frühling und im Herbst, hat man das Gefühl, alle Bäume seien unterirdisch miteinander verbunden, auch alle Blumen, Gräser und Sträucher. Fast gleichzeitig beginnt das Aufblühen, das Hervorschieben der Blätter, und ebenso gleichzeitig setzt überall der Herbst ein. Fluchtpunkt für diese Gleichzeitigkeit ist die Sonne. Ihre Strahlen »ziehen« die Blätter und Blüten hervor, ihr Verschwinden hinter den Herbstnebeln läßt das allgemeine Absterben einsetzen.

In the seasons of growth and of passing away, in the spring and in the autumn, there is a feeling that all trees could be connected together under the ground, and so could all flowers, grasses and bushes. Leaves start to push their way out at almost the same time, and autumn begins everywhere at almost the same time as well. The vanishing point for all this simultaneity is the sun. Its rays ›draw‹ out the leaves and plants, and its disappearance behind the autumn mists starts the general process of dying away.

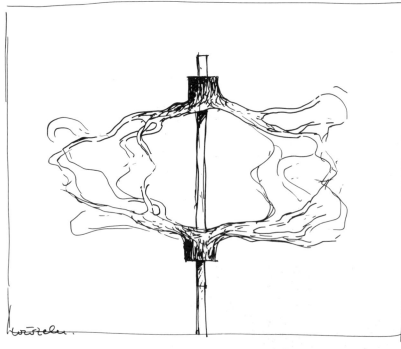

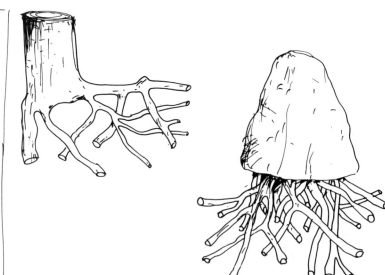

Wurzeln: negative, unsichtbare Spiegelform des sichtbaren Baums unter der Erde. Nährstoffe werden dem Boden entnommen und bis in die Baumkronen transportiert (Osmose).

*Roots: negative and invisible mirror image of the visible tree under the ground.
Nutrients are taken from the soil and transported to the crown of the tree (osmosis).*

Baum-Heiligtümer: Vor allem der große, alte Einzelbaum wurde zu allen Zeiten wie ein Natur-Tempel verehrt (Dorflinde, Gerichtseiche).

Tree shrines: large, ancient individual trees in particular have been worshipped as temples of nature throughout the ages (village lime tree, judgement oak).

Der Wald als Ansammlung von Bäumen ist – zusammen mit Sträuchern, Kräutern, Vögeln und Tieren – das eigentliche Erscheinungsbild der Landschaft. Dem ursprünglich überall vorhandenen Urwald mußten die Menschen erst die freien Flächen, die Wiesen und Felder abtrotzen. Würden heute die Bauern ihre Arbeit einstellen, wäre das Land in einigen Jahren wieder ganz mit Wäldern bedeckt.
Dem undurchdringlichen Urwald steht der gepflanzte Kulturwald gegenüber. Der Urwald in unseren Breiten bestand aus Laubbäumen. Die Buche herrschte vor. Nadelbäume wuchsen vor allem in den Mittelgebirgen und den Alpen.
Der Kulturwald besteht heute bis zu 70% aus Fichten und Kiefern.

Der Wald: Ort der zunehmenden Dunkelheit, der versteckten Geheimnisse, der Gefahren, der Hexen und Räuber, der möglicherweise doch wahren Märchenfiguren. Labyrinth und letzter Zufluchtsort von Flüchtenden und Ausgestoßenen. Fluchtpunkt der Wünsche und Ängste, der geheimen Schauer, der Religion. Der Wald: romantische Naturkirche, Ort der Begegnung mit sich selbst.

The forest: a place of increasing darkness, hidden secrets, dangers, witches and robbers, fairytale figures who might be real after all. Labyrinth and last resort of people rejected and on the run. The vanishing point of desires and fears, of secret horror, of religion. The forest: a romantic natural church, a place of confrontation with oneself.

The forest, as an accumulation of trees – with bushes, herbaceous plants, birds and animals – is the actual appearance of the landscape. Man had to wrest open spaces, the meadows and fields, from the jungle that was originally everywhere. If farmers were to stop work today the countryside would be completely covered with woods again in a few years.
Planted and cultivated woods are a contrast with the impenetrable primeval forest. In our latitudes the primeval forest consisted of deciduous trees. Beeches predominated. Coniferous trees grew principally in the lower mountain ranges and the Alps. 70 % of today's cultivated forests is made up of pines and spruces.

Jahreszeiten: Von der ungeheuren Bewegung
der Erdkugel durch den Weltraum spüren wir
nichts, aber wir sehen die indirekten Auswirkungen auf die Natur, wir sehen die Veränderung der
Tages- und Jahreszeiten.
Die Rhythmen der Natur. Die Kreisläufe der Zeit.
Frühling, Sommer, Herbst, Winter, Frühling, Sommer ... Kalenderbilder. Symbole für das Leben,
die Geburt und den Tod.

Seasons: we sense nothing of the enormous
movement of the globe through space, but we
see indirect effects on nature, we see the chang-
ing days and seasons.
The rhythms of nature. The cycles of time.
Spring, summer, autumn, winter. Spring, summer
... Calendar pictures. Symbols of life, birth and
death.

Phänomenologie der Landschaft
Wasser: Quellen, Bäche, Flüsse, Meere, Kreisläufe

Phenomenology of landscape
Water: springs, streams, rivers, seas, cycles

Wasser, H$_2$O, ist eine chemische Verbindung aus Sauerstoff und Wasserstoff, eine an sich geruch- und geschmacklose Flüssigkeit.

Die Pflanzen bestehen bis zu 95%, die höheren Tiere und der Mensch zu 60–70% aus Wasser. Es ist das am meisten gebrauchte Lösungs- und Transportmittel in der Natur. Ohne Wasser gäbe es kein Leben.

Wasser befindet sich in ständiger Metamorphose und Zirkulation. Über dem Meer verdunstet es durch Sonnenwärme, steigt auf, wird von Winden auf das Land weitergetragen und fällt als Regen oder Schnee auf die Erde zurück. Ein Teil verdunstet wieder, ein anderer Teil fließt dem Meer oder den Binnenseen zu.

Das Wasser hat keine Form, ist formlos und weich. Es kann als Tropfen erscheinen, als Pfütze, als Teich, Tümpel, See, Bach oder Fluß. Es kann stehen, fließen, fallen, stürzen und auch steigen. Man kann es in ein Glas füllen (nimmt dessen Form an) oder in ein Schwimmbassin. Wasser ist naß, es kann kalt sein, warm, gefroren (Eis) oder kochend.

Für den Menschen hat es zwei Aspekte: einen positiven und einen negativen. Man kann es trinken, sich erfrischen, sich waschen, man kann darin schwimmen, und man kann darin ertrinken. Es löscht das Feuer, und es zerstört Gebirge, baut Felsen ab und spült sie ins Meer. Man kann damit Brunnen anlegen, Teiche, Kaskaden, Fontänen, Wasserfälle, es zersetzt Hauswände, wenn es sich darin festgesaugt hat. Man kann die Wasserfläche als Straße nutzen, Fische aus der Tiefe fangen, die Felder bewässern. Es kann durch Überschwemmungen das Land verwüsten.

Im Wasser wirken unsichtbare Kräfte, man kann damit Arbeiten verrichten: Wasserrad, Mühle, Elektrizität; bei einem Unwetter aber wird es unheimlich, peitscht wild gegen Häuser und Fenster, zerstört die Felder.

In der religiösen Mythologie hatte das Wasser von Anfang an auch einen Lebens- und Todesaspekt. Wasser des Lebens, Weihwasser, Taufe und der Totenfluß, der die Grenze zum Jenseits markiert.

In der Psychologie, insbesondere bei Jung, wird das Wasser mit dem Unbewußten gleichgesetzt. Das Ich wird zu einem tiefen See, über dessen Oberfläche das Bewußtsein als winzige Insel herausragt.

Meerwasser, Grundwasser, Quellwasser, Regenwasser, Flußwasser, Chlorwasser, Süßwasser, Salzwasser, Hochwasser, Niedrigwasser, Heilwasser, Schmelzwasser, Mineralwasser, Thermalwasser, Badewasser, Trinkwasser, Kaffeewasser, Feuerwasser, Fruchtwasser, Kühlwasser, Leitungswasser, Brunnenwasser, Abwasser … Metamorphosen des Wassers. Kreisläufe durch die Welt, die Atmosphäre, die Vegetation, die Körper, die Köpfe und die Sprache.

Sea water, ground water, spring water, rainwater, river water, chlorinated water, fresh water, salt water, high water, low water, healing water, melt water, mineral water, thermal water, bath water, drinking water, coffee water, fire water, womb water, cooling water, tap water, spring water, waste water … metamorphoses of water. Cycles through the world, the atmosphere, vegetation, bodies, heads and language.

Water, H$_2$0, is a chemical combination of oxygen and hydrogen, an essentially odourless and tasteless liquid.

Plants consist of up to 95 % water, and man and the higher animals of up to 60–70 %. It is nature's most used means of solution and transport.

Without water there would be no life. Water is in a state of constant metamorphosis and circulation. Over the sea it evaporates in the warmth of the sun, rises, is carried on to land by the wind and falls back on to the earth as rain or snow. Some of this evaporates again, the rest flows into the sea or inland lakes.

Water has no form, it is shapeless and soft. It can appear as drops, as a puddle, as a pool, pond, lake, stream or river. It can stand, flow, fall, plunge and also rise. It can be poured into a glass (will adopt its shape) or into a swimming pool. Water is wet, it can be cold, warm, frozen (ice) or boiling. For man it has two aspects: positive and negative. He can drink it, use it as a source of refreshment, wash in it, he can swim in it and he can drown in it. It puts out fires and destroys mountains, breaks down rocks and washes them into the sea. It can be used to make wells, ponds, cascades, fountains, waterfalls, it destroys the walls of houses when it has penetrated them. The surface of the water can be used as a road, fish can be caught from its depths, it can be used to irrigate fields, and it can destroy the land by flooding.

Invisible forces are at work in water, and they can be put to work: water wheels, mills, electricity; but when there is a storm it can be threatening, whipping wildly against houses and windows, destroying fields.

In religious mythology water has had a life and death aspect from the very beginning. Source of life, holy water, baptismal water and then the river of the dead that marks the border of the beyond. In psychology, especially in Jung, water means the subconscious. The ego becomes a deep lake above whose surface consciousness towers as a tiny island.

Wasser ist die Grundvoraussetzung für jede Siedlung, jedes Dorf und jede Stadt. In mittelalterlichen Städten wurden die Brunnen an zentralen Orten aufgestellt und erhielten kostbare steinerne Fassungen.

Water is the basic prerequisite for any settlement, every village and every town. In medieval towns the wells were set up in central places and surrounded with costly stone.

Flüsse sind wie Adern in der Haut der Erde. Nur fließt dieses Blut offen, offen zum Licht, zum Himmel und zur Luft.

Rivers are like veins in the earth's skin. But this blood flows open, open to the light, the sky and the air.

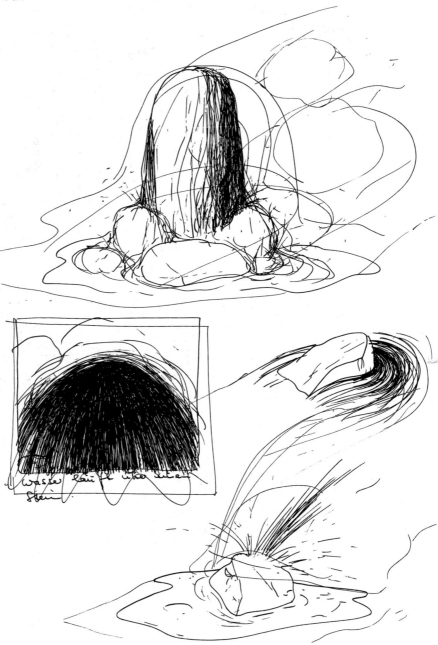

Die Kraft des Wassers durch das Fließen von einem höheren Niveau zu einem tieferen bewegt Räder von Mühlen und Turbinen. Am Anfang der Industrialisierung spielte der Wasserdampf, die Dampfmaschine eine entscheidende Rolle.

The power generated by water flowing from a higher to a lower level turns mill wheels and turbines. In the early stages of industrialization steam and the steam engine played a crucial role.

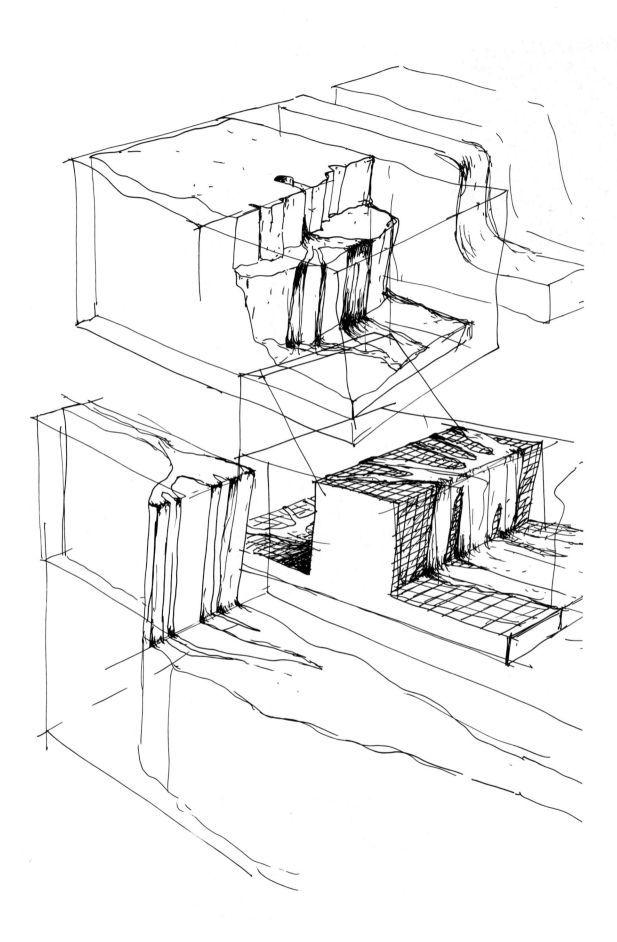

Seenflächen als Augen der Landschaft, als Über-
gangsbilder zur Innenwelt der Natur. Metaphysik
der Natur. Blickverbindungen.
Die Schönheit des Sees besteht einerseits in
seiner Leere, andererseits in seinen spiegeln-
den Veränderungen. Die Seefläche wird so zu
einem idealen Bild. Sie malt ihre Umgebung und
verfremdet das Dargestellte durch Rasterung,
Schraffierung, Verschlingung oder durch einge-
streute Blätter, die auf der Oberfläche treiben.

Stilles, lautloses Dahingleiten des Flusses. Die
Oberfläche ist fast glatt, nur an manchen Stellen
ein sanftes Aufwellen, eine leichte Verwirbelung,
dann wieder die ruhige Fläche. Wie achtlos spiegeln sich das Ufer, die Weiden und Pappeln in
dieser Fläche. Die Bilder bleiben am gleichen Ort,
das Wasser fließt durch sie hindurch. Wie unter
einer Glasplatte sieht man Kiesel, Felsbrocken
und sich windende Wasserpflanzen. Der Fluß
strebt still einem fernen, unbekannten, aber tiefer
liegenden Ziel zu.
»Vielleicht sind die Bäume die einzigen, die das
Geheimnis des Wassers von Grund aus kennen.«
(Jules Renard)

*The river glides by, still and silent. The surface is
almost smooth, with just a gentle wave rising in
places, a slight swirl, and then the surface is calm
again. The bank, willows and poplars are so heed-
lessly reflected in this surface. The images remain
in the same place, the water flows through them.
Gravel, rocks and twining water plants are seen
as if under a sheet of glass.
The river is quietly striving towards a distant, unknown but lower-lying goal.
»Perhaps the trees are the only ones that know
the secret of water from the very depths.«
(Jules Renard)*

Lakes as the landscape's eyes, as transitional images to the inner world of nature. Metaphysics of nature. Visual connections.
The beauty of the lake derives partly from its emptiness, and partly from its reflecting changes. The surface of the lake becomes an ideal image in this way. It paints its surroundings and alienates what is presented by scanning, hatching, intertwining or by fallen leaves floating on the surface.

Wasserflächen sind die größten und stärksten Stimmungsträger der Landschaft.
»Endlich das Wasser, als viertes Hauptelement des Naturlebens, inwiefern aus ihm alles Lebendige dieser Erde sich erschließt, in ihm die Unendlichkeit des Himmels sich widerspiegelt (recht eigentlich der Himmel auf Erden zu nennen), zieht uns mit doppelten Banden an, wie es lebenstätig erbrandend und rauschend das Gefühl erregt und belebt, erweckt in uns sein heiterer oder dunkler Spiegel das Gefühl unendlicher Sehnsucht.« (Carl Gustav Carus)

Water is the greatest and most powerful carrier of the landscape's mood. »Finally water, as the fourth principal element of natural life, as every living thing on the earth derives from it, and the infinity of the sky is reflected in it (properly to be called heaven on earth). It draws us with double bonds, as it stimulates and enlivens our feelings, living and active, foaming and rushing, and its bright or dark mirror awakes in us a feeling of endless longing.« (Carl Gustav Carus)

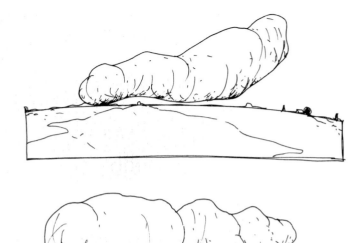

Das durch Sonneneinstrahlung verdunstete Wasser schwebt in Wolkenform über der Landschaft. Architekturen aus Wassertropfen und Eiskristallen, die sich durch thermische Zirkulation und Luftdruckschwankungen permanent verändern und fortbewegen. Die Formensprache der Wolken ist genauso vielfältig wie die der Blätter, Blüten, Bäume, Steine oder Wellen. Es gibt hingehauchte Schlieren, zarte Fasern, gerasterte Tupfer, Flocken, Walzen, Baldachine, wogende Hügel und Türme und gewaltige Gewittergebirge. Manche Wolkenarchitekturen ereichen eine Höhe von bis zu 18 000 m.

Water evaporated by the rays of the sun hovers over the landscape in the form of clouds. Architecture made up of drops of water and ice crystals, constantly changing and moving as a result of thermal circulation and changes in the temperature of the air. The formal language of clouds is just as diverse as that of leaves, blossoms, trees, stones or waves. There are breaths of schliere, delicate threads, scanned dots, tufts, rollers, baldacchinos, swelling hills and towers and mighty thunder mountains. Some cloud architecture reaches a height of 18,000 metres.

Bei Regen wird die Welt schraffiert und in Punkte aufgelöst. Rasterungen und Linierungen wie auf den Bildern Seurats und wie auf einem Fernsehbildschirm.
Dann sinkt die Temperatur. Die Wassertropfen vereisen oder gefrieren zu Schneekristallen. Langsam schweben Milliarden dieser Kristalle aus den grauen Wolken zur Erde. Alle Farben werden ausgelöscht. Die Landschaft ist nur noch ein sanftes, weißes Auf- und Abschwellen. Monochromie der Verhüllung.

When it rains the world is hatched and dissolved into dots. Grids and lines like a picture by Seurat or a television screen.
Then the temperature falls. The drops of water freeze or form snow crystals. Slowly hundreds of thousands of these crystals float to the ground from these grey clouds. All colours are extinguished. The landscape is now nothing but a gentle, white swelling up and down. A monochrome disguise.

»Mit sehr unterschiedlichem Gang kommt der Regen herab, in den Hof, wo ich ihn fallen sehe. Mittendrin ist er ein feiner, diskontinuierlicher Vorhang (oder Netz), ein unversöhnlicher, doch relativ langsamer Fall vermutlich ziemlich leichter Tropfen, ein immerwährendes Herabstürzen ohne Nachdruck, ein sehr feines Zerbröckeln des reinen Meteors. In geringer Entfernung von den Mauern rechts und links fallen geräuschvoller die schwereren, vereinzelten Tropfen. Hier sind sie an Größe einem Weizenkorn gleich, dort einer Erbse, anderswo fast einer Murmel.«
(Francis Ponge)

»The rain falls into the yard in which I see it in many different ways. Right in the middle it is a fine, discontinuous curtain (or net), an irreconcilable but relatively slow fall of drops that are presumably quite light, a constant, unemphatic fall, a very gentle crumbling of the pure meteor. Not far away from the walls to the right and left the heavy individual drops fall more noisily. Here they are about the same size as a grain of corn, there as big as a pea, elsewhere almost as big as a marble.« (Francis Ponge)

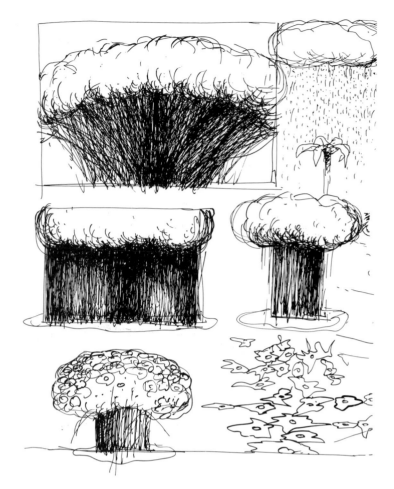

Langsame Vereisung der Natur.

Slowly nature changes into ice.

Gletscherzungen schieben sich über die Landschaft. Eiszeit.

Glacier tongues push across the landscape. Ice age.

Meer: Obwohl das Wasser nur einen geringen Teil der Erd-Masse ausmacht, bedeckt es fast dreiviertel der Erdoberfläche.
Küsten, Strände, steil, flach, sandig, felsig, geröllig, mit Kies bedeckt, paradiesisch gesäumt von riesigen Kokospalmen oder von gewaltigen Eisbergen begrenzt.

Sea: although water makes up only a small part of the earth's mass it covers almost three quarters of the earth's surface.
Coasts, beaches, steep, shallow, sandy, rocky, pebbly, covered with shingle, edged with gigantic coconut palms like paradise, or bordered with icebergs.

Die Ränder: Seit Jahrmillionen schlagen die Brandungswellen gegen Felswände, stürzen sich auf Sandstrände, fallen in sich zusammen und werden vom großen Meerblock wieder geschluckt. Immer wieder die gleiche lustvolle, hoffnungsvolle, gierige, dann verzweifelte, letzten Endes absurd-sinnlose Bewegung.
Dennoch wird hier Arbeit verrichtet. Felsen werden zu Steinen verkleinert, Steine zu Sand. Sand wird in die Meeressenken gespült. Irgendwann wird sich das Meer die Länder einverleibt haben und ohne Grenzen und Strände in sich selbst kreisen und zucken.

The edges: for millions of years waves have been beating against rocky walls, crashing on to sandy beaches, breaking, then swallowed again by the great block of the sea. Always the same pleasurable, hopeful, greedy, then desperate, ultimately absurd and senseless movement.
Nevertheless work is done here. Rocks are broken down into stones, stones into sand. Sand is washed into the hollows of the sea. The time will come when the sea will have swallowed the land and will circle and twitch without borders or beaches.

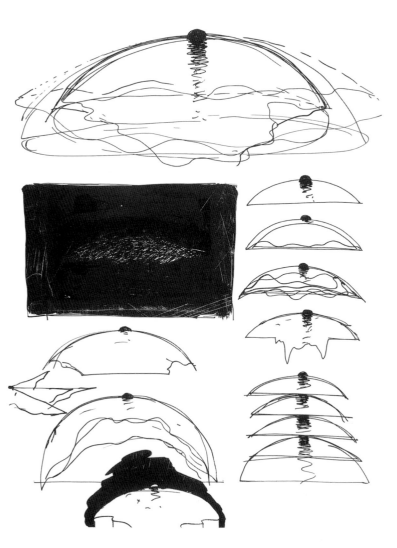

42

Phänomenologie der Landschaft
Steine und Gebirge

Phenomenology of landscape
Rocks and mountains

Alle Steine sind stumme Zeugen der Erdentste-
hung und der Erdgeschichte. Steine stehen auch
am Anfang der kulturellen Entwicklung des Menschen: Mit ihnen wurden die ersten Mauern
errichtet, und aus ihnen wurden die ersten Werk-
zeuge (Steinkeil) und Waffen gemacht.
»Im Stein ruht das erste Wort der Erde, das Endlose des Zeichens. Vielleicht ist das All aus dieser
gewagten Lektüre hervorgegangen.«
(Edmond Jabès)

*All stones bear silent witness to the origins of the
earth and its history. Stones also mark the beginning of man's cultural development: they were
used to build the first walls and the first tools
(stone wedge) and weapons were made from
them.*
*»The first word on earth rests in stone, the infinity
of the sign. Perhaps the universe emerged from
this daring reading matter.« (Edmond Jabès)*

Stein und Blatt am Wegrand in einer Wasser-
pfütze. Das Blatt mit seiner gezahnten Form, seinen Adern, abgefallen von der Hauptader, dem
Baum, zum Austrocknen, zur Verfaulung, zur Verwesung verurteilt. Es hat nur ein halbes Jahr
gelebt. Jetzt wird es sich auflösen, in kleine
Stücke zerfallen, zu Erde, zu Humus werden.
Dagegen der Stein. Er ist Jahrmillionen alt, einst
vom Gletscher aus dem Gebirge hierher gerollt
worden, immer wieder zerkleinert, immer wieder
geschliffen. Er ist Teil eines größeren Teils gewesen. Er liegt hier geduldig, verharrend zwischen
Leben und Tod. Ein Dasein für die nächsten Jahrmillionen.
Im Innern bewahrt er die Zeit, wer ihn aufschlägt,
sieht Millionen Jahre zurück, sieht etwas, was
noch kein Auge gesehen hat.

*Stone and leaf at the wayside in a puddle of
water. The leaf with its denticulate shape, its
veins, fallen off the main veins, the tree, condemned to dry out, to decay, to rot. It has only lived
for half a year. Now it will dissolve, break down
into small pieces, and become soil, humus.*
*The stone forms a contrast. It is millions of years
old, once rolled here from the mountains by a
glacier, becoming smaller and smoother. It was
once part of a greater whole. It lies here patiently,
poised between life and death. Existence for the
next millions of years.*
*Inside it time is preserved, anyone who breaks
it open will look back millions of years, will see
something that no eye has yet seen.*

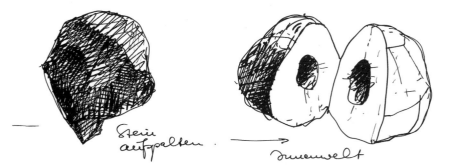

»Was bist du, finstere Nacht im Innern eines Steins.« (Henri Michaux)

»*What are you, dark night in the middle of a stone.*« *(Henri Michaux)*

Der Berg. Etymologisch verwandt mit gebären, bergen, verbergen, Herberge und Burg. Ein Steinblock, ein Riesenkristall. Aufwerfung, Aufbäumung der Erde.
Annäherung an das Gebirge: Die Landschaft beginnt sich zu wellen, die Bäume schaukeln an schiefen Hängen entlang. Wege winden sich steil empor. Perspektiven steigen und stürzen. Es gibt keine Waagrechte mehr. Die Landschaft ist in die Schräge gekippt. Dagegen steht die Vertikalstruktur der Vegetation.

The mountain. The German word for mountain, Berg, is etymologically related to gebären, to bear, bergen, to shelter, verbergen, to hide, Herberge, a refuge and Burg, a castle. A block of stone, a gigantic crystal. Thrown up, rearing up from the earth.
Approach to the mountains: the landscape starts to move in waves, the trees rock along steep slopes. Paths wind steeply up. Perspectives rise and fall. There are no more horizontals. The landscape has tipped over at an angle. The vertical structure of the vegetation stands in contrast with this.

Gebirge: die Dramatik der Landschaft, die Tragödie, das Scheitern. Das Gebirge verkörpert den barocken Gegenentwurf der Erdkruste zum radikalen Nihilismus der gekrümmten Meeresfläche. Hier haben sich die Gesteinsmassen aufgetürmt, übereinandergeschoben, aufgefaltet und abgesenkt. Die einstigen Bewegungen sind erstarrt und versteinert. »Die Alpen wirken einerseits als das Chaos, als die ungefüge Masse des Gestaltlosen, das nur zufällig und ohne eigenen Formsinn einen Umriß bekommen hat, das Geheimnis der Materie schweigt heraus, von der man an den Konfigurationen der Berge mehr mit einem Blick erfaßt, als in irgendeiner anderen Landschaft. Wir fühlen hier das Irdische als solches in seiner ungeheuren Wucht, das noch ganz fern von allem Leben und Eigenbedeutung der Form ist. Andrerseits aber sind die übergroß aufsteigenden Felsen, die durchsichtigen und schimmernden Eishänge, der Schnee der Gipfel, der keine Beziehung mehr zu den Niederungen der Erde hat – alles dies sind Symbole des Transzendenten, den seelischen Blick aufführend, wo über dem mit höchster Gefahr noch Erreichbaren das liegt, zu dem keine bloße Willenskraft mehr hin-

auflangt. Darum verschwindet der ästhetische Eindruck zugleich mit dem mystischen, von dem er hier durchwachsen ist, sobald der Himmel über den Schneebergen dicht bezogen ist; denn nun werden sie von den Wolken zur Erde herabgedrückt, sie sind eingefangen und mit aller anderen Erde zusammengeschlossen. Erst wenn nichts als Himmel über ihnen ist, weisen sie grenzenlos und ununterbrochen in das Überirdische hinauf und können einer anderen Ordnung als der der Erde angehören. Soweit man von einer Landschaft sagen kann, daß sie transzendent wäre, gilt es von der Firnlandschaft – freilich nur dort, wo nur noch Eis und Schnee, aber kein Grünes, kein Tal, kein Pulsschlag des Lebens mehr besteht. Und weil das Transzendente, das Absolute, in dessen Stimmung uns diese Landschaft verwebt, über alle Worte hinaus ist, so liegt es auch, wenn es nicht kindlich vermenschlicht wird, über aller Form.« (Georg Simmel)

Mountains: the drama of the landscape, the tragedy, the collapse. Mountains are the baroque reply by the crust of the earth to the radical nihilism of the curved surface of the sea. Here the masses of stone have risen in towers, pushed one over the other, folded and sunken. Former movement has become paralysed and petrified. »On the one hand the Alps seem chaotic, a towering formless mass that has acquired an outline only by chance and without its own sense of shape, the secret of the material is a silent presence, and more can be grasped from one glance at the configuration of this material than in any other landscape. Here we feel earthliness as such in its enormous power, still a long way away from all life and inherent significance of form. But on the other hand there are the rocks, soaring up in their excessive size, the transparent and shimmering ice slopes, the snow of the summits, that no longer relates to the lowlands of the earth – all these are symbols of the transcendent, leading the eye of the soul upwards, where above that which is only accessible with the greatest degree of danger there lies that which no mere strength of will can reach. For this reason the aesthetic impression disappears together with the mystical one with which it is steeped here as soon as the sky is thickly covered above the snow-capped mountains; for now they are being pushed down to the earth by the clouds, they are captured and put together with all the rest of the earth. Only when there is nothing but sky above them do they point unlimited and uninterrupted into the celestial and are able to belong to an order other than that of the earth. If it is ever possible to say of a landscape that it is transcendent then this is true of the firn landscape – though of course only where there is only ice and snow, but nothing green, no valley, no pulse of life any more. And because the transcendent, the absolute, into the mood of which this landscape binds us, is beyond all words, then it is also, if it is not anthropomorphized in a childlike way, beyond all form.« (Georg Simmel)

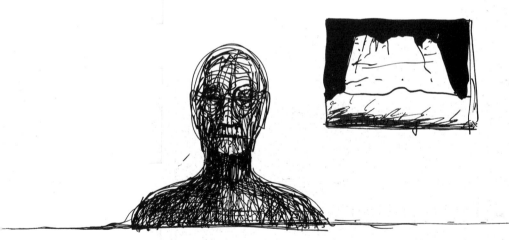

Verwitterung: zum Extrem der Formen kommt das Extrem des Klimas. Starke Sonneneinstrahlung und lange, strenge Winterfröste sprengen die Felsen. Wasserfälle und Gebirgsbäche spülen die Steine in die Täler hinab. Irgendwann werden alle Gebirge verwittert, zerfallen und abgetragen sein.

Weathering: extremes of form are joined by extremes of climate. Strong sunlight and long, severe winter frosts crack the rocks. Waterfalls and mountain streams wash the stones down into the valleys. The time will come when all mountains will be weathered, broken down and carried away.

47

Die Wildheit der Gebirge wurde über Jahrhunderte gemieden. Man betrachtete sie mit Angst, Ehrfurcht oder Abscheu. Italienreisende verhängten beim Durchqueren der Alpen ihre Kutschenfenster. Heute wird das Gebirge als Erlebnis-, Freizeit- und Sportlandschaft benutzt und verbraucht.

The wildness of the mountains was avoided for centuries. They were looked at with fear, reverence or abhorrence. Travellers to Italy used to cover the windows of their coaches when crossing the Alps. Today the mountains are used and consumed as a landscape for experience, leisure and sport.

»Und welch ein Hochgenuß, so hinauszuziehen in Berg und Wald, wenn nach Sturm und Wetter sich der Himmel klärt, wenn in der Ferne dumpf die Donner verrollen, wenn der letzte Entscheidungskampf der Wolken um die Zinnen der Berge wogt, wenn ein kräftiger Erdgeruch, vermischt mit süßem Blumenduft, die Lüfte füllt und die ganze Natur so recht von Herzen aufzuatmen scheint in Erquickung und Frische! Oder vor Anbruch des Tages die gemütliche Hütte zu verlassen und hineinzuschreiten in die stille Dämmerung, wenn fern über den westlichen Bergen die letzten Sterne erlöschen, wenn im Osten das wachsende Frühlicht in farbigen Bändern emporschwimmt über den Himmel, wenn der Tau wie ein grauer, seidenartig schimmernder Schleier über allem Grunde liegt, wenn die steigende Helle in den zahllosen Tropfen, unter denen sich die schlanken Gräser tief zur Erde neigen, ein buntes Glühen und Blitzen weckt, wenn aus Bäumen und Büschen sich die ersten schüchternen Vogelstimmen hören lassen und wenn der volle Tag erwacht in seiner leuchtenden Glorie! Und welchen Reichtum an stillen Reizen bietet am Abend das stundenlange Verweilen an einer Stelle, wo dem Jäger zu Häupten sich die wild zerrissenen Felsen über den Bergwald türmen, während ihm zu Füßen das tiefe Tal gebettet liegt in sanfter Schönheit! Dieser Reichtum erschöpft sich nicht und wird nicht ausgenossen, da er mit jedem Abend sich neu erzeugt in neuer Form. Jeder einzelne Abend hat seinen eigenen Reiz, jeder andere ein anderes Gesicht.« (Ludwig Ganghofer)

»Der leere Berg im Regen, die leeren Wege: immer deutlicher, immer klarer, immer mehr Antwort-genug erscheint mir die Leere; so jetzt auch die Gewißheit, auf dem leeren See etwas zu erblicken – und wenn es nur die Leere wäre.« (Peter Handke)

»And what a pleasure it is to go out like that into mountain and forest, when the skies clear after tempest and storm, when thunder is rolling dully in the distance, when the last struggle for supremacy rolls the clouds over battlements of the mountains, when a strong smell of earth, mingling with the sweet fragrance of flowers, fills the air and the whole of nature seems to breathe a heartfelt sigh of relief of refreshment and freshness! Or leaving the comfortable hut before daybreak and striding into the silent gloaming, when the last stars finally go out over the western mountains, when in the east the growing early light swims up over the sky in coloured bands, when the dew lies over all the ground like a grey, silky-shimmering, when the increasing brightness brings out a colourful glow and flash in the countless drops under which the slender grasses bend low to the ground, when the first shy birdcalls are heard from the trees and bushes, and when the full day awakens in its glowing glory! And what a wealth of quiet pleasures can be had from lingering for hours in the evening in a spot where the wildly broken rocks tower over the mountain wood above the huntsman's head, while at his feet the deep valley lies bedded in gentle beauty! This wealth cannot be exhausted and never fails to provide enjoyment as it is produced every evening anew. Every single evening has its own charm, every new one a different face.« (Ludwig Ganghofer)

»The empty mountain in the rain, the empty paths: emptiness seems to me ever more distinct, more clear, increasingly ›answer enough‹; and now also the certainty of catching sight of something on the empty lake – and even if it is only emptiness.« (Peter Handke)

Phänomenologie der Landschaft
Natur – Mensch und Natur. Anatomien und Bewußtsein

Phenomenology of landscape
Nature – man and nature. Anatomies and consciousness

Der umfassende Begriff für alle beschriebenen Phänomene ist »Natur«. Sie produziert nicht nur die Pflanzen, die Erde, die Steine, das Wasser, die Luft, sondern auch die Tiere und den Menschen. Das Bewußtsein des Menschen ist der Ort, an dem alle Linien zusammenfließen. Von hier aus wird beobachtet, beschrieben, befragt, untersucht, seziert und eingeteilt.

The all-embracing concept for all described phenomena is »nature«. It not only produces plants, earth, stones, water, air, but also animals and man. Man's consciousness is the place at which all lines meet. From this point observation takes place, description, questions, examination, dissection and classification.

Natur. Natur-Natur. Alles ist Natur. Anatomie der Natur. Bewußtsein der Natur. Bewußtsein von der Natur. Beschreibungen. Hinterfragungen. Kindliche Annäherungen, Annäherungen eines Naturwissenschaftlers. »Natur ist unser Unterbewußtsein.« (Louis Aragon)

»Natur ist, was wir nicht gemacht haben.« (Robert Spaemann)

Nature. Nature-nature. Everything is nature. Anatomy of nature. Awareness of nature. Consciousness of nature. Descriptions. Questioning. Childlike approaches, scientific approaches. »Nature is our subconscious.« (Louis Aragon)

»Nature is what we have not made.« (Robert Spaemann)

»Die Natur aber ist ungläubig, rechtsfeindlich, alogisch und anarchisch. Sie und das Universum, das All, der Kosmos werden analog zu einer irdischen Herrschaftsordnung behandelt. Durch die Umkehrung dieser soziomorphen Projektion werden die Erde, die Zivilisation und ihre politischen Systeme über sozunennende monarchisch-absolute Verhältnisse des Kosmos verantwortet. Die Natur ist so, und wir? fragt der Diktator und lächelt.

Diese Projektion trifft wie ein Projektil mit seinen Querschlägern alles. Die Menschen, die Dinge. Alles gehorcht und sagt, ohne es auszusprechen: Die Natur ist so, wir sind natürlich, oder? Ich lache und gehorche, horche und lache und gehorche. Auch Erkenntnis hilft nur wenig.

Ich weiß, auch die reine Vernunft ist im Grunde nur das artikulierte Lachen über sich selbst. So ist es, aber?

Wir sitzen vor der Natur wie ein Kind im Theater vor dem bunten, aber geschlossenen Vorhang. Das Kind bewundert ihn, das Bild, die Farben und glaubt, das sei alles; deswegen sei es hierhergekommen.

Die Wirklichkeit hinter dem Vorhang sehen wir nie. Wir vermuten, sie über eine gemessene Realität, über Daten, Indikatoren, Annahmen, Axiome, Theoreme, Gesetze, Hypothesen zu entdecken. Genau darin drückt sich unsere Vermessenheit aus: im Vermessen und Messen. Gesetze, welche immer, sind die jüngste Mythologie, die der Mensch über die Natur und sich gelegt hat. Die Legislatur des Menschen tritt gegen die Natur an. Das sogenannte Naturgesetz bedeutet eine Rechtsordnung der Welt, der Zivilisation, im moral-theologischen Sinne.«
(Helmut Eisendle)

»But nature is disbelieving, inimical to law, illogical and anarchic. It and the universe, the cosmos are treated analogously to an earthly order of rule. By reversing this sociomorphic projection the earth, civilization and its political systems take responsibility for what can be called the monarchist-absolutist conditions of the cosmos. Nature is like this, and we? asks the dictator, and smiles.

This projection hits everything like a ricocheting projectile. People, things. Everything obeys and says, without speaking it aloud: nature is like that; we are natural, or aren't we?

I laugh and obey, hear and laugh and obey. Insight helps very little either.

I know that even Pure Reason is essentially only articulated laughter about oneself. So it is, but?

We sit before nature like a child in the theatre before the colourful but closed curtain. The child admires it, the picture and colours, and thinks that is all; that is why it came here.

We never see the reality behind the curtain. We assume that we are discovering it through a measured reality, through data, indicators, assumptions, axioms, theorems, laws and hypotheses. It is precisely in this that our arrogance is expressed: in surveying and measuring. Laws, of whatever kind, are the most recent mythology that man has placed upon himself and nature. Human legislature sets itself against nature's legislature. The so-called law of nature means a law-ordering of the world, of civilization, in the moral and theological sense.« (Helmut Eisendle)

Nach Erkenntnis der Evolutionstheorie ist alles Natur-Leben und alle Natur-Form aus einfachen Grundstrukturen entstanden.

According to insights into the theory of evolution all nature-life and nature form emerged from simple basic structures.

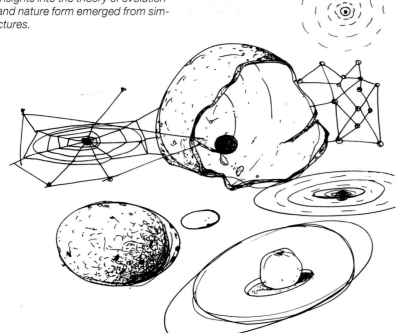

Wie die Natur in ihrer Evolution hin- und herpendelt zwischen chaotischen und geordneten Strukturen, wie sie Zusammenhänge ausprobiert und wieder verwirft, wie sie schließlich dauerhafte Programme hervorbringt und sie von Generation zu Generation weitervererbt, vergleichbar dazu arbeitet auch das menschliche Gehirn, die gesamte Vorstellungswelt. Alles ist denkbar und wird als Gedanke von der Natur wertfrei angeboten: Liebe und Haß, Eifersucht und Mord, Gier und Sanftmut, Klarheit und Romantik. Alle Bewußtseinsinhalte schweben in der Schwerelosigkeit des Vorstellungs-Weltalls umher wie Raumschiffe und Meteore. Logische Verknüpfungen, sinnvolle Weltbilder liegen zwar im Bereich der Möglichkeit, müssen aber gesucht und »künstlich« konstruiert werden. Diese Konstruktionen – Gesetze, Kultur, Ethik, Wirtschaft, Architektur – bringen die Ordnung in das Chaos. Erinnerungsvermögen, Erziehung und Tradition erfüllen die Funktion der dauerhaften Programme. Inwieweit diese Konstruktionen als Vorgänge der Natur definiert werden können, darüber mag man unterschiedlicher Meinung sein. Letzten Endes jedoch ist auf der Welt nichts denkbar, was nicht bereits in ihr – als Möglichkeit – enthalten ist.

The way in which nature swings to and fro in its evolution between chaotic and ordered structures, the way in which it tries out connections and rejects them again, the way it finally produces durable programmes and passes them down from generation to generation, all this has a parallel in the human brain, the whole world of imagination.
Everything is conceivable and is offered neutrally by nature as a thought: love and hate, jealousy and murder, greed and gentleness. Clarity and romanticism. All the contents of our consciousness hover in the weightlessness of the universe of imagination like space ships and meteors. Logical connections, meaningful perceptions of the world may be within the bounds of the possible, but they have to be sought out and »artificially« constructed. These constructions – laws, culture, ethics, economy, architecture – bring order into chaos. Memory, education and tradition fulfil the function of durable programmes. The extent to which these constructions can be defined as processes of nature may produce differing opinions. But in the last resort nothing is conceivable in the world that is not already contained within it – as a possibility.

Apfel und Welt, Auge und Sonne, Zelle und Gehirn, Atomaufbau und Planetensystem: Überall scheint man auf Ähnlichkeiten und verwandte Strukturen zu stoßen.

Apple and world, eye and sun, cell and brain, atomic structure and planetary system: we seem to come across similarities and related structures everywhere.

Je größer der Bewußtseinsraum des Ich, umso größer seine Entfernung und Entfremdung von der sich dumpf ereignenden Natur. Die fraglose Einheit von Baum und Welt, von Tier und Natur sehen und den tiefen Riß spüren, der durch Auge, Geist und Sprache in die Welt gekommen ist. Sehnsucht nach Berührung, nach Einheit mit der Natur und der Landschaft.

The larger the consciousness of the ego, the greater the distance and alienation from dully occurring nature. Seeing the unquestionable unity of tree and world, of animal and nature, and sensing the profound break that has come into the world through eye, mind and language. Longing for contact, for unity with nature and landscape.

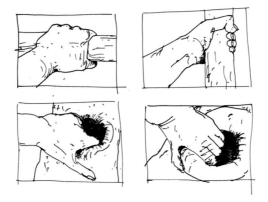

Blick in die Geschichte der Landschafts- und Gartenarchitektur
Mensch und Landschaft

A look at the history of landscape and garden architecture
Man and landscape

Ein Ort zum Leben, ein Ort zum Sterben. Die frühen Kulturen haben die Natur-Landschaft mit ihren Vorstellungen, Sehnsüchten und Ängsten beseelt. Animismus und Mythologie. Überall trieben Erdgeister, Nymphen, Waldfeen, Baumgespenster, Götter und Göttinnen ihr Unwesen. Die Erde war die ›Ur-Mutter‹, der man mit Opfern und Riten Verehrung entgegenbringen mußte.

A place to live, a place to die. Early cultures animated landscape with their imaginings, longings and fears. Animism and mythology. Earth spirits, nymphs, woodland spirites, tree spirits, gods and goddesses got up to their mischief everywhere. Earth was the ›primeval mother‹, who had to be honoured with sacrifice and ritual.

Die Landschaft wurde über Jahrtausende als umfassender Außenraum empfunden. Der Innenraum war die Siedlung, das Dorf, die Burg, das Kloster, das Gehöft, das Haus. Alle dauerhaften Eingriffe in die Landschaft hatten landwirtschaftliche (Ackerbau, Weinbau usw.) oder verkehrstechnische Gründe (Wege und Straßen). Ästhetisch gestaltete Landschaftsbereiche beschränkten sich auf wohnhausnahe Zonen, auf Innenhöfe.
Bei Schlössern nahmen die Anlagen später größere Dimensionen an. Schneisen mit Wasserbecken und Alleen wurden in unwegsames Gelände geschlagen, Fühler, Ausleger in eine andere Welt hinein.

For thousands of years landscape was perceived as an all-embracing external space. Internal space was the settlement, the village, the castle, the monastery, the farmstead, the house. All permanent interventions into the landscape were for agricultural (farming, viticulture etc.) or transport (paths and roads) purposes.
Aesthetically designed landscapes were limited to zones near residences and courtyards.
Palace gardens later acquired larger dimensions. Aisles with pools and avenues were cut into impassable territory, feelers, interpreters of another world.

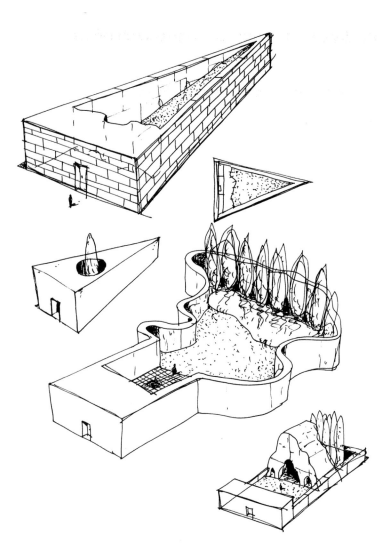

Der Garten hat im Verhältnis Mensch und Natur eine besondere Bedeutung. Er setzt jemanden voraus, der ein Stück Land umzäunt und es nach seinen Vorstellungen anlegt – und nicht den Gesetzen der Natur überläßt. Garten (aus indogermanisch = Flechtwerk, umzäunter Platz, Hof, Weide) wird von Anfang an als ein erweiterter Wohnraum (als Ziergarten) mit landwirtschaftlicher Nutzung (Nutzgarten, Feld, Tierhaltung usw.) angesehen. Während in fernöstlichen Bereichen (Japan und China) meditativ-religiöse Betrachtungsweisen überwogen – die Landschaft wurde symbolisch an das Haus geholt, mit Kies, Sand, Steinen, Wasser und Pflanzen – suchte man im europäisch-mediterranen Garten mehr das Vergnügen und die Erholung.

Gardens have a special meaning in man's relationship with nature. They require someone to fence in a piece of land, and to lay it out according to his ideas – and not the purposes of nature. Gardens (from the Indo-Germanic wicker, fenced place, court, pasture) were from the beginning conceived as an extended living area (as decorative gardens) with some agricultural features. While in the Far East (Japan and China) the meditative-religious point of view predominated – the landscape was symbolically brought towards the house, with gravel, sand, stones, water and plants – pleasure and recreation were sought in European and Mediterranean gardens.

Garten und Wohnhaus als Einheit. Ideale Lebensform zu allen Zeiten. Der Bewohner sieht immer das gleiche Naturbild, den gleichen kleinen Landschaftsausschnitt. Er erlebt die jahreszeitlichen Veränderungen, Blühen, Wachstum und Zerfall als das Leben mit der Natur.

Garden and house as a unit. An ideal form of life at all times. The resident always sees the same little landscape detail. He experiences seasonal change, flowering, growth and decay: living with nature.

»Wenn der Park eine zusammengezogene idealisierte Natur ist, so ist der Garten eine ausgedehnte Wohnung.«
(Hermann Fürst zu Pückler-Muskau)

*»If a park is a drawing together of idealized nature, then a garden is an extended residence.«
(Hermann Fürst zu Pückler-Muskau)*

Blick in die Geschichte der Landschafts- und Gartenarchitektur
Gartensysteme

A look at the history of landscape and garden architecture
Garden systems

Klostergärten, Philosophengärten, Wassergärten, Ziergärten, Nutzgärten, Blumengärten, Innenhofgärten, Bauerngärten, italienische Gärten, französische Gärten.

Monastery gardens, philosophers' gardens, water gardens, ornamental gardens, vegetable gardens, flower gardens, courtyard gardens, peasants' gardens, Italian gardens, French gardens.

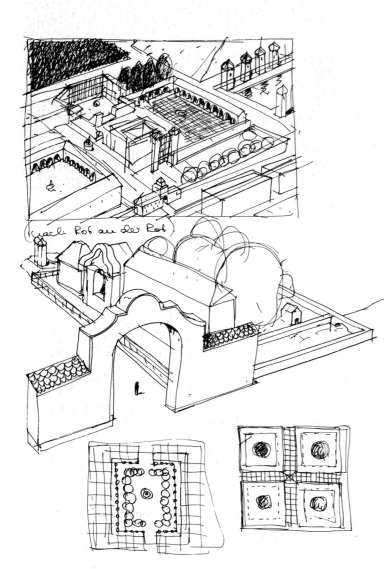

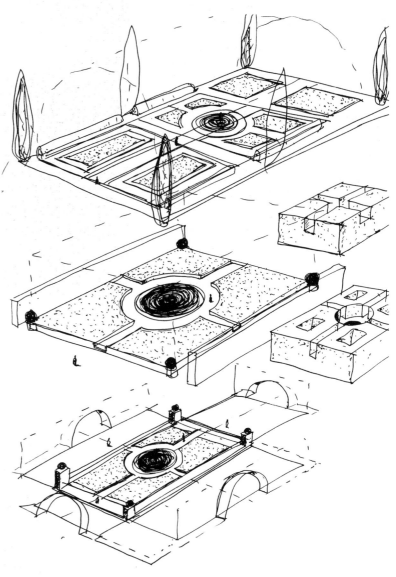

Die Kulturgeschichte des Gartens zeigt, daß es von Beginn an zwei Gestaltungsarten gegeben hat: die geometrische und die frei organische. Die geometrischen, streng symmetrischen Anlagen sind die ursprünglichen. Sie waren in Ägypten, Griechenland, Rom und dann wieder im Italien der Rennaissance und im Barock Frankreichs verbreitet. Der asymmetrische, malerisch-freie Stil wurde früh in China entwickelt und beeinflußte im 18. Jh. die englische Gartenbaukunst.

The cultural history of the garden shows that there were two kinds of design from the beginning: geometrical and free organic. Geometrical, strictly symmetrical layouts came first. They were widespread in Egypt, Greece, Rome and then again in Renaissance Italy and baroque France. The asymmetrical, freely picturesque style was developed at an early stage in China and influenced English gardening in the 18th century.

Der geometrische Garten fand seinen Vollender in Le Nôtre. Die Anlagen von Vaux-le-Vicomte und Versailles fassen alle Motive zusammen, die für einen geometrischen Garten wichtig sind: die gerade Achse, die spiegelsymmetrisch den Park in zwei gleiche Hälften teilt, und die beschnittene Natur.

Alles sieht aus wie der Idealentwurf einer fiktiven Ordnung, nichts bleibt dem Zufall überlassen. Die Schönheit der Anlagen ergibt sich aus dem Triumph der Geometrie über das Chaos. Die Schlösser wirken nur noch wie eine ferne Zutat zum liegenden Bild, ein gebauter Hügel, ein bewohnter Fluchtpunkt.

Le Nôtre perfected the geometrical garden. The gardens at Vaux-le-Vicomte and Versailles bring together all the motifs that are important for a geometrical garden: the straight axis, dividing the park into two equal halves with mirror symmetry, and the clipped nature.

Everything looks like an ideal draft of a fictitious order, nothing is left to chance. The beauty of the layout arises from the triumph of geometry over chaos. The palaces look like a distant addition to the horizontal image, a built hill, an inhabited vanishing-point.

Wasser – Perspektive. Idealisierung der Ferne. Fluchtpunkteuphorie. Landebahnen für Götter, Lichtstrahlen und Vögel.

Water – Perspective. Idealization of distance. Vanishing-point euphoria. Landing strips for gods, beams of light and birds.

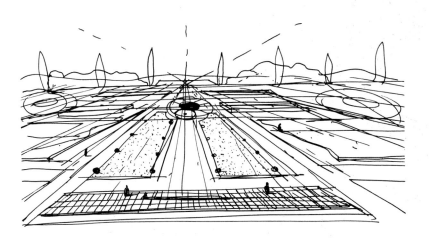

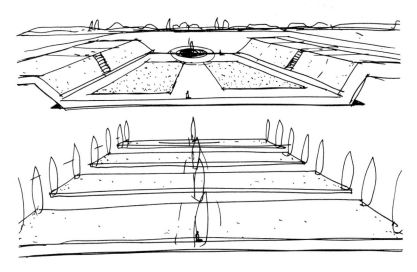

Es ist klar, daß auf dem Höhepunkt des geometrischen Stils die Gegenkräfte hervorkommen und diesen Zwang als Vergewaltigung verurteilen.

It is clear that at the climax of the geometrical style counter-forces occur and condemn this constraint as rape.

Der neue Stil, der organisch-malerische englische Garten, fand in Rousseau einen philosophischen Apologeten. Sein »Zurück-zur-Natur« war der Schlachtruf, der nach Ermenonville und in die Französische Revolution führte. Die Pappelinsel, auf der man Rousseau beerdigte, wurde in den neuen romantischen Gärten zum oft zitierten Motiv.

The new style, the organic and picturesque English garden, found a philosophical apologist in Rousseau. His ›back to nature‹ was the battle-cry that led to Ermenonville and the French Revolution. The island with poplars on which Rousseau was buried is a motif that was often quoted in the new, Romantic gardens.

Diese Insel verkörpert Paradies und Jenseits in einem. Sie ist das unerreichbare Urbild der Natur, der Anfang und das Ende. Ein Naturtempel, ein Stonehenge aus gewachsenen Bäumen, ein treibendes Floß im Nebel des romantischen Ungefähr. Während die Achse Le Nôtres die Sonne im Visier hatte (Apollos Wagen erhebt sich aus dem Seė in Versailles), also den Tag, das Überbelichtete, das Helle und Klare, bevorzugt Rousseaus Grabinsel die Nacht und den Tod, die nebelige Ursuppe mit Schilf und Seerosen. Der romantische Garten liebt das Krumme, das Gebogene, das Unklare, die Grotte, die Höhle, das undurchdringliche Dickicht, das Dämmerlicht und den Sonnenuntergang. Der Kampf zwischen den beiden Sehweisen und Gestaltungsmöglichkeiten hat sich in den nachfolgenden Zeiten fortgesetzt und hält bis heute an.

This island embodies paradise and the hereafter in one. It is the unattainable primeval image of nature, the beginning and the end. A natural temple, a Stonehenge of grown trees, a drifting raft in the mists of Romantic vagueness. While Le Nôtre's axis had the sun in its sights (Apollo's chariot rises from the lake in Versailles), and thus the day, the overexposed, the bright and clear, Rousseau's island tomb prefers night and death, a misty primeval soup of reeds and water-lilies. The Romantic garden likes things that are crooked, curves, lack of clarity, grottoes, caves, impenetrable thickets, twilight and sunset. The struggle between the two approaches and design possibilities continued in subsequent periods and still persists today.

Blick in die Geschichte der Landschafts- und Gartenarchitektur
Poetik und Motive

A look at the history of landscape and garden architecture
Poetics and motifs

Gerahmte Durchblicke. Landschaftsbilder, mit
Achsen und Fernblicken (Horizontlinie), mit
Spiegelungen und fernen Baumgruppen.

*Framed views. Landscape pictures, with axes
and distant views (horizon), with reflections and
distant groups of trees.*

Tore, Portale, Pforten, Durchgänge, Eingänge. In der Ferne das Traumland, das »Ende der Welt«, das Paradies.

Gates, portals, openings, corridors, entrances. In the distance the land of dreams, the »end of the world«, paradise.

Laubengänge. Halb Flur (Architektur), halb Waldweg.

Arbours. Partly halls (architecture), partly woodland paths.

Grotten, Alleen, Seen, Wasserläufe, Brunnen, Grabmäler, Wiesen, Wälder, Haine, Laubengänge, Ruinen, Baumgruppen, Blumenbilder, Follies.

Grottoes, tree-lined a avenues, lakes, watercourses, fountains, tombs, lawns, woods, groves, arbours, ruins, groups of trees, flower pictures, follies.

Wiesenstücke. Flach, geneigt, gewölbt. Mit
Bosketten, mit beschnittenen Hecken, mit Figu-
ren und Brunnen. Unter dem Rasen zerfallene
Gebäude, unterirdische Ruinen.

*Lawns. Flat, sloping, rolling. With boscages,
clipped hedges, statues and fountains.
Under the lawn are decaying buildings, subter-
ranean ruins.*

Blumenbilder, flach ausgebreitet wie Teppiche,
durchgehbar, überblickbar.

*Flower pictures, spread out flat like carpets,
available for walking through, to be overlooked.*

Beschnittene Heckenwände.
Grüne Architekturen.

Trimmed hedge walls. Green architecture.

Terrassen, Bastionen, höhergelegene Alleen,
Treppen und Wege. Überall Bänke. Ruhezonen,
gebaute Blicke.

*Terraces, bastions, avenues, steps and paths on
a higher level. Benches everywhere. Quiet areas,
built views.*

Tempel als Aussichtspunkte und Ruheorte. Treff-punkte für geheime Rendezvous. Garten und Erotik.

Temples and viewing points and resting places. Meeting-points for secret rendezvous. Gardens and eroticism.

Versteinerte und vergrößerte Naturformen: Muscheln, Schnecken, Stämme, Felsbrocken.

Petrified and enlarged natural forms: shells, snails, trunks, fragments of rock.

Große Steinvasen auf Mauern und Pfeilern, in den Bäumen. Immer wird Natur mit künstlichem Schmuck verwoben.

Large stone vases on walls and pillars, in the trees. Nature is always interwoven with artificial decoration.

Wasserfälle, Wasserkaskaden. Fließendes Wasser, stehendes Wasser, aufsteigendes Wasser und fallendes Wasser, jeder Aggregatzustand wird verwendet. Geräusche.
Seen, Wasserbassins, rund, quadratisch, mit Fontänen und Springbrunnen. Mit Inseln oder Figurengruppen.

Waterfalls, cascades. Running water, still water, rising water and falling water, every aggregate condition is used. Noises.
Lakes, pools, round and square, with fountains and cascades. With islands or groups of figures.

Brücken.

Bridges.

Teiche, Seen, Tümpel: Romantische ›Seele‹ des Gartens. Hier die Lichtspiele und subtilen Reflexe der Natur wie Monet in Giverny studieren.

Pools, lakes, ponds: Romantic ›soul‹ of the garden. Study the play of light and nature's subtle reflections like Monet in Giverny.

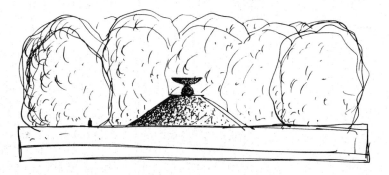

Ruinen, täuschend echt.
Oder künstlich, mit aufgemalter Mauerstruktur.
Zitiert werden Situationen aus dem Mittelalter,
aus der griechischen und römischen Antike, aus
Italien.

Ruins, deceptively genuine.
Or artificial, with painted masonry structures.
Medieval situations are cited, and situations from
Greek and Roman antiquity, from Italy.

Waldstücke mit Gräbern (fiktiv und real).

Wooded areas with tombs (fictitious and
genuine).

Figuren. Mythologische Szenen. Hier taucht der Gott auf, hier entkommt die Nymphe in den Wald. Frühes Kino, Theater auch.

Figures, mythological scenes. Here a god appears, there a nymph is escaping into the wood. Early cinema, theatre too.

Steinerne Götter und Nymphen zwischen Ruinen, auf Inseln, im Schilf.

Stone gods and nymphs among the ruins, on islands, in the reeds.

Putten schweben vorbei.

Putti float past.

Götter im Wasser. Stumm. Nur das Zwitschern der Vögel ist zu hören.

Gods in the water. Silent. Nothing to be heard but twittering birds.

Jede nackte Figur in der Gartenlandschaft läßt den Traum vom Paradies anklingen. So sein, nackt gehend über die feuchten Wiesen, zwischen den Ästen der Bäume hindurch, hinein ins helle Licht der Sonne.

Every naked figure in the garden landscape sounds a note of the dream of paradise. To be like this, walking naked over the damp lawns, through the branches of the trees, into the bright sunlight.

Alle Motive sind Versuche, die Landschaft aus ihrem bloßen Naturzustand zu entführen, sie umzuformen in einen anderen Aggregatzustand, ihr mögliches Unterbewußtsein oder ihr Überbewußtsein zu zeigen. Jeder Gang durch den Garten, den Park wird so zu einem Weg durch einen Text, ein Bilderbuch, einen Comic, einen Film und zu einer Reise.

Dieser Ansatz wird im folgenden immer wieder aufgegriffen. Die klassischen Motive sind heute noch verwendbar, auch wenn die Umwelt brutaler und die Fiktionen perfekter geworden sind. Der Dialog zwischen Entwerfer – Betrachter und Natur ist durch die klassischen Motive vorgeformt und teilweise in faszinierender Weise ausformuliert worden. Jeder, der die wichtigen Gärten der Welt gesehen und erlebt hat (Villa d'Este, Viterbo, Schwetzingen, Herrenhausen, Versailles, Vaux-Le-Vicomte, Potsdam, Buttes-Chaumont usw.), wird sich an die poetische Kraft dieser Orte erinnern. Sie sitzen fest im Gedächtnis und wollen in neuen Zonen, in neuen Gärten und Parks wiederauferstehen.

All motifs are attempts to wrest landscape out of its merely natural condition, to reshape it into another aggregate condition, to show its possible subconscious or enhanced consciousness. Every walk through the garden, through the park, thus becomes a way through a text, a picture book, a comic, a film; the walk becomes a journey.

This approach will be constantly returned to in what is to follow. Classical motifs can still be used today, even though the environment has become more brutal and the fictions more perfect. The dialogue between designer – viewer and nature is shaped in advance by classical motifs and has been formulated in a fascinating way in places. Anyone who has seen and experienced the world's important gardens (Villa d'Este., Viterbo, Schwetzingen, Herrenhausen, Versailles, Vaux-le-Vicomte, Potsdam, Buttes-Chaumont etc.) will remember the poetic force of these places. They sit firmly in the memory and intend to rise again in new areas, in new parks and gardens.

Mit verwestem Blick in die Ferne lächeln.

Smiling into the distance with a decomposing gaze.

Landschaft heute
Landschaft als Verkehrsraum

Landscape today
Landscape as a Space for transport

Seitdem es die Raumfahrt gibt und wir Bilder der Erde, vom All aus gesehen, besitzen, hat sich der Begriff »Landschaft« verändert. Man kennt die Erde jetzt als eine von blauen Wolken verhangene Kugeloberfläche in der schwarzen Unendlichkeit des Alls. Begriffe wie Weite und Ferne sind ins Taumeln geraten und explodiert.

Die Ferne, die früher hinter der Stadtgrenze, in der nächsten Stadt, im nächsten Land, in Italien vielleicht oder in Amerika gesucht wurde, diese Ferne, alle Ferne ist jetzt auf diese Kugeloberfläche begrenzt oder verliert sich zwischen Milliarden von Galaxien.

Landschaft ist heute wissenschaftlich untersucht, in ihren Einzelteilen katalogisiert, bis in den Atomkern hinein erforscht und in ihren Vernetzungen beschrieben. Landschaft ist heute nicht mehr nur Naturlandschaft, viele Landschaften überlagern einander: Stadtlandschaften, Seelenlandschaften, Müllandschaften, Verkehrslandschaften, künstliche Landschaften, Phantasielandschaften, Reklamelandschaften, Photolandschaften, Filmlandschaften, Medienlandschaften, Ausstellungslandschaften, Wohnlandschaften, Zeitungslandschaften, Sportlandschaften, Vergnügungslandschaften, Computerlandschaften, Wolkenlandschaften, Touristenlandschaften.

Blicke von oben.

Blicke von unten.

Simulation. Wahrheit ist von Fiktion und Fälschung nicht mehr zu unterscheiden.

Since the start of space travel and since the image of the earth seen from outer space has become familiar the concept of ›landscape‹ has changed completely. We now know the earth's surface as a sphere hanging with blue clouds in the black infinity of outer space. Concepts like distance and being a long way away have started to shake and been exploded.

Being far away, which used to mean beyond the town boundary, in the next town, in the next country, in Italy perhaps or in America, this distance, all distance is now limited to this spherical surface or lost between thousands of millions of galaxies.

Today landscape is examined scientifically, catalogued in its individual sections, explored down to the nucleus of the atom and described in its interlacements. Landscape today is no longer just natural landscape, many landscapes are superimposed upon each other: city landscapes, grassy landscapes, industrial landscapes, water landscapes, psychic landscapes, refuse landscapes, traffic landscapes, artificial landscapes, fantasy landscapes, advertising landscapes, photographic landscapes, film landscapes, media landscapes, exhibition landscapes, residential landscapes, newspaper landscapes, sport landscapes, pleasure landscapes, computer landscapes, cloud landscapes, tourist landscapes.

Views from above.

Views from below.

Simulation. Truth can no longer be distinguished from forgery and fiction.

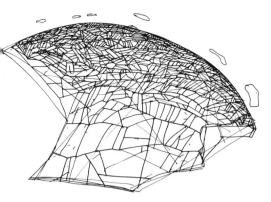 

Die Erdoberfläche ist vermessen, in Karten erfaßt. Die Landschaften sind verteilt, sie werden bewirtschaftet, bebaut oder abgebaut, sie werden bewohnt und verbraucht. Noch niemals in der Geschichte dieses Planeten lebten so viele Menschen auf der Erdoberfläche wie heute. Und es werden immer mehr.
Die Erdoberfläche ist überzogen mit Linien, Grenzen, mit Wegen und Straßen, mit Spuren und Bewegungen.

The surface of the earth has been surveyed and recorded on maps. Landscapes are divided, they are cultivated, planted or mined, they are lived in and consumed.
Never before in the history of this planet have so many people lived on the earth's surface as today. And numbers are increasing continuously.
The surface of the earth is covered with lines, borders, with paths and roads, with tracks and movements.

Straßennetz als Verbindungsnetz, als Adernsystem der Zivilisation. Kommunikation.
Der Gegensatz zwischen städtischer Landschaft und »Natur-Landschaft« ist heute verschwommen, es gibt kaum noch Ränder. Alles ist Stadt, alles Landschaft. Die Straßen sind Durchgangs- und Verbindungskorridore.
Die Radikalität des Straßenbaus! Ohne Schnörkel, ohne Umschweife das Ziel ansteuern. Sehnsucht nach der direktesten Verbindung, nach der geraden Linie.

Road network as a connecting network, as a vein system for civilization. Communication.
The contrast between urban landscape and »natural landscape« is blurred today, there are hardly any borders left. Everything is town, everything landscape. Roads are thoroughfares and connecting corridors.
Radical road-building! Heading for a destination without flourishes or detours. Longing for the most direct connection, for the straight line.

Das Asphaltband liegt in der Landschaft. Gewißheit des klaren Verlaufs. Keine Hindernisse. Leichte Bögen, Kurven, Zeichen, Verbote, Gebote. Leitplanken. Geschwindigkeit zwischen Linien.

The asphalt band lies across the landscape, levelling it out; certainty of a clear course. No obstacles. Gentle bends, curves, signs, bans, commands. Crash barriers. Speed between lines.

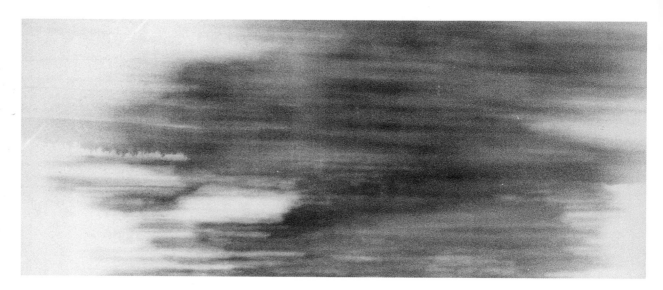

Landschaft fliegt vorbei, löst sich auf in Einzelteile, in Atome. Masten tauchen auf, fallen zurück in den Raum der Vergangenheit.

The landscape flies past, dissolves into individual parts, into atoms. Masts appear, fall back into the space of the past.

Bewegung der Autos gegen das starre Stehen der Architektur.

Movement of cars against the rigid stance of architecture.

Neue Gärten auf Verkehrsinseln, auf Grünstreifen zwischen den Autobahnen, an Tunneleinfahrten, an Schallschutzwänden und an riesigen Böschungen. Gärten nicht zum Verweilen, sondern zum Vorbeifahren mit zweihundert Kilometern in der Stunde.

New gardens on traffic islands, on green strips between the motorways, by tunnel entrances, by sound-absorbing walls and gigantic embankments. Gardens not intended to linger in, but to drive past at two hundred kilometres an hour.

Kreuzungen: Überlagerung zweier verschiedener Strömungsrichtungen. Die Gleichzeitigkeit des Verkehrs wird zeitlich auseinandergerissen, Ampeln rhythmisieren das Strömen. Überschneidungen führen zum Zusammenstoß.
Die Idee der Ampel, die Idee der weißen Striche und die Idee der Kreuzung überhaupt.

Junctions: two different traffic directions superimposed. The simultaneity of the traffic is torn apart in terms of time, the stream is given rhythm by traffic lights. Intersections lead to collision. The idea of the traffic lights, the idea of the white lines and the junction in general.

Ruhender Verkehr. Parkplätze und Parkhäuser. Garagen. Die neue Ästhetik dieser Orte. Die Tristesse, die Ordnung.
Das Ersticken in der Masse: Die Mobilität endet hier, stehend, ruhend, ohne Bewegung, aufgestaut. »Die parkenden Autos standen da als eine Versammlung verschiedener, verschieden großer, in verschiedenem Winkel zueinander stehender Konserven, aus denen kein Entkommen mehr war (nur ein paar Inhalte entrannen).« (Peter Handke)

Traffic at rest. Car parks and multi-storeys. Garages. The new aesthetic of these places. The melancholy, the order.
Suffocating in the mass: mobility ends here, standing, at rest, motionless, jammed. »Parked cars stood there as an assembly of different tin cans, of varying sizes, at different angles to each other, and it was no longer possible to escape from them (it was just that some of the contents ran out).« (Peter Handke)

Straßen aus Asphalt und Beton oder Schienen aus Stahl: Eisenbahn. Die Bewegung ist genau vorgegeben, es gibt keine Abweichung. Immer höhere Geschwindigkeiten sind möglich. Fahrpläne, Bahnhöfe.

Roads made of asphalt and concrete or rails made of steel: railway. The movement is precisely prescribed, there can be no deviation. Ever higher speeds are possible. Timetables. Stations.

Dann das Fliegen: Sich über die Landschaft erheben, erst wenige Meter, dann höher und höher, die Wolkendecke durchstoßen, in den ewigen Sonnentag hinein. Städte und Landschaften von oben sehen, zum ersten Mal werden Stadtpläne und Grundrisse wahrhaftig.
Überblick als Strukturerkenntnis. Zusammenhänge sehen, Verbindungen, Zusammenballungen und Zerstreutheiten.

Then flying: rising above the landscape, first a few metres, then higher and higher, thrusting through the cloud covering into the day of eternal sun. Seeing cities and landscapes from above, town plans and ground plans become real for the first time.
An overview as perception of structure. Seeing links, connections, concentrations and dispersions.

Landschaft heute
Landschaft als Fabrikationsraum

Landscape today
Landscape as a space for manufacture

Die Landwirtschaft teilt die Landschaftsfreiflächen in Felder ein, die mit Pflügen bearbeitet werden. Auf jedem Feld ist nur eine Frucht zugelassen: Weizen, Gerste, Raps, Dinkel, Mais oder Sonnenblumen beispielsweise.

Agriculture divides open landscape space into fields that are then ploughed. Only one crop per field is permitted: wheat, barley, rape, spelt, maize or sunflowers, for example.

Felder: Gleichheit wird mit einem Blick sichtbar. Millionen von Körnern sind in die Erdfurchen gestreut worden. Jetzt steht hier die aufgegangene Saat wie in einer Fabrikhalle. Fließbänder für den Wind. Monokultur für einsilbige Denker. Die Vielfalt wird bekämpft, die Einfalt verherrlicht. Nur diese eine Sache will man haben, nur diesen Weizen, diesen Hafer, sonst nichts. Das weiße Quadrat auf weißer Fläche. Die Radikalität der Kunst. Feld an Feld, Quadrat an Quadrat. Dazwischen die asphaltierten und betonierten schnurgeraden Feldwege für den Betrachter und den angreifenden Landwirt.

Fields: their identical nature is visible at a glance. Millions of grains have been sown in the furrows. Now the grown seeds stand as though they are in a factory hall. Conveyor belts for the wind. Monoculture for monosyllabic thinkers. Diversity is resisted, simplicity extolled. Only this one thing is wanted, only this wheat, this oats, nothing else. The white square on a white surface. The radicality of art. Field after field, square after square. In between asphalted, dead straight field paths for observers and the attacking farmer.

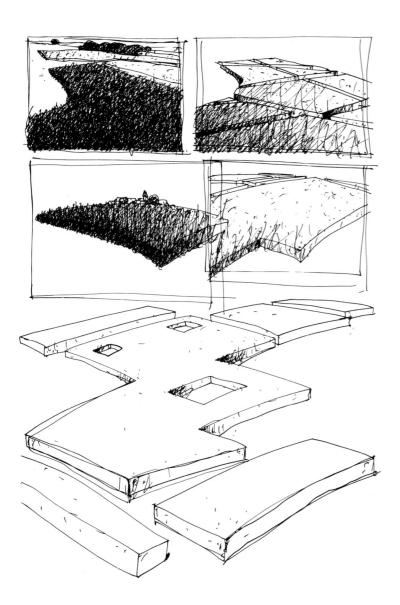

Ernte: Das Säen erfolgt durch den Menschen (den Landwirt), die eigentliche Wachstumsarbeit führt die Natur aus, das Ernten geschieht wieder durch den Menschen beziehungsweise seine Maschinen.

Harvest: sowing is the work of man (the farmer), the actual work of growth is carried out by nature, harvesting is again done by man, and his machines respectively.

Instrumente des Beschneidens, des Zerteilens, des Durchfurchens, des Pflügens. Was zu Beginn der landwirtschaftlichen Nutzung noch handliches, kleines Gerät war, wächst im Laufe der Zeit zum Maschinenpark aus, der fast militärischen Charakter hat.

Instruments for cutting, for dividing, for making furrows, for ploughing. In the early days of agricultural use of landfarming this equipment was small and easily carried, but it has grown in the course of time in a machine of an almost paramilitary character.

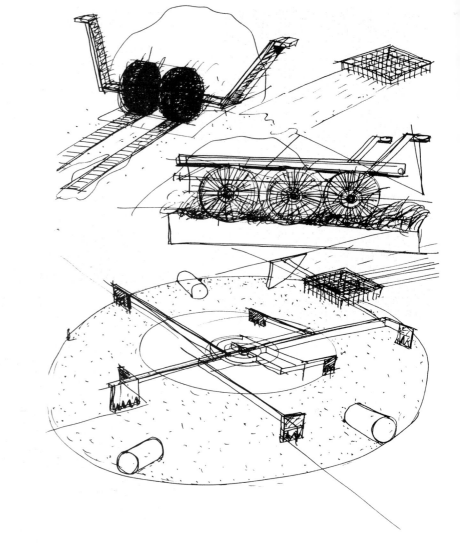

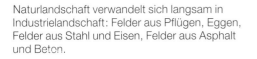

Naturlandschaft verwandelt sich langsam in Industrielandschaft: Felder aus Pflügen, Eggen, Felder aus Stahl und Eisen, Felder aus Asphalt und Beton.

Natural landscape slowly changes into industrial landscape: fields of ploughs, harrows, fields of steel and iron, fields of asphalt and concrete.

Andere Fabrikationsformen in der Landschaft: Viehwirtschaft, Gartenbau, Fortwirtschaft.

Jede Nutzung, jeder Anbau und Abbau bringt eine eigene Ästhetik in die Landschaft. Grundtendenz ist überall die Begradigung, der leichte Zugang und der bequeme Abtransport.
Der ursprünglich chaotische Wald, der undurchdringliche Urwald wird von der Forstwirtschaft zu einer geordneten Fabrikationshalle umgebaut.

Other forms of manufacture in the landscape: livestock farming, market gardening, forestry.

Every use, every planting and cropping brings its own aesthetic to the landscape. The basic tendency everywhere is straightening, ease of access and transport.
The originally chaotic forest, the impenetrable jungle is reshaped by forestry to make an ordered manufacturing hall.

Landschaftsabbau: Steinbrüche, Kieswerke, Salzbergwerke, Kohlebergwerke, Uranbergwerke, Ölquellen usw. Alles, was für den Menschen verwendbar ist, wird seit Jahrhunderten rücksichtslos abgebaut. Erst seit einigen Jahrzehnten breitet sich die Gewißheit aus, daß der Vorrat begrenzt ist, daß die Ressourcen bald zu Ende gehen. Bestrebungen, erneuerbare Quellen zu nutzen, gibt es in allen Bereichen.

Extraction from the landscape: quarries, gravel pits, salt mines, coal mines, uranium mines, oil wells etc. Everything that is useful to man has been ruthlessly mined for centuries. It is only a few decades since a certainty has spread that supplies are limited, that the resources will soon be exhausted. Attempts are being made to use renewable sources in all spheres.

Zentrales Thema in diesem Zusammenhang ist die Energiefrage. Bis heute verheizt die Bevölkerung der nördlichen Halbkugel noch immer Kohle und Öl, beides Naturstoffe, die in absehbarer Zeit nicht erneuert werden können. Die Atomenergie ist bekanntlich umstritten, und neue Technologien befinden sich im Experimentalstadium. Der Blick auf die Natur, ihre Strukturen und ihre Verarbeitungsweisen, der Sonnenenergie beispielsweise, ist wichtig geworden. Ähnliches gilt für Techniken, die heute mit, an und parallel zur Natur arbeiten: Physik, Chemie, Biochemie, Pharmazie und Medizin. Überall ist man heute bestrebt, Kreisläufe nach dem Modell der Natur zu entwickeln.

The central theme in this context is the energy question. Today the population of the northern hemisphere is still burning oil and coal, both natural materials that will not be renewable in the foreseeable future. Atomic energy is known to be controversial, and new technologies are at the experimental stage. Looking at nature, its structures and processing methods, solar energy for example has become important. The same is true of technologies that work today with, on and parallel to nature: physics, chemistry, biochemistry, pharmacy and medicine. Everywhere attempts are being made to develop cycles modelled on nature.

Landschaft heute
Stadtlandschaften

Landscape today
City landscapes

Stadt: das gebaute, rein vom Menschen gemachte Gegenbild zur Landschaft. Natur ist bedeckt von Asphalt, Stein und Beton. Nur in kleinen Oasen tritt sie in Erscheinung, wird zum besonderen, fremden Ereignis. Ein Hauch von Urzeit, von Urwald weht durch jeden Stadtpark. Stadt ist heute und jetzt. Überall hängen Uhren. Informationen erscheinen auf großen Bildschirmen.

City: the built counter-image to landscape, made by man alone. Nature is covered by asphalt, stone and concrete. It appears only in little oases, becomes a special and alien event. A breath of primeval times, of jungle, wafts through every urban park. Cities are today and now. Clocks hang everywhere. Information appears on large screens.

Die Elemente der Landschaft –, Hügel, Tal, Fluß, Fels, Berg – haben sich in geometrische Körper verwandelt. Die Stadt als geometrisierte Wiederholung der Landschaft. Künstliche Natur.

The elements of the landscape – hill, valley, river, rock, mountain – have transformed themselves into geometrical bodies. The city as a geometrized repetition of the landscape. Artificial nature.

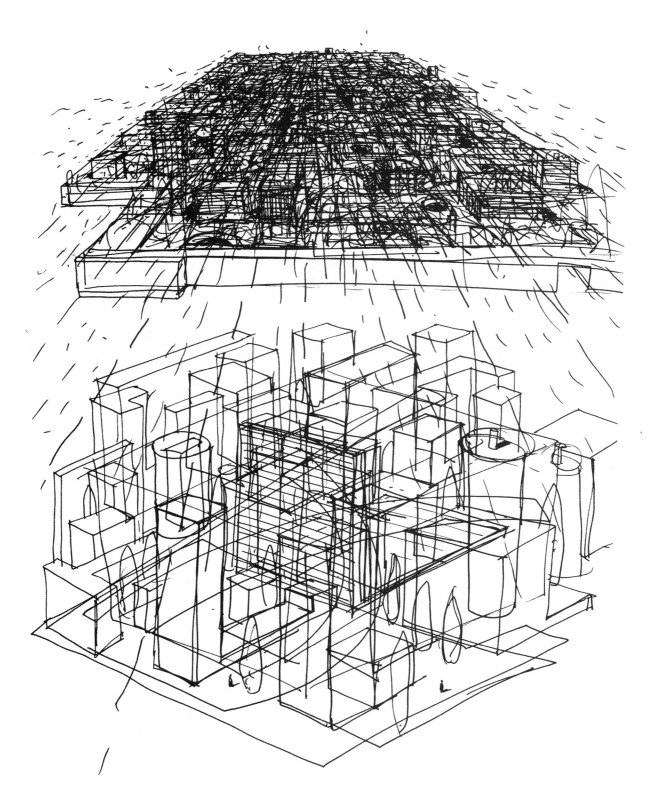

Wie aus einem Stein gehauen.

As if hewn from a single stone.

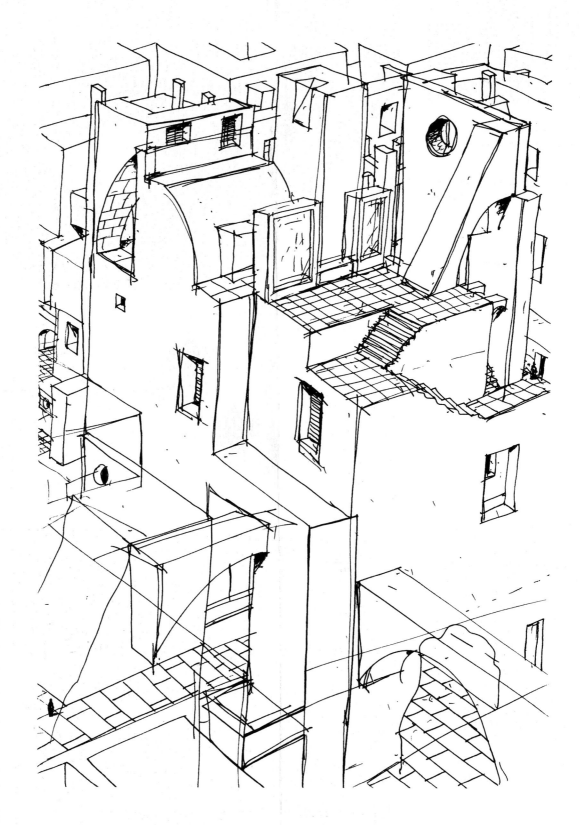

Dachlandschaften: Vor allem der Blick von oben auf eine Stadt zeigt die Ähnlichkeit mit gewachsener Landschaft.

Roof landscapes: looking down on a city in particular shows the similarity to natural landscape.

Abgründe, Höhlen, Täler, Felsschluchten.

Abysses, caves, valleys, rocky gorges.

Wege, Straßen, Spuren: »Die ›Krise der Stadt‹ tritt im Verkehrsproblem banal und drastisch zutage. Hier zeigt sich, daß die ›Krise‹ in einem Selbstwiderspruch besteht, der sich in vielen Formen und Verkleidungen wiederholt: Mobilität ist ein Ideal des städtischen Lebens. Aber die uferlose Zunahme an Mobilität führt zur Immobilität. Der überbordende Verkehr stellt sich selbst still. Darin verrät sich viel. Es wird bildhaft deutlich, daß die Mobilität in sich selbst – und von Anfang an – eine Form der Immobilität gewesen ist. Weil es sich um einen inneren Widerspruch handelt, müssen alle am äußeren Symptom ansetzenden Maßnahmen auf die Dauer scheitern.« (Heinrich Rombach)

Paths, roads, tracks: »The ›crisis of the city‹ is revealed in a banal and drastic manner in the traffic problem. Here it can be seen that the crisis consists of a self-contradiction that is repeated in many forms and disguises: mobility is an ideal of urban life. But boundless increases in mobility lead to immobility. Overflowing traffic brings itself to a standstill.
This gives a lot away. It is vividly clear that mobility as such – and from the beginning – has been a form of immobility. Because we are dealing with an internal contradiction, all measures aimed at the external symptoms will ultimately come to nothing.« (Heinrich Rombach)

Geometrie des Alltags. Choreographie des Verkehrs. Dynamik. Sichtbares und Unsichtbares. Blicke, die sich kreuzen. Handlungsfragmente, unerklärbar, die herausgeschnitten auftauchen und wieder verlöschen. Wie vorbeihuschende Autos: Man erfährt nichts über den Anfang und nichts über das Ende der Fahrt. Kreisläufe, jeden Tag aufs neue, nie gleichen sie einander. Keine exakten Wiederholungen, keine Spiegelungen. Zufall. Labyrinth im Labyrinth. Tautologie.

Geometry of every day. Choreography of traffic. Dynamics. Visible things and invisible things. Glances that meet. Fragments of action, inexplicable, that crop up as something cut out and then disappear again. Like cars swishing past: we do not discover anything about the beginning or end of the journey. Cycles, new every day, never exactly the same. No exact repetitions, no reflections.Chance. Labyrinth in the labyrinth. Tautology.

Im Strömen wenige Inseln der Ruhe, Haltestellen beispielsweise. Sie stehen da wie Fragmente einer anderen Zeit. Menschen kauern darin, mit leeren Blicken, in Erwartung der Erlösung. Tempel vielleicht, Heiligtümer des Ortswechsels.

Very few islands of peace in the streams, for example bus or tram stops. They stand there like fragments of another age. People cower in them with empty looks, expecting redemption. Temples perhaps, shrines to changing places.

Dagegen die Banalität der Häuser, der Fassaden, der Straßen und Plätze.

And in contrast the banality of the buildings, façades, roads and squares.

Die Städte sind durchzogen von sichtbaren und unsichtbaren Grenzlinien: Zäune, Mauern, Linien, Ketten, Geländer, Stützen, Randsteine, Gestänge, Tresen, Drehtüren, Worte, Bestimmungen, Tafeln, Anweisungen, automatische Lichtschranken. Wer die Grenzen übertritt, läuft Gefahr, überfahren oder verhaftet zu werden. Dazu kommen Reklametafeln mit Bildern und Schriften: Aufforderungen und Empfehlungen zum Kauf. Ein Labyrinth aus Zeichen und Codes.

Cities are traversed by visible and invisible borderlines: fences, walls, lines, chains, railings, joists, kerbstones, struts, counters, revolving doors, words, regulations, tables, instructions, automatic light barriers. Anyone who fails to toe the line is in danger of being run over or arrested. Advertising spaces with images and writing appear, invitations and recommendations to buy. A labyrinth of signs and codes.

Gehäuse für das Leben, übereinandergestapelt.
Wände, Fenster.
Davor die Fassaden als Zeitschichten. Hinter
jeder Haut liegt eine andere Haut, ein weiterer
Körper, die nächste, die ältere Zeit. Archäologie.

Casings for life, piled one on top of the other.
Walls, windows.
In front of them the façades as layers of time.
Behind each skin is another skin, another body,
the next, the earlier time. Archaeology.

Löcher im Boden geben den Blick frei ins Innere
des Stadtkörpers, in die Eingeweide. Man sieht
die Nerven, das Blut, die verdrängten Aspekte.

Holes in the ground give a glimpse of the interior
of the urban body, into the entrails. You see the
nerves, the bloodied, and suppressed aspects.

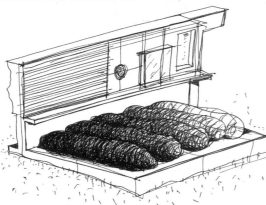

91

Wenn es dunkelt, zeigt die Stadt ihr bedrohliches Gesicht. Sie wird nicht mehr von der Sonne beleuchtet, sondern leuchtet selbst, aus sich heraus. Aus allen Ritzen quillt das Böse, es kommt aus Kellern und finsteren Gängen, entsteigt schummrigen Bars und schleimigen Peep-Shows. In den Straßen lauert Mord und Überfall, Gefahr und Angst.

When it starts to get dark the city shows its threatening face. It is no longer lit by the sun, but shines itself, from within itself. Evil pours out of every crack, comes out of cellars and dark corridors, slips out of gloomy bars and slimy peepshows. In the streets lurk murder and assault, danger and fear.

Die Fußgängerzonen werden zu Bereichen des Übergangs. Unter den Steinplatten glüht die verdrängte Innenwelt, glüht das Jenseits, die Hölle.

Pedestrian areas become realms of transition. Below the stone slabs glows the suppressed world of the interior, glows the hereafter, and hell.

Die nächtlichen Stadtparks sind die surrealsten Orte. Im grellen Licht der Straßenbeleuchtung scheint es, als seien die Äste aus Eis und Schnee. Vielleicht ist die Welt hier ein Röntgenbild oder ein Fernsehbild, übertragen aus dem Weltall. Eine neue Romatik entsteht, giftig und künstlich, grell und scharf. Der ferne Autolärm klingt wie das Rauschen der Meeresbrandung.

Nocturnal urban parks are the most surreal places. In the harsh light of the street lamps the branches seem to be made of ice and snow. Perhaps the world here is an x-ray or a television picture, broadcast from outer space. A new Romanticism is born, poisonous and artificial, harsh and sharp. The distant noise of cars sounds like the rustle of surf.

Am hellen Tag sind diese Stadtparks Ersatz-Natur für Kinder und alte Menschen. Hier wird gespielt, man führt Hunde aus, füttert Tauben und Enten.

By daylight these parks are substitute nature for children and old people. Here games are played and dogs taken for walks, pigeons and ducks are fed.

Parks heute, in Paris beispielsweise, den Strömen der Menschen ausgesetzt, dem Vandalismus, den parkenden Autos, den Hunden. Natur überlebt nur noch, wenn sie durch Zäune und Käfige geschützt wird. Blumen blühen in gefangenen, unbetretbaren, abgesenkten Gartenfragmenten, Efeu wächst nur noch in gesicherten höheren Regionen, Wasser plätschert in immer gleichen stereotypen Formen und verströmt statt Naturgeruch einen Gestank aus Chlor und Urin. Keine Algen wachsen mehr, alles ist clean wie in einem Stadtbad. Hygiene auch hier.

Im Grunde sind in den Großstädten nur noch Gartenfestungen möglich oder vandalensichere Steingärten, gegossen aus Beton. Natur mit Video-Überwachung. Architektur und Natur als Waffe gegen die Brutalität der rücksichtslos gewordenen Stadtmenschen.

Parks today, in Paris, for example: exposed to streams of people, to vandalism, to parking cars, to dogs. Nature survives only when protected by fences and cages. Flowers bloom in captured sunken garden fragments, on which it is not possible to tread, ivy grows only in secured higher regions, water splashes in stereotyped forms that are always the same and instead of a natural smell exudes a stench of chlorine and urine. No water-weed grows any more, everything is as clean as the municipal swimming pool. Hygiene here as well.

Fundamentally all that is now possible in large towns are garden fortresses, or vandal-proof stone gardens, cast in concrete. Nature with video surveillance. Architecture and nature as a weapon against the brutality of city people who have become ruthless.

Natur- und Dorfleben als TV-Direktübertragung in die städtischen Wohnzimmer. Das Rauschen der Wälder, das Zwitschern der Vögel, das Klatschen der Brandung, das Plätschern der Gebirgsbäche, das Heulen des Windes: alle Naturgeräusche werden im Radio gesendet.

Nature and village life as a direct television transfer into an urban living-room. The rustle of the woods, the twittering of the birds, the crash of the surf, the splashing of mountain streams, the howling of the wind: all the noises of nature are broadcast on the radio.

Landschaft heute
Markante Einzelorte innerhalb des Stadtgefüges

Landscape today
Striking individual places within the structure of the city

Sportlandschaften: Jede Sportart hat durch ihre Funktionsbedingtheiten und ihre Regeln eine eigene Landschaftsarchitektur hervorgebracht: Fußballplätze, Stadien, Laufbahnen, Weitsprunganlagen, Hochsprunganlagen, Speerwurf- und Hammerwurfanlagen, Golfplätze, Rennbahnen für Autos, Fahrräder, Motorräder, Bobs usw. Sprungschanzen, Reiterparcoure, Minigolfanlagen usw.
Die Grenzlinien und die dabei entstehenden Architekturen sind oft so interessant und absurd, daß sie in zukünftigen neuen Gartenanlagen aufgegriffen werden sollten.

Sport landscapes: every kind of sport has produced landscape architecture of its own as a result of its structural nature: football pitches, stadiums, running tracks, long jump pits, high jump pits, javelin- and hammer-throwing facilities, golf courses, racing tracks for cars, bicycles, motorbikes, bob sleighs etc., ski-jumping hills, riding courses, mini-golf courses etc.
The borderlines and the architecture they produce are often so interesting and absurd that they should be taken up for the garden designs of the future.

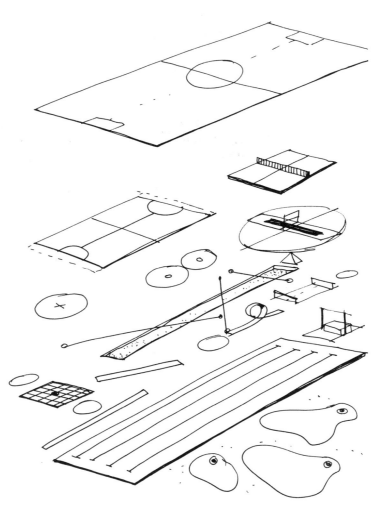

Funktionslandschaften: Industriegebiete:
Gehäuse um Maschinen. Ziel ist die klare Funkti-
onserfüllung. Alles ist nach dem Prinzip der kür-
zesten Wege und der größten Wirtschaftlichkeit
angelegt.
Die Verhüllungen sind nur partiell. Surreale Städte
und Landschaften entstehen, Zementwerke und
Raffinerien.

*Functional landscapes. Industrial estates: cas-
ings around machines and conveyor belts. The
aim is clear fulfilment of function. Everything is
arranged according to the principle of shortest
routes and maximum economy.
The masking is only partial. Surreal cities and
landscapes are produced, cement factories and
refineries for example.*

Tankstellen – Landschaften
Bahnhofslandschaften.

Petrol station landscapes.
Station landscapes.

Umspannwerke. Technische Landschaften.
Transformer stations. Technical landscapes.

Container, Silos, Kräne.
Containers, silos, cranes.

Botanische Gärten: Immer schon dienten sie weniger der Unterhaltung als dem wissenschaftlichen Interesse. Jede Universität hatte seit dem Ende des Mittelalters ihren eigenen botanischen Garten. Glashäuser: Orangerien usw.

Botanical gardens: they served less for entertainment than for scientific interest all along. Every university had its own botanical garden from the late Middle Ages. Glasshouses: orangeries etc.

Zoologische Gärten: Ausstellung von wilden Tieren in Käfigen und Gehegen.

Zoos: exhibitions of wild animals in cages and enclosures.

Was mit Bären im Zwinger und in Gruben (seit dem Mittelalter) begann und zu Menagerien auswuchs, wird heute parkartig präsentiert: die gesamte Tierwelt wie in einem Lexikon. Der Aspekt des Gefängnisses ist heute vom Aspekt der Arche Noah ersetzt worden: Viele Tierarten können nur noch im geschützten Bereich der Zoologischen Gärten überleben, in freier Wildbahn sind sie längst vom Aussterben bedroht.

It all started with bears in enclosures and pits (from the Middle Ages), then grew into menageries and is now presented in a park-like fashion: the whole of the animal as if in a dictionary. Prison has now been replaced by Noah's Ark: many species can survive only in the protected sphere of the zoological garden, in the wild they were threatened with extinction long ago.

Friedhofslandschaften: Hier findet alles menschliche Leben ein Ende. Die Idee der Stadt wiederholt, verkleinert zwar, aber klar erkennbar. Friedhöfe waren von Anfang an Orte zwischen Stadt und Landschaft. Übergangsräume.

Cemetery landscapes: here all life comes to an end. The idea of the city is repeated, reduced in size, but clearly recognizable. Cemeteries have been places between town and landscape from the earliest days. Transitional spaces.

Stadtrandlandschaften: die Städte haben heute keine klare Begrenzung mehr wie zu Zeiten von Stadtmauer und Stadttor. Die Ränder sind unklar, zerfranst, die Bebauung wird niedriger, Industriehallen und Schrebergärten sind hier angesiedelt, große Parkplätze, Supermärkte, Friedhöfe und Müllplätze.

Landscapes on the urban periphery: today cities have no clear boundaries, unlike the times of city walls and gates. The edges are unclear, frayed, buildings become lower, industrial halls and allotments are sited here, large car parks, supermarkets, cemeteries and refuse dumps.

Müllhalden. Müllawinen. Müllgletscher. Berge aus Glas, Flaschen, Berge aus Blech, Berge aus Kleidern und Zeitungen.

Müll-Landschaften: Weiter draußen vor der Stadt türmen sich Müllgebirge, Deponien und Müllverbrennungsanlagen. Die Müllbeseitigung ist zum zentralen Problem unserer Zivilisation geworden. Was in den Städten für Sauberkeit und Hygiene, für eine glänzende Oberfläche aufgewendet wird, zeigt hier seine häßliche Kehrseite: die leeren Hüllen, die Dosen, Flaschen, die Tüten und Kartons. Die Archäologen des nächsten Jahrtausends werden bei ihren Grabungen vor allem auf Müll stoßen.

Aus den Rohren der Kanalisation fließt das Abwasser der Städte, giftig und stinkend. Würden unsere Weltmeere weniger groß sein, wäre unsere Zivilisation schon längst im eigenen Müll und am selbst produzierten Schmutzwasser erstickt.

Vorstellung: Pompejis Schicksal, nicht von Lava, sondern von Müll begraben, übertragen auf die großen Metropolen dieser Welt.

Refuse dumps. Refuse avalanches. Refuse glaciers. Mountains of glass, bottles, mountains of tin, mountains of clothing and newspapers.
Refuse landscapes: further out of the city mountains of refuse tower up, dumps and refuse incineration plants. Refuse disposal has become a central problem of our civilization. What in the city is used to provide a shiny surface in the name of cleanliness and hygiene shows its ugly other face here: the empty covers, tins, bottles, bags and cartons. Archaeologists of the next millennium will come across refuse more than anything else in their excavations.
Sewage from the cities flows through the pipes of the sewerage system, poisonous and stinking. When the world's oceans were not so large our civilization would long since have suffocated in its own refuse and the dirty water it produces itself. Imagine: the fate of Pompeii, buried not in lava but in refuse, transferred to the world's metropolises.

Landschaft heute
Landschaftsausstellungen – Ausstellungslandschaften

Landscape today
Landscape exhibitions – exhibition landscapes

Landschaften mit Industriemessen, Jahrmärkten, Weltausstellungen, Vergnügungsparks, Filmstädten, Gartenschauen, Disney-Worlds, Epcots: Alle diese Ausstellungen haben mehr oder weniger bizarre Gebilde zwischen Landschaft und Architektur hervorgebracht.

Landscapes with trade fairs, markets, world fairs, pleasure parks, film cities, garden shows, Disney worlds, Epcots: all these exhibitions have come up with more or less bizarre structures – somewhere in between landscape and architecture.

Vergnügungs-Landschaften. Elemente der Stadt und der Natur werden ineinandercollagiert, gemalt, kulissenartig gebaut, aus Neon-Röhren nachgebildet.

Pleasure landscapes. Elements of the city and nature are made into a collage, painted, built like a stage set, imitated by neon tubes etc.

Theater-Landschaften. Film-Landschaften. Studio-Landschaften.

Theatre landscapes. Film landscapes. Studio landscapes.

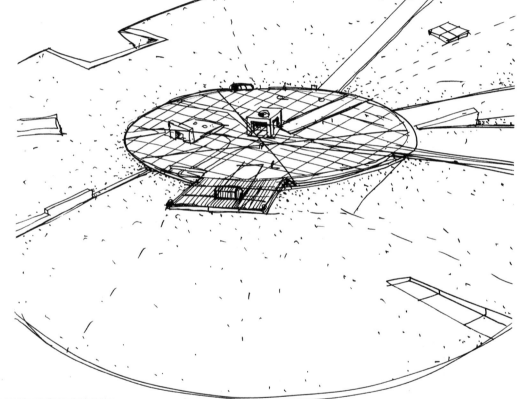

Science-fiction-Landschaft. Mischung aus utopischen Elementen und urwaldartiger Vegetation. Halbinsel vom Meer umgeben.

Science-fiction landscape. Mixture of utopian elements and jungle-like vegetation. A peninsula, bounded by the sea.

Zukünftige Gärten? Rotierend in neonbeleuchteten Trommeln oder hängend an künstlichen Gerüsten.

Gardens of the future? Rotating in neon-lit drums or hanging in artificial scaffolding.

Landschaft heute
Künstliche Landschaften, Medien

Landscape today
Artificial landscapes, Media

Heute hat man die Welt gesehen, alle Landschaften photographiert und abgefilmt. Vor die reale Natur hat sich die fiktive Natur der Medien geschoben. Zum Erlebnis muß man die realen Orte nicht mehr ansteuern, man kann sich die Sonnenuntergänge als Direktübertragungen ins Wohnzimmer flimmern lassen, bequem im Sessel sitzend, oder man kann sie synthetisch produzieren.

Today we have seen the world, photographed and filmed all the landscapes. The fictitious nature of the media has been placed in front of real nature. It is no longer necessary to make for the real places to have an experience, sunsets can come flickering into our living-rooms as direct broadcasts, and you can watch them sitting comfortably in your chair, or they can be produced synthetically.

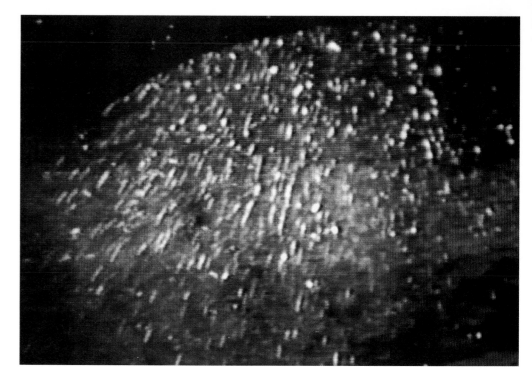

Jahreszeiten als Pausenzeichen. Verwischungen, Austauschungen, Collagen. Schnitte. Alles ist reproduzierbar. Realität wird konserviert. Zeit und Leben aufbewahrt. Der Tod erhält eine andere Realität.
Das Bild des Gartens gegen die Realität des Gartens. Gerasterte Wirklichkeit. Wirklichkeit, wie durch einen Rechen gezogen. Stehende Bilder, laufende Bilder, verlangsamte Bilder, beschleunigte Bilder. Rückwärtslaufende Zeit.

Seasons marking a break. Smudges. Exchanges. Collages. Cuts. Everything can be reproduced. Reality is preserved. Time and life stored up. Death is given a different reality. The image of the garden as opposed to the reality of the garden. Scanned reality. Reality as if drawn through a rake. Still pictures, moving pictures, sloweddown pictures, speeded-up pictures. Time moving backwards.

Die Tagesschau liefert jeden Abend eine Weltreise mit den wichtigsten Ereignissen. Die Wetterkarte zeigt den Blick von oben. Man sieht das eigene Land und hat den Überblick.

The television news provides a journey round the world each evening, with the most important events. The weather map shows a view from above. You can see your own country, and get a general view.

Landschaft heute
Tourismus

Landscape today
Tourism

Bevor sich die Medien entwickelten, war der Tourismus die wichtigste Form der Welterfahrung. Der Tourist zog seine Kreise, erst kleine, dann immer größere. Heute gibt es kaum einen Winkel in der Welt, in dem nicht Touristen anzutreffen sind. Wie alle Evolutionen hat auch die Evolution des Tourismus zwei Aspekte, einen positiven und einen negativen. Der positive besteht darin, daß der Tourist andere Landschaften, andere Völker und andere Sitten kennengelernt hat, wodurch er meist an Weltläufigkeit und Toleranz gewinnt. Kehrseite dessen ist die Vernichtung regionaler Eigenarten durch Hotel- und Tourismusfolgeneinerlei. Im Massentourismus erstickt jede Landschaft und jede schöne Stelle.

Before the media developed tourism was the most important way to experience the world. Tourists described their circles, first small ones, then they got bigger and bigger. Today there is scarcely a corner of the world where there are no tourists. Like all evolution the evolution of tourism has two aspects, a positive and a negative one. The positive one is that tourists get to know different landscapes, different peoples and different customs, thus usually gaining awareness of the world and tolerance. The other side of this is the destruction of the particular regional characteristics by the monotony produced by hotels and tourists. Every landscape and every ›beauty spot‹ is suffocated by mass tourism.

Sonnenuntergänge auf Capri, Sonnenaufgänge
in Florida und Manhattan, Regenwetter in Stockholm und Schnorcheln auf den Malediven.
Wohnen in Hotels.

Sunsets on Capri, sunrise in Florida and Manhat-
tan, rainy weather in Stockholm and snorkelling in
the Maldives. Living in hotels.

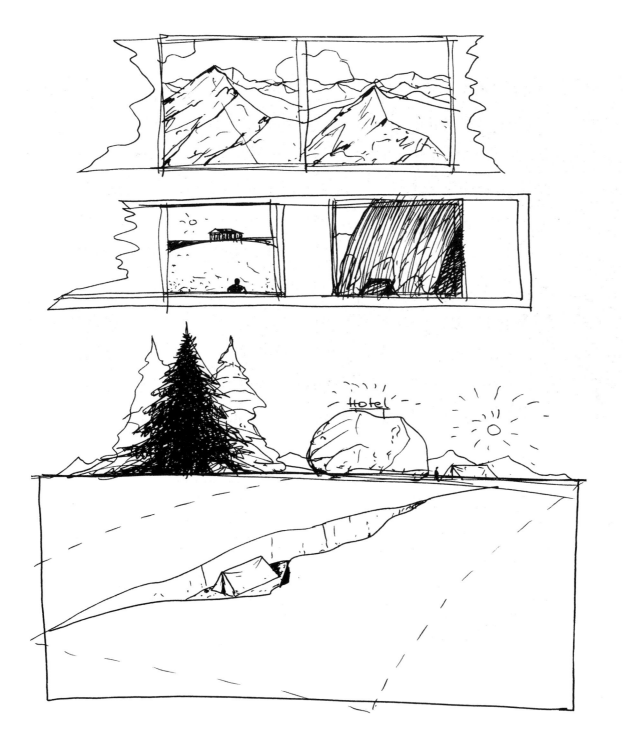

Foto-Landschaften: Der Tourismus führt dazu,
daß die Menschen immer mehr Bilder von extre-
men Landschaften in sich tragen und sie mit der
bestehenden Realität vergleichen.
Heute wandert der Touristenstrom vorbei an allen
schönen Stellen der Welt.

*Photo-landscapes: Tourism means that people
carry increasing numbers of extreme landscapes
within themselves and compare them with exist-
ing reality.*

*Today the stream of tourism wanders past every-
thing beautiful.*

Neue Landschafts- und Gartenarchitektur
Strukturen der Gestaltung

New landscape and garden architecture
Structures of design

Die Überflutung mit Zivilisationsstrukturen hat die Landschaft zu einem Labyrinth aus Innen und Außen, aus Müll und Bildern, aus Lärm und Kommunikation, aus Geometrien und versteinerten Spuren, aus Ampeln und Rolltreppen, aus Landebahnen und klimatisierten Unterführungen, aus neonbeleuchteten Schaufenstern und automatischen Anrufbeantwortern, aus Zeichenwäldern und Fernsehcollagen gemacht. Die Erdoberfläche erträgt dieses wahnwitzige Geflecht in schweigender Duldsamkeit. Der Himmel überwölbt die Wiesen, Autobahnen und Städte wie zu Beginn der Geschichte. Der Jahreszeitenrhythmus ist immer noch der gleiche, die Vorgänge der Natur, Wachstum und Absterben, vollziehen sich wie am Anfang.

Annäherungen an die Natur sind heute wie ein Griff hinaus aus einer technisch-geometrisierten Umwelt, aus Taumel, Wirbel, kreisendem Reden am Rand eines Trichters, in den Anfang der Welt, in den »letzten Wahrheits-Bereich«.

Nach mehreren Phasen der exzessiven Landschaftszerstörung hat sich in den letzten Jahrzehnten ein ökologisches Bewußtsein durchgesetzt, das heute allerdings Züge hysterischer Übertreibung trägt.

Das Interesse an Natur und Landschaft ist nach dem Verschwinden der globalen Ost-West-Konfrontation ins Zentrum des öffentlichen Bewußtseins gerückt. Alle Medien berichten täglich über die »Umwelt«, wie der umfassende Oberbegriff lautet.

Meist sind es negative Berichte über Umwelt-Verschmutzungen (Müll, Wasser, Baumsterben usw.) und Umwelt-Katastrophen. Aber auch künstliche Befruchtung, Organtransplantation, Gen-Manipulation und Ernteergebnisse interessieren. Gartenschauen erzielen Besucherrekorde. Natur und Landschaft sind wieder zu geachteten Gütern geworden. Man trägt gemeinsam die Verantwortung. Parteigrenzen zählen nicht. Die am Horizont drohende Zerstörung der Welt läßt die Menschheit zu einer Einheit, zu einer Familie werden.

Thema der folgenden Kapitel ist es, die Landschaft als künstlerischen Gestaltungsbereich zurückzugewinnen. Die Sprache der Natur mit ihren Elementen und Erscheinungsformen soll dabei als Ausdrucksmittel eingesetzt werden, ergänzt durch Elemente der Architektur, der Kunst, der Literatur, der Musik und des Theaters. Die Wiesen als riesige Leinwände, die Hügel und Täler als durchgehbare Skulpturen, die Gebirge als Natur-Museen, die Wälder als architektonische Raumfolgen, die Pflanzen, Bäume und Steine als Notationen einer neuen Musik, die Brunnen als Münder der Natur, die Seen als Augen der Landschaft. Zunächst werden die Elemente und Strukturen im einzelnen vorgestellt: Punkt, Linie, Fläche, Feld, Erde, Steine, Pflanzen, Wasser, Wind usw. In diesen Kapiteln wird versucht, das Wesen der Elemente zu beschreiben und die Gestaltungsmöglichkeiten, die sich mit ihn verbinden, zu ermitteln. In den darauf folgenden Kapiteln werden die Elemente zueinander in Beziehung gesetzt, miteinander konfrontiert und miteinander verflochten. Die abschließenden Kapitel beschreiben mögliche Gesamtkompositionen, ergänzt durch Fragmente der heutigen Verkehrs- und Stadtlandschaften. Der Landschaftsraum wird als der umfassende Gestaltungsraum der Zukunft gesehen, die Landschaftsarchitektur selbst als das alle Medien verbindende Gesamt(kunst)werk.

Flooded with the structures of civilization has become the landscape a labyrinth of interior and exterior, of rubbish and images, of noise and communication, of geometries and petrified tracks, of traffic lights and escalators, of runways and air- conditioned underpasses, of neon-lit shop windows and telephone answering machines, of forests of signs and television collages. The surface of the earth supports this crazy tangle with silent patience. The sky arches above the meadows, motorways and cities as it did when history began. The rhythm of the seasons is still the same, and the processes of nature, growth and death, happen as they have done from the beginning.

Today approaches to nature are like putting out a hand between a technical and geometrized environment, a mixture of frenzy, hubbub, circling speeches on the edge of a funnel, into the beginning of the world, into the ›last realm of truth‹. After several phases of excessive landscape destruction, ecological awareness has started to make itself felt in the last few decades, though this is starting to carry traits of hysterical exaggeration.

Interest in nature and landscape has moved to the centre of public awareness since the disappearance of the global confrontation between East and West. All the media carry daily reports about the ›environment‹, as the all-embracing generic term has it.

Usually they are negative reports about environmental pollution (refuse, water, dying trees etc.) and environmental catastrophes. But interest is also aroused by artificial insemination, organ transplants, genetic engineering and harvest statistics. Garden shows have record numbers of visitors. Nature and landscape have become valued goods again. General responsibility is taken. Differences in political parties count for nothing. Destruction threatening on the horizon has made mankind into a unit, into a single family.

The subject of the following chapter is the regaining of the landscape as an area for artistic design. The language of nature with its elements and manifestations is intended to be used as a means of expression here, complemented by elements of architecture, art, literature, music and theatre.

Meadows as gigantic canvases, hills and valleys as sculptures to be walked through, mountains as museums of nature, forests as sequences of architectonic space, plants, trees and stones as notation in a new music, springs as the mouths of nature, lakes as eyes in the landscape. First the elements and structures are introduced individually: point, line, area, fields, earth, stones, plants, water, wind etc. In these chapters an attempt will be made to describe the nature of the elements and to discover the design possibilities associated with them. In the following chapters the elements are related to each other, confronted with each other and interwoven. The concluding chapters describe possible overall compositions, complemented with fragments of today's transport and urban landscapes. Landscape space is seen as the comprehensive design space of the future, and landscape architecture itself as the overall (art) work joining all the media.

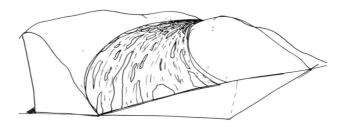

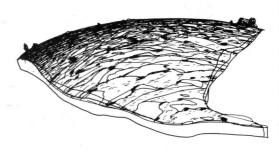

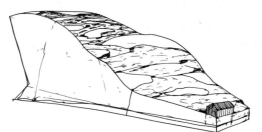

Punkt, Ort, Platz, Garten

Dot, place, square, garden

Geometrische Bausteine der Landschaftsarchitektur in der Fläche sind Punkte, Linien und Felder.

Landscape architecture's geometrical building bricks on the surface are points, lines and fields.

Der Punkt ist das geometrisierte Kürzel des Hier und Jetzt. Kleinstmögliche Markierung des Da-Seins. Zeitlich gesehen zum Beispiel eine Sekunde, räumlich gesehen ein Atom oder eine Zelle, musikalisch ein Schlag, eine Note, landschaftlich ein Stein, ein Busch, ein Baum, ein Stück Wiese.
Vergrößert wird der Punkt zur Stelle, zum Ort, zur kleinsten Einheit im Landschaftsgeflecht. Ein Stück Erdoberfläche, ein Stück Garten, ein kleines Haus.

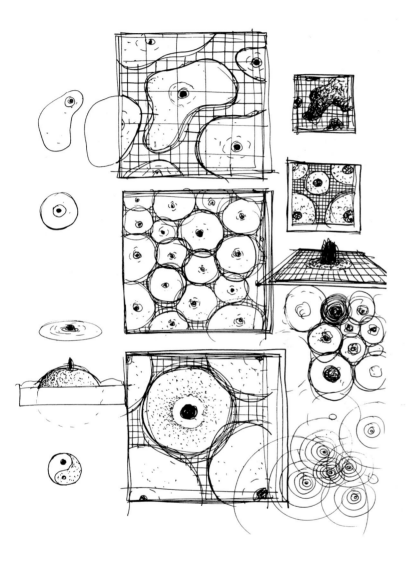

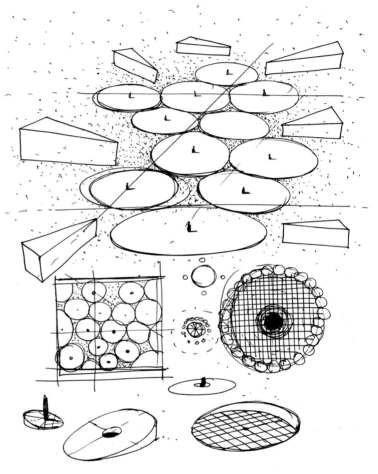

*The dot is the geometrical abbreviation for here and now. The smallest possible marker for existence, for being there. Seen in terms of time for example a second, in terms of space an atom or a cell, musically a beat, a note, in the landscape a stone, a bush, a tree, a piece of lawn.
Enlarged, the dot becomes a spot, a place, the smallest unit in the landscape network. A piece of surface, a piece of garden, a little house.*

Geometrischer Ort, Wohnort, Standort, Denkort, Tatort, archäologischer Ort, Zukunftsort, technischer Ort, Badeort, astronomischer Ort, Ortschaft, Örtchen, Örtlichkeit … Orte der Stille, des Lärms, der Expression, der Konzentration, der Vertiefung, der Erklärung, des Verstummens, des Erstarrens, der Angst, der Freude, des Glücks. Orte der Verhüllung, der Rätselhaftigkeit, der Realität, der Romantik, der Schönheit, der Häßlichkeit, der Armut, des Reichtums, Orte der Geschichte, kein Ort, nirgends …

Geometrical place, place to live, place to be, thinking place, the place where the deed was done, archaeological place, future's place technical place, bathing place, astronomical place, private little place, a feeling for place … places where it is quiet, noisy, expressive, where there is concentration, absorption, enlightenment, falling silent, paralysis, fear, joy, happiness. Places of concealment, mystery, enigma reality, romanticism, beauty, ugliness, poverty, wealth, places steeped in history, no place at all, nowhere …

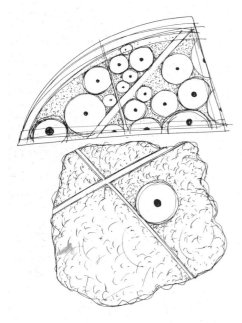

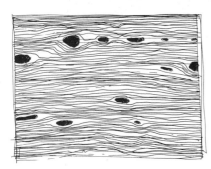

Der Ort im Zeitfluß, im Wegenetz, in der offenen Landschaft.

A place in the flow of time, in the network of paths, in the open landscape.

Der Ort als ausgezonte Fläche.
Das Fließen der Zeit sehen.
Das Wachsen des Grases ringsum hören.

The place as a separate zone. Seeing the flow of time. Hearing the grass grow all around.

116

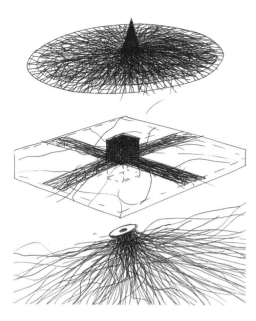

Der Ich-Punkt, der Ich-Ort und der kreisende
Horizont. Hier ist die Mitte der Welt. Schnittpunkt
der vertikalen und der horizontalen Linien.
Sich einlassen auf einen Ort, Wurzeln schlagen.

*The point of the I, the plane of the self and the
circling horizon. This is the centre of the earth.
The point where the vertical and the horizontal
line intersect.
Becoming involved in a place, putting down
roots.*

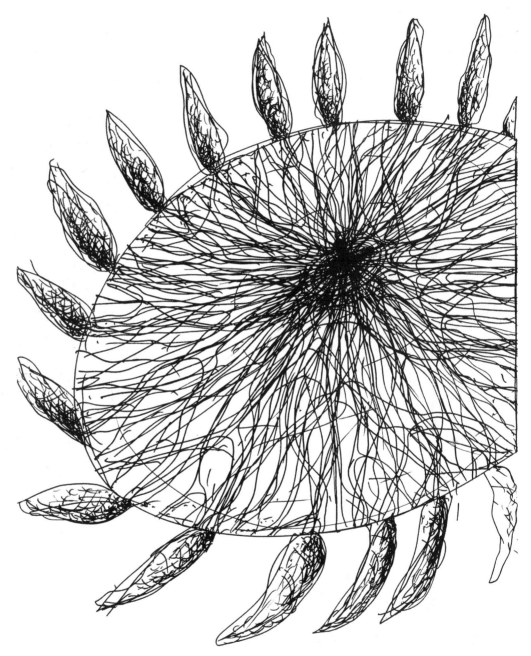

Der Ort als Garten. Wohnen. Der geschützte Ort.
Haus. Ein architektonisch gefaßtes Gefäß für ein
Stück Natur, ein Stück Landschaft. Das Paradies
des Anfangs klingt wieder an. An die Außenwand
brandet Lärm, Gefahr, Gestank und Zersplitte-
rung.

*The place as garden. Living. The protected
place. House. An architectonically shaped vessel
for a spot of nature, a piece of landscape. The
paradise of the beginning resounds again. Noise,
danger, stench and splintering surge against the
outer wall.*

Einkreisung der Natur.
Versuche der Annäherung.
Leben mit der Natur.
Leben in ihr.
Eindringen, Eintreten in die Natur.

*Encirclement of nature.
Attempts to come closer together.
Living with nature.
Living in nature.
Penetrating, stepping into nature.*

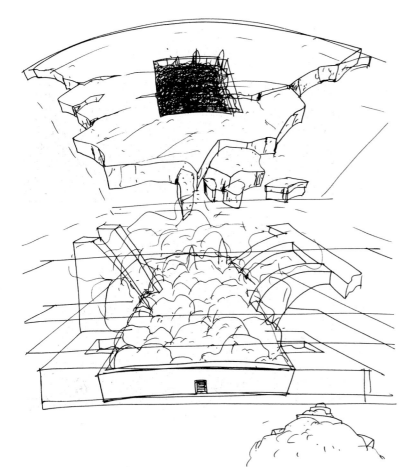

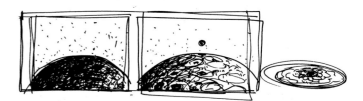

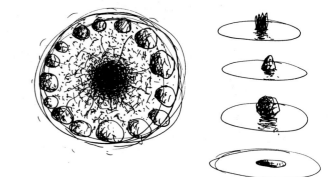

Meditationsort. Konzentration. Alle Linien zielen auf eine Mitte. Energiepunkt. In der Ferne die Krümmung des Horizonts. Darüber das Ziehen der Wolken. Dasein als Pendeln zwischen Wegen nach innen und Wegen nach außen. Einatmen und Ausatmen.

Place of meditation. Concentration. All lines aim at a centre. Focus of energy.
In the distance the curve of the horizon. Above that the procession of the clouds. Existence as a swinging between ways to the inside and ways to the outside. Breathing in and breathing out.

Der Gartenort ist eine Möglichkeit, sich in die Natur zu versenken und in sie einzudringen. Dieser eine Punkt der Erde wird zur Tür, zum Tor, zum Spalt, zur Grotte, zur Höhle, zum Gang nach innen.

The garden place is a possibility of immersing oneself in nature and penetrating it.
This one spot on the earth becomes a door, a gate, a crack, a grotto, a cave, a corridor leading inwards.

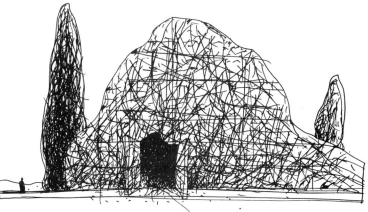

119

Linie, Weg

Line, way

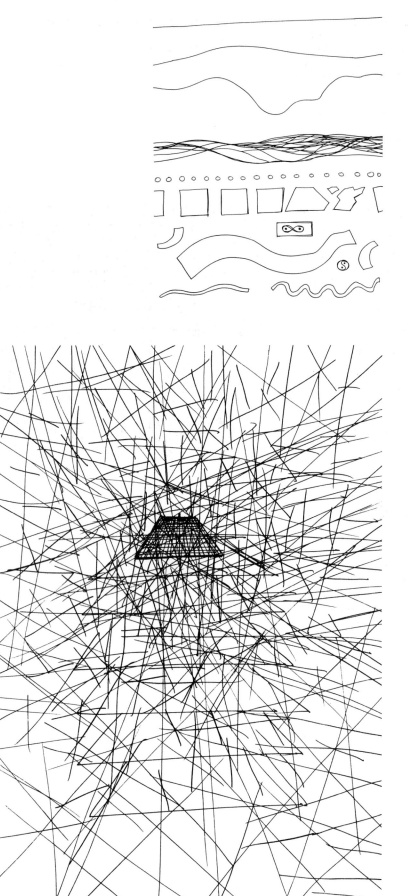

Die Linie ist eine Aneinanderreihung von Punkten. Hier beginnt die Bewegung, das Fließen. Eine Linie kann zwei auseinanderliegende Punkte verbinden, gerade (kürzeste Verbindung) oder geschwungen sein. Vergrößert wird die Linie zum Weg, zur Wegverbindung, zur Straße. Musikalisch gesehen wird sie zur Melodie.
Linien: einsam, gerade, gebogen, gewellt, geschwungen, schmal, breit, zu mehreren, gesellig. Linien-Geflecht. Linien-Mäander. Linien wie Adern.
Monotonie einer Linie. Das langsame Entstehen einer Melodie. Klänge. Cluster. Rhythmen. Quadrate kommen dazu. Zerfallen wieder, Kurven, breite, schmale, sanfte, gewalttätige …

A line is a sequence of juxtaposed dots. Here movement, a flow begins. A line can connect two separate points, be straight (the shortest connection) or curved. Enlarged, the line becomes a path, a connecting path, a road. Seen in terms of music it becomes a melody. Lines: lonely, straight, bent, wavy, curved, narrow, broad, in larger numbers, sociable. Line-network. Line meander. Lines like veins. Monotony of a line. The slow emergence of a melody. Sounds. Clusters. Rhythms.
Squares are added. Break down again, curves, broad, narrow, gentle, violent . . .

Linien-Labyrinth.

Line-labyrinth.

Mit der Linie beginnt die Ordnungsstruktur. Übertragen auf die Landschaft wird mit der Linie eine
Richtung gegeben, werden Zeit und Raum aus
der gleichgültigen Richtungslosigkeit in eine
Richtung gezwungen. Denklinie, Bedeutungskor-
ridor.

*Structural order begins with the line. When trans-
ferred to landscape, a line is used to give direction; time and space are forced out of indifferent
lack of direction into a particular direction. Line of
thought, corridor of meaning.*

Die Linien werden zu Wegen und zu Straßen.

Lines become paths and roads.

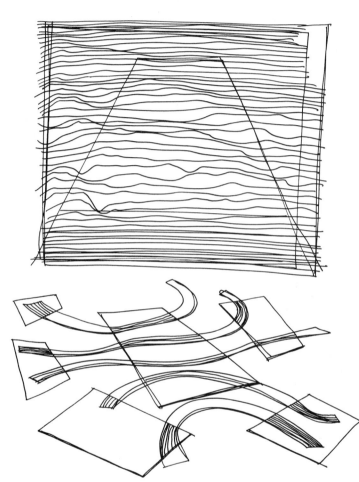

Gerade Wege, gebogene Wege, krumme Wege.
Wege mit begleitenden Hecken und Büschen,
mit Bäumen (Alleen), Wege mit Zielen.
Wege, die zwei Orte miteinander verbinden,
Wege, die eine Landschaft zerschneiden.
Wege mit Treppen, Wege über Hügel und Berge.
Wege, die durch Wälder und Städte führen.
Wege, die am Meer enden.
Kreiswege.
Unendliche Wege.

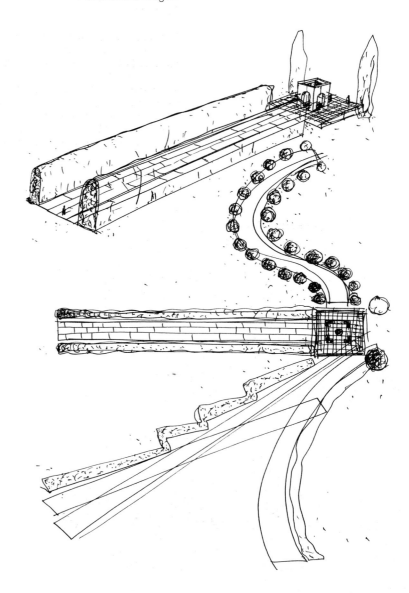

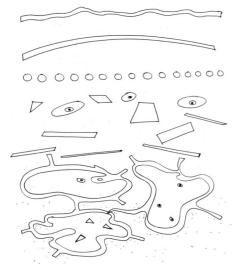

Gehen, Rhythmen, Geschwindigkeit, Bilder.
Wegformen, Wegverläufe, offene und geschlossene Systeme.

Walking, rhythms, speed, images.
Shapes of paths, courses of paths, open and
closed systems.

Straight paths, bent paths, crooked paths. Paths
with accompanying hedges and bushes, with
trees (avenues), paths that lead somewhere.
Paths that connect two places together.
Paths that dissect a landscape.
Paths with steps, paths over hills and mountains.
Paths that lead through woods and towns.
Paths that end at the sea.
Circular paths.
Endless paths.

Felder

Fields

Felder sind vergrößerte Orte, sind verbreiterte Linien, Felder sind Flächen mit aneinandergefügten Orten oder aneinandergefügten Linien. Orteversammlungen und Linienversammlungen. Ortfelder und Linienfelder. Vergrößert werden sie zu Ausschnitten der Erdoberflächen mit topographischen, geologischen und klimatischen Bedingtheiten. Felder aus Schnee und Eis, aus Sand und Wasser, Steinfelder, Wiesenfelder, Erdfelder, Felsfelder, Buschfelder, Blumenfelder, Waldfelder, Hausfelder.

Fields are enlarged places, they are broader lines, fields are areas with places or lines added together. Collections of places and collections of lines. Place fields and line fields. They are enlarged to form sections of the earth's surface with topographical, geological and climatic characteristics. Fields of snow and ice, of sand and water, stone fields, meadow fields, earth fields, rock fields, bush fields, flower fields, wood fields, house fields.

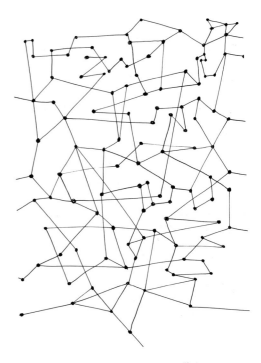

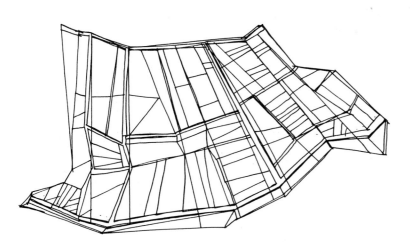

Felder sind flächige (gekrümmt, gewellt oder eben) Ausgangsgebiete einer Entwurfskonzeption und – als begrenzte Formelemente – Teile eines größeren Geflechts, einer größeren Komposition (zusammen mit Punkten, Orten und Linien).

Fields are extensive (curved, rolling or even) starting points for design conception and – as limited elements of form – parts of a larger network, a larger composition (together with dots, places and lines).

Organisation dieser Flächen mit Dingen (Wände, Architekturen, Büsche, Bäume, Hecken, Fontänen, Möbel usw.). Die Dinge gliedern die Fläche. Ihre Ränder bilden die Architektur des Sichtbaren. Die Zwischenräume beginnen zu strömen und zu pulsieren.

Organization of these areas by objects (walls, architecture, bushes, trees, hedges, fountains, furniture etc). Things structure the area. Their edges form the architecture of the visible. The gaps begin to stream and pulsate.

Ding-Felder.

Thing-fields.

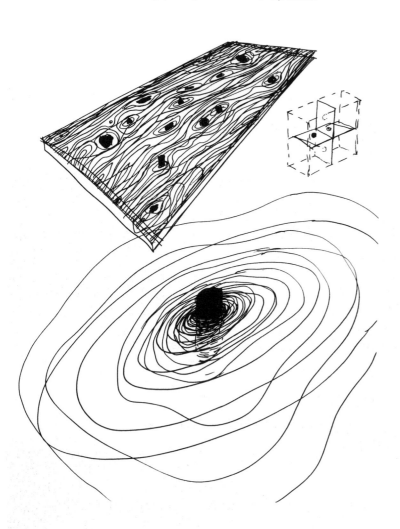

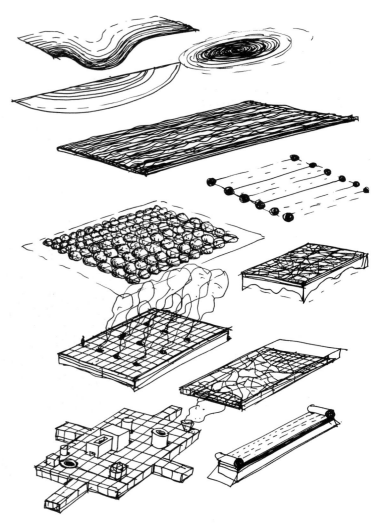

Felder als Ausgangsebenen für Plätze und Gärten. Ansätze von Handlungen und Szenen.

Fields as starting-planes for squares and gardens. Beginnings of action and scenes.

Organisation der Feldflächen:
Zufallsstrukturen

Organization of the field areas:
random structures

Landschaftsarchitektur heißt Organisation von Feldflächen, heißt Komposition von Wegen, Wegteilen, Plätzen, Wiesenflächen, Hügeln, Tälern, Hainen, Hecken, Waldstücken, Bächen, Seen, Rändern, Architekturen, Szenen usw. Struktur meint immer Gefüge, Aufbau, innere Gliederung, Zusammenhang, Bezugssystem im Aufbau des Ganzen, »Lage und Verbindung der Teile eines nach einheitlichem Zweck sich bilden- den Organismus.« (Immanuel Kant) Am Anfang steht der Zufall, stehen die beliebig über die Feld- fläche verteilten Formen. Ein Wirrwarr aus Innen- und Außenräumen.

Landscape architecture means organizing field areas, means composition of paths, parts of paths, squares, meadow areas, hills, valleys, groves, hedges, pieces of forest, streams, lakes, edges, architecture, scenes etc.
Structure always means construction, building up, inner articulation, context, reference system in the build-up of the whole, »situation and con- nection of the pieces of an organism evolving towards a uniform purpose« (Immanuel Kant). At the beginning is chance, and forms are distribut- ed randomly over the field area. A tangle of inter- nal and external spaces.

Zufallsbilder der Natur.

Random images from nature.

Alle in der Natur vorkommenden Formen und Anordnungen (auch in der beschriebenen Feld- fläche) pendeln zwischen Chaos und Ordnung.

All forms and arrangements occurring in nature (in the described field area as well) swing be- tween chaos and order.

Im strengen Raster der Zeitrhythmen, des Herzschlags, des Atmens entfalten sich die wirren Gedankenströme des Ich, die chaotischen Bewegungen des Alltags, die Flugbahnen der Wolken, der Vögel und der Insekten. Kaum etwas läßt sich vorhersagen. Nur die Vergangenheit ist dokumentierbar.

Aus einem Durcheinander von Gedanken und Ideen formt sich langsam eine Struktur, eine Linie, ein Raster heraus. Alles Entwerfen ist so gesehen immer auch Nachvollziehung des Ur-akts: Aus dem Chaos entwickeln sich Ordnungen und Strukturen.
Das Belassen des Wirrwarrs und des anfänglichen Durcheinanders ist ein Hinweis auf die Künstlichkeit von Ordnungen, auf die idealisierte Setzung: Unter jeder Ordnung brodelt die Lava des Chaos. Mögliche Ordnungen halten das Chaos in Schach, sind Schutzwälle gegen Wirbel und Durcheinander, leuchtende Zeichen über den schwarzen Löchern.

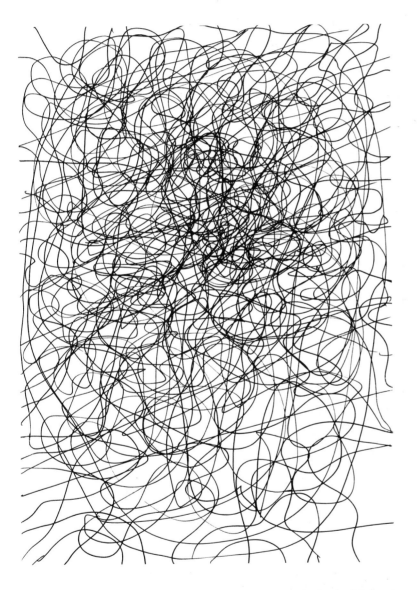

Within the strict grid of time rhythms, of the heartbeat, of breathing, the muddled thought-streams of the ego unfold, the chaotic movements of every day, the flight paths of the clouds, of the birds and insects. Hardly anything can be foretold. Only the past can be documented.

A structure, a line, a grid slowly forms from the chaos of thoughts and ideas. Seen in this way, all designing is also reconstruction of the primeval act: order and structure emerge from chaos. Revelation of muddle and of the initial chaos is an indication of the artificiality of orders, of the idealized setting: under every order seethes the lava of chaos. Possible orders keep chaos in check, are protective walls against hurly-burly and muddle, glowing signs above the black holes.

Organische Strukturen

Organic structures

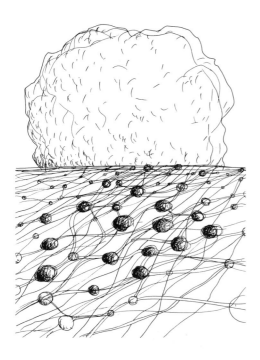

Diese Natur-Formen und Formationen auf neue Entwürfe anwenden: Gärten wie Blätter, wie Flecken, wie Tropfen, wie Strömungsturbulenzen, wie Wasserwirbel, wie Mäander, wie Verästelungen, Deltas, wie Baumkronen.

Apply these nature-forms and formations to new designs: gardens like leaves, like spots, like drops, like turbulence in the current, like whirlpools, like meanders, like branch systems, deltas, like the crowns of trees.

Die Evolution hat unendlich viele Strukturen hervorgebracht. Immer geht es um die Organisation von Flächen, von Körpern, von Raum und von Welt. Die Idee einer Architektur aus Atomen und Molekülen, die Idee der Adern und Nerven, die Idee der Kreisläufe!

Evolution has produced an infinity of structures. Areas, bodies, space and world are always being organized. The idea of an architecture of atoms and molecules, the idea of veins and nerves, the idea of cycles!

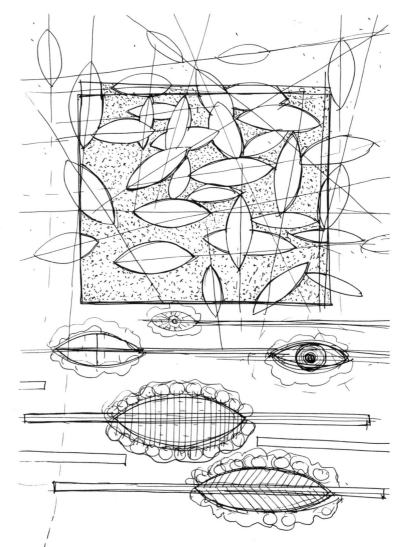

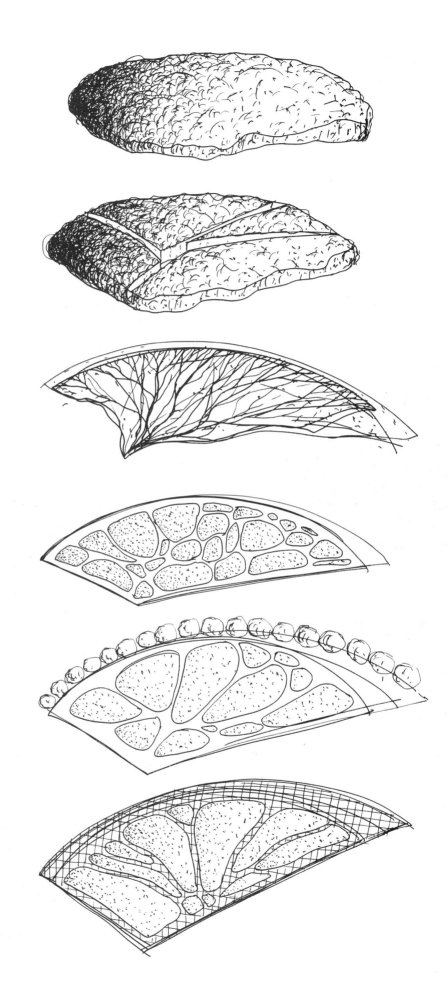

Organische Landschaftsarchitektur.

Organic landscape architecture.

Geometrische Strukturen

Geometrical structures

Die Geometrie des gleichmäßigen Rasters ist der äußerste Gegenpol zum anfänglichen Zufalls-Chaos. Jeder Punkt in diesem System ist vorhersehbar, ist in seiner Lage genau beschreibbar und immer wieder auffindbar.

Auch diese Art von Struktur ist in der Welt enthalten (sonst könnten wir sie nicht denken und nicht verwenden).

The geometry of the even grid is the extreme counter-pole to the original random chaos. Every point in this system is predictable, can be precisely described in terms of its position and always is found again.

This kind of structure is also contained in the world (otherwise we could not think it and apply it).

Strukturüberlagerungen

Structural superimpositions

Das klassische Bild des gerasterten Gartens, des geometrisierten Platzes mit dem Bild einer organischen Anlage überlagert. (Flußmäander oder Wiesenmäander).

The classic image of the garden on a grid pattern, of the geometrical place with the image of an organic layout superimposed. (River meander, or meadow meander).

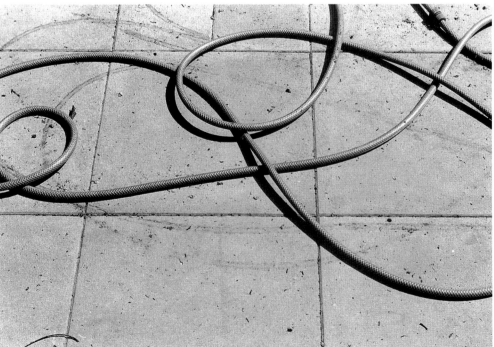

Linien, Punkte, Raster, Felder mit Blättern und Blüten.
Organisch geformte Flächen mit geometrischen Fragmenten und Rastern.

Lines, dots, grids, fields with leaves and blossoms.
Organically formed areas with geometrical fragments and grids.

Überlagerungen.

Superimpositions.

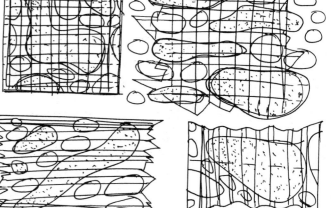

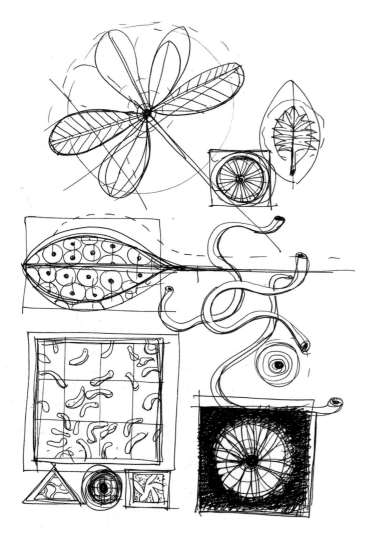

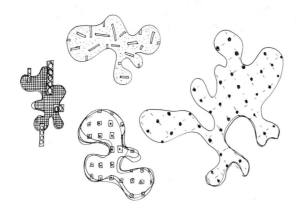

132

Ausschnitte möglicher Ordnungen.

Details of possible orders.

Chaos und Ordnung. Konfrontationen. Störungen. Transformationen. Explosionen. Implosionen. Abfolgen.

Chaos and order. Confrontations. Disturbances. Transformations. Explosions. Implosions. Sequences.

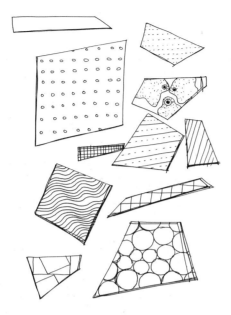

Die Natur selbst zerbricht die auferlegte Geometrie durch Verwitterung zu einem Bild der Überlagerung.

Nature itself breaks imposed geometry down to an image of superimposition by weathering.

Vorgriff mit Vegetation: gepflanzte Linien, Alleen. Felder aus Rastern, Punkten, Wellen, Formtrümmern, aus Büschen und Bäumen. Plätze und Gärten wie liegende Bilder. Formen werden durchgehbar. Geometrie wird erlebbar. Klare Flächen in wuchernder Landschaft.

Die Weichheit der Landschaft verzahnt mit der Starrheit von Wegen und Architekturfragmenten. Langsames Einwachsen und Verschwinden der Geometrie in der sommerlichen Wiese.

The softness of the landscape linked with the stiffness of paths and architectural fragments. Slow ingrowing and disappearance of geometry in the summery meadow.

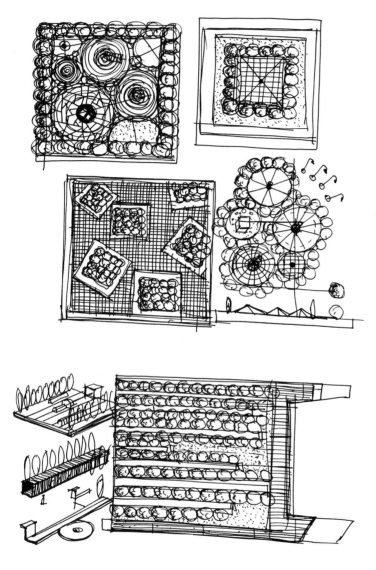

Anticipation, with vegetation: planted lines, avenues. Fields made up of grids, dots, waves, formal rubble, of bushes and trees.
Squares and gardens like pictures lying down. It becomes possible to walk through form. Geometry can be experienced. Clear areas in a teeming landscape.

Neue Landschafts- und Gartenarchitektur
Elemente der Landschaftsarchitektur mit möglichen Eingriffen

New landscape and garden architecture
Elements of landscape architecture with possible interventions

Zu den beschriebenen Elementen und Strukturen kommen die konkreten Elemente der Landschaft: Erde, Stein, Vegetation, Wasser und Luft. Es sind die »natürlichen« Baustoffe der Landschaftsarchitektur. Anschließend treten die »künstlichen« Elemente und Baustoffe ins Bild: die Steinflächen der Plätze, die Wände der Architekturen, die Zäune und die Antennen. Die immateriellen Elemente und »Baustoffe« schließen sich an: die literarischen Texte, die Beschreibungen und die inszenierten Situationen, die Landschaft zu einem Handlungsort mit Bedeutung erheben.

The elements and structures described are joined by the concrete elements of the landscape: earth, stone, vegetation, water and air. These are the »natural« building materials of landscape architecture. Subsequently the »artificial« elements and building materials come into the picture: the stone surfaces of squares, the walls of the various buildings, fences and aerials. Immaterial elements and »building materials« follow: literary texts, descriptions and staged situations that make landscape into a significant place for action.

Neue Landschafts- und Gartenarchitektur
Erdbewegung

New landscape and garden architecture
Earth movements

Erde ist die Grundkomponente der Landschafts-architektur. Aus ihr werden die Hügel und Täler geformt, aus ihr heraus wachsen Gras und Bäume.

Earth is the basic component of landscape architecture. Hills and valleys are formed from it, grass and trees grow out of it.

Die nackte, nasse oder trockene Erde als Teil der Erdkugel-Oberfläche gibt es ohne Vegetation nur in Steppen- und Wüstengebieten, überall sonst ist sie überzogen von Gras, Stauden, Büschen oder Bäumen.
Körperlich gesehen ist die Erde die Muskulatur der Landschaft, ihr Fleisch. Die Vegetation zieht sich darüber wie eine Haut mit Haaren.

Bare, wet or dry earth as part of the surface of the globe exists without vegetation only in steppe and desert conditions, otherwise it is covered with grass, shrubs, bushes or trees.
Physically speaking earth is the muscles of the landscape, its flesh. Vegetation covers it like a skin with hair.

Erdbaustelle, Erdplatz. Diese aufgeworfenen Stellen der Erdoberfläche haben etwas von Wun-den, von blutendem Dreck, von Geburt und ver-schmiertem Anfang. Eine Situation des Noch-nicht, des Ungestalteten – man möchte hineingehen, im Schlamm wühlen, Gestalten dar-aus formen, kleine Häuser, Burgen, kleine Bäume, Waldstücke, Alleen bauen. Aber man hat Angst, im Sumpf zu versinken. Aus diesem Lehmklumpen ist man entstanden, zu diesem Lehmklumpen wird man wieder werden.

Earth building site, earth place. These dug-up patches of the earth's surface are to an extent like wounds, like bleeding dirt, of birth and a smeared beginning. A not-yet situation, an unfor-med situation – you are tempted to go in there, to burrow in the mud, to make shapes with it, build little houses, castles, small trees, woods, ave-nues, but you are afraid of sinking into the marsh. We came from this piece of clay, and to this clay we will return.

Die umgepflügten Äcker im Herbst zeigen in geo-
metrisierter Form die Unterseite der Erdoberfläche: die dampfenden Schollen als immer wieder-
kehrendes Bild des Anfangs.

*Ploughed fields in the autumn show the under-
side of the earth's surface in geometricized form:
steaming clods as a constantly recurring image
of the beginning.*

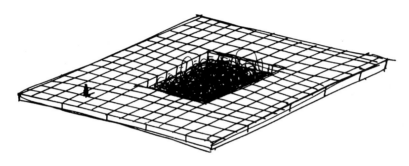

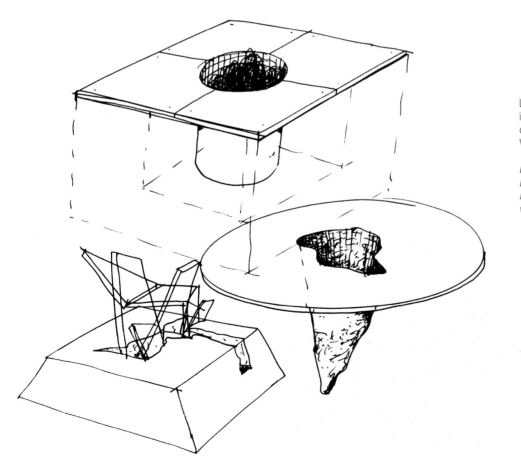

Löcher im Boden: Aufreißen der Erde. Der Blick
in das Innenleben: Humus, Wurzel, Steine, Knochen, Luftblasen, Käfer und Würmer, Reich der
Würmer und Maulwürfe.

*Holes in the ground: tearing the earth open.
Looking into its inner life: humus, root, stones,
bones, air bubbles, insects and worms, empire of
worms and moles.*

Die Vorgänge und Motive der Landwirtschaft aufgreifen: Linien ziehen, Kerben schneiden, kleine Täler anlegen, gerade und krumme Verläufe, kurvige und gezackte. Mulden graben, die Erde zu kleinen Hügeln aufschütten, dieses Motiv mehrfach wiederholen, kleine Landschaften aus Berg und Tal formen. Wellen.

Erd-Einschnitte. Die Schnittflächen verglasen oder mit Metall-Flächen überziehen.

Incisions in the earth. Glaze the cut surfaces or cover them with metal.

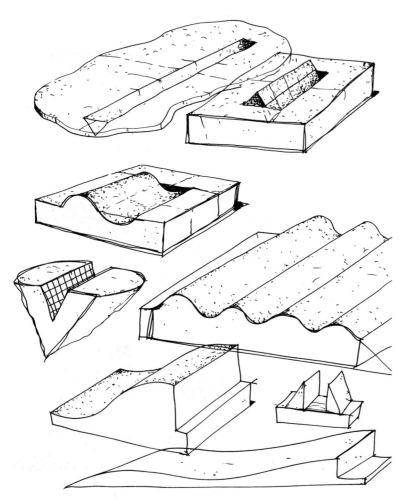

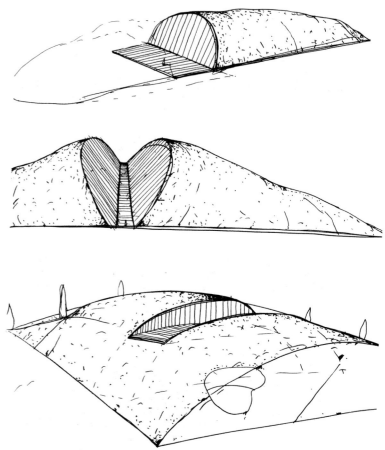

Picking up the processes and motifs of agriculture: drawing lines, cutting notches, making little valleys, straight and crooked courses, curved and zig-zag ones. Digging ditches, piling up little hills with the earth you dig out, repeating this motif a number of times, making little landscapes of mountain and valley. Waves.

Ebene, Berg und Tal. Positive und negative
Pyramiden.

*Plain, mountain and valley. Positive and negative
pyramids.*

Hügel als Fragment der Erdwölbung (Kugel-
segment)?

*Hill as a fragment of the earth's curvature (sphere
segment)?*

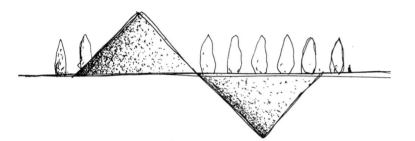

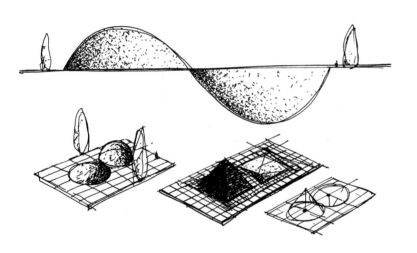

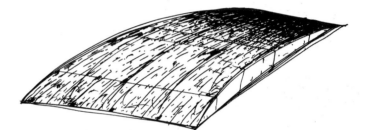

Erd-Pyramiden, massiv aufgebaut oder aus Erd-klumpen, aus Erdkugeln, aus Erdscherben aufgetürmt. Sichtbare Erd-Archäologie.

Earth pyramids, solid or made of piled up clods of earth, balls of earth, fragments of earth. Visible earth archaeology.

Erdhügelreihungen. Rund, eckig, Richtung Kugel, Richtung Kegel. Erde nackt belassen, rauh, ruppig oder mit einer Lehmschicht glatt gestrichen, mit Gras eingesät oder von Spontanvegetation überzogen. Mit Bäumen bepflanzt oder von einem Baum (Pappel, Zypresse) gekrönt.

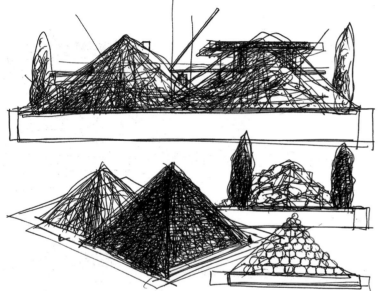

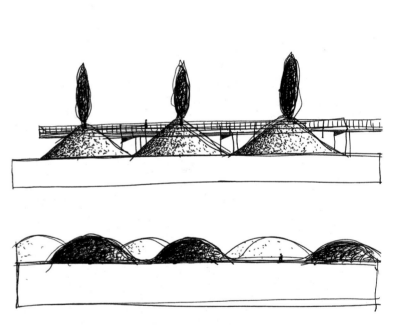

Sequences of mounds of earth. Round, with corners, tending towards the sphere, tending towards the cone. Earth left bare, raw, rough or smoothed over with a layer of clay, sown with grass or covered with spontaneous vegetation. Planted with trees or topped with a single tree (poplar, cypress).

Erdhügel. Erdmulden. Mischungen von verschlossenen und offenen Bodenbereichen.

Mounds of earth. Troughs in the earth. Mixtures of closed and open ground areas.

Sich aufbäumende Erde. Erd-Brandung. Geologische Formationen. Die Bewegungen zeigen, den Schmerz hörbar machen. Übertragungen aus dem Inneren der Erde: das Brodeln der Lava, ihr Eingesperrtsein, ihr Kochen, ihre Wut.

Earth towering up. Earth-surf. Geological formations. Showing the movements, making the pain audible. Communications from the centre of the earth: seething lava, its trapped nature, its boiling, its fury.

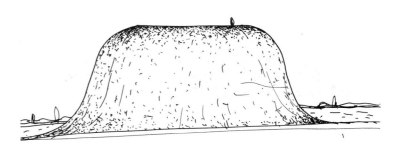

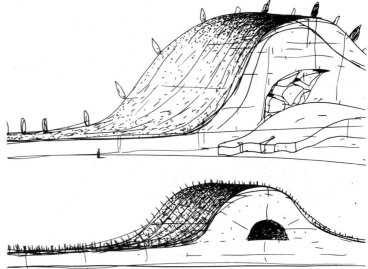

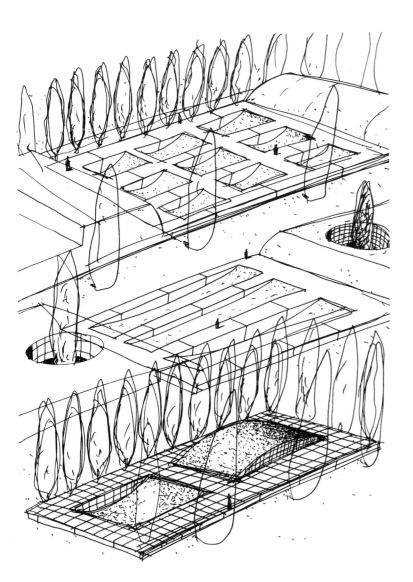

Grabungen, Aufwerfungen, Vertiefungen, Aufschichtungen, Begradigungen, Verweichlichungen, Öffnungen, Verschließungen, Einkreisungen, Ummauerungen, Überdachungen, Überbrückungen, Verkleinerungen, Vergrößerungen, Umwandlungen.

Excavations, piles, hollows, stacks, straightenings, softenings, openings, closures, encirclements, surrounding walls, roofing over, bridging, reduction, enlargement, transformation.

Erd-Gefäße, Erd-Vasen. Erd-Teller. Erd-Tassen. Erd-Gläser. Erd-Beete. Erd-Felder. Erd-Labyrinthe, Erd-Schluchten, Erd-Zimmer, Erd-Fenster, Erd-Türen, Erd-Keller.

Earth vessels. Earth vases. Earth plates. Earth cups. Earth glasses. Earth beds. Earth fields. Earth labyrinths, earth gorges, earth rooms, earth windows, earth doors, earth cellars.

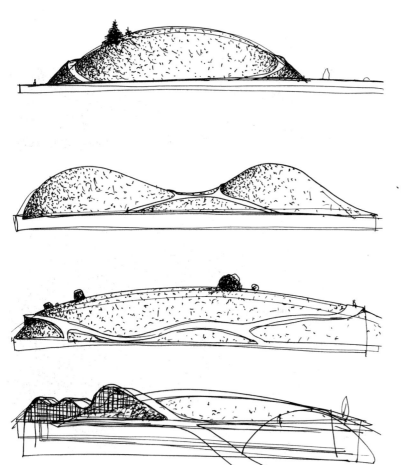

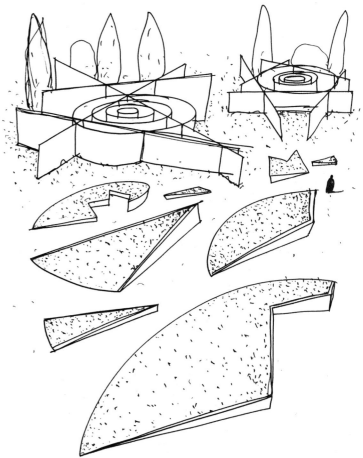

Erdhügel und Erdwellen mit Mauern aus Stein, Stahl oder Glas. Erdstaudämme. Wiesen wie Wasserfälle.

Earth mounds and earth waves with walls of stone, steel or glass. Earth dams. Meadows like waterfalls.

Erdhügel-Plantage.

Earth mound plantation.

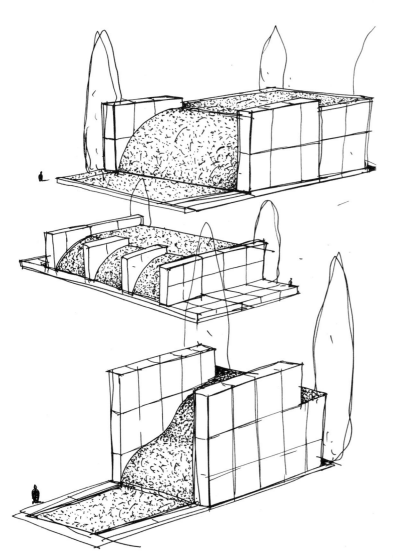

Erdwälle, Erdmauern, Erdtürme, mit Gras
bewachsen.

*Earth ramparts, earth walls, earth towers, planted
with grass.*

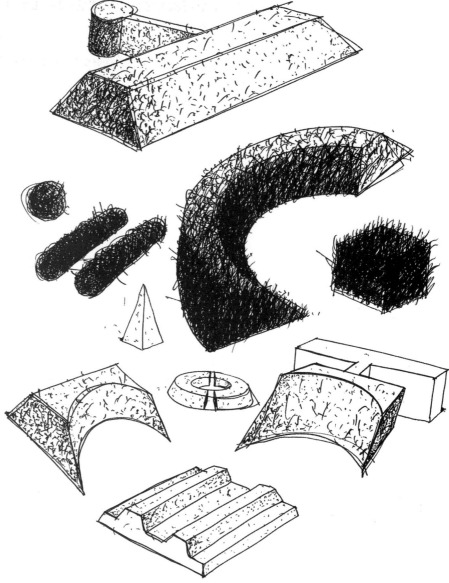

Langsame Austrockung des Bodens.
Versteppung. Der Wind bläst den entstehenden
Staub über die Landschaft. Staublandschaften.

*Slow desiccation out of the earth. Turning into
steppe.*
*The wind blows the dust that is produced across
the landscape. Landscapes of dust.*

Neue Landschafts- und Gartenarchitektur
Steinbewegungen

New landscape and garden architecture
Stone movements

Während Erde, Lehm und Dreck die leicht verformbare, potentiell lebensstiftende Komponente der Landschaftsarchitektur darstellt, ist der Stein, der Fels, der Kiesel das unerbittlich Harte, das trotzig auf sein millionenjähriges Alter hinweist. Die Zeit seiner Bewegung, seines Flüssigseins liegt weit zurück. Er ist schwer verformbar und symbolisiert »versteinert« den Beginn. Alles, was mit ihm und aus ihm gemacht wird, will dauern und hat Anspruch auf Ewigkeit.

Earth, clay and dirt are the easily shaped, potentially life-giving elements of landscape architecture, whereas stone, rock, gravel is remorselessly hard, defiantly indicating that it is millions of years old. The time when it could move, when it was liquid, is deep in the past. It is difficult to shape and is a »petrified« symbol of the beginning. Everything that can be made with it and from it intends to last and has a claim to eternity.

Jeder Stein ist – wie am Anfang beschrieben – Teil des großen Steins, der Erdkugel, er ist herausgebrochen – durch Wettereinfluß oder von Menschenhand – aus dem Körper der Erde, dem Berg, dem Felsen, dem Steinbruch.

Every stone is – as described above – part of the great stone, the globe, it has been broken – by the effects of the weather or the hand of man – from the body of the earth, the mountain, the rock, the quarry.

Steine zu Mauern aufgeschichtet, zu Häusern verarbeitet, Steine in Scheiben geschnitten, zu Kugeln geformt. Steinwolken, Steinmöbel, Steinbetten, Steinkissen, Steinstraßen, Steinplätze, Steinvorhänge, Steinmeteore, Stein-Werkzeug, Grenzsteine, Denkmalsteine, Steinschleudern, Steinmenschen – jede Form und fast jede Funktion scheint im Stein, im Felsblock verborgen zu sein.

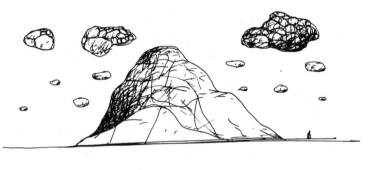

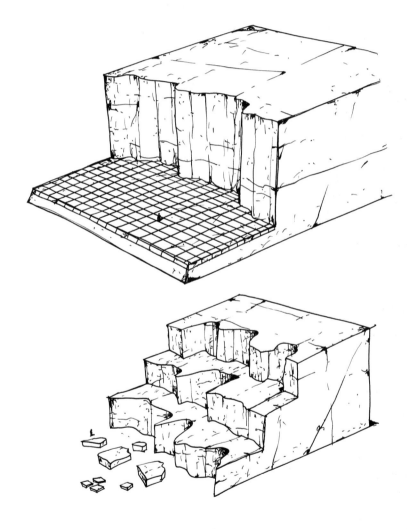

Stone piled up to form walls, made into buildings. Stone cut into discs, shaped into spheres. Stone clouds, stone furniture, stone beds, stone cushions, stone roads, stone squares, stone curtains, stone meteors, stone tools, boundary stones, memorial stones, stone catapults, stone people – every form and almost every function seems to be concealed in stone, in the block of rock.

149

Felsbrocken, Stein mit verwitterten Kanten, runder Stein, Kiesel, Edelstein. Steinkreise, Steinfelder, Steinnester, Steinquadrate, Stein-Moleküle. Jede Steinsetzung erinnert an archaische Zeiten, an Steinzeit, an Stonehenge und Höhlenbewohner. Stein-Landschaften sind ernst und würdevoll. Ein Hauch von Friedhof umweht sie.

Lumps of rock, stone with weathered edges, round stone, gravel, precious stones.
Stone circles, stone fields, stone nests, stone squares, stone molecules.
Every stone setting is reminiscent of ancient times, of the Stone Age, of Stonehenge and cave-dwellers. Stone landscapes are serious and dignified. A breath of the cemetery wafts around them.

Das Gewicht der Steine.

The weight of stones.

150

Aufgespaltene Steine mit Anbauten, mit Zwischenbauten, mit Löchern und Hohlräumen.

Split stones with things built on to or between them, with holes and hollows.

Versteinerungen: sich ganze Landschaften versteinert vorstellen, Wälder, Seen, Felder oder Häuser, Autos, Straßenbahnen, Flugzeuge und Rolltreppen. Ganze Ladeneinrichtungen und Kaufhausinnereien: von einem Moment zum andern erstarren alle Bewegungen, erlöschen alle Farben, ist alles wie aus Marmor gemeißelt.

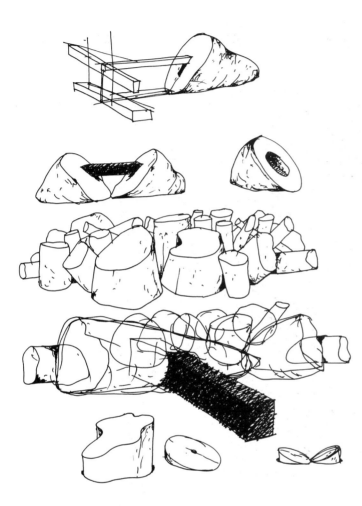

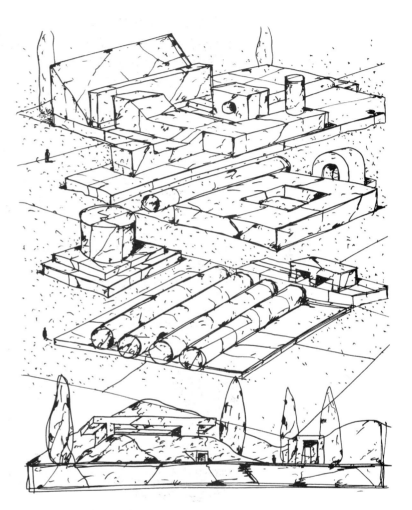

Petrifaction: imagine whole landscapes petrified, woods, lakes, fields or houses, cars, trams, aircraft and escalators. Whole shop fitments and department store interiors: from one moment to another all movement is petrified, all colours are extinguished, it is as though everything is chiselled from marble.

Stadtplätze mit Steinsetzungen. In die Felsbrocken sind Telefonzellen oder Schaufenstervi-
trinen eingelassen.

City squares set with stones. Telephone boxes or
show cases are set into the lumps of rock.

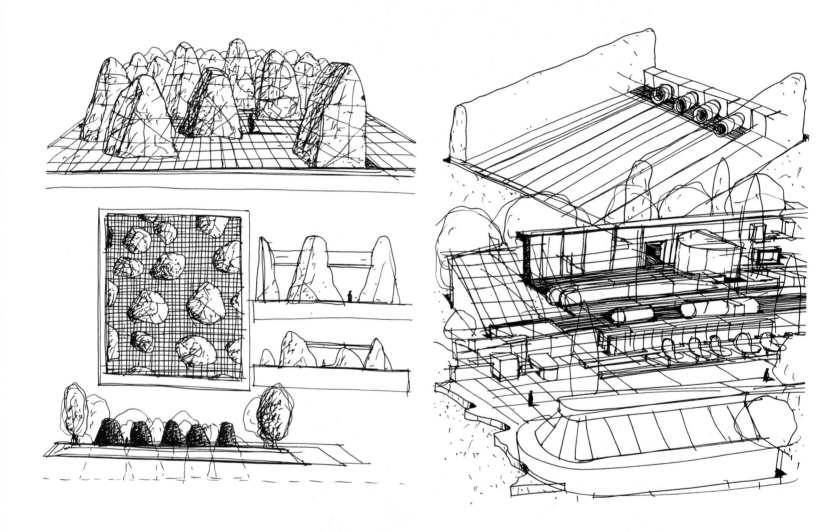

Steine liegen an den Straßen, stehen mitten auf den Kreuzungen: Prellböcke im Fluß. Verwirbelungen des Verkehrs. Potentielle Ruhepunkte, absoluter Stillstand gegen das Verströmen der Zeit.

Stones lie in the streets, stand in the middle of junctions: buffers in the river, swirls in the traffic. Potential points of rest, absolute stillness against the streaming away of time.

Steinfelder quer durch Städte gelegt. Über Plätze und Kreuzungen, durch Wohnungen und Kirchen, durch Museen und Schwimmbäder, durch Bibliotheken und Fabriken, durch Kindergärten und Schulen, durch Krankenhäuser und Friedhöfe.

Fields of stone running straight through cities. Across squares and junctions, through flats and churches, through museums and swimming pools, through libraries and factories, through kindergartens and schools, through hospitals and cemeteries.

Stein-Einbauten in Hauszwischenräume und auf
Kreuzungen.

*Stone built in the gaps between houses and at
junctions.*

Steingärten, Felsgärten.
Die klassischen Motive klingen an.

*Stone gardens. Rock gardens.
The classic motifs can be discerned.*

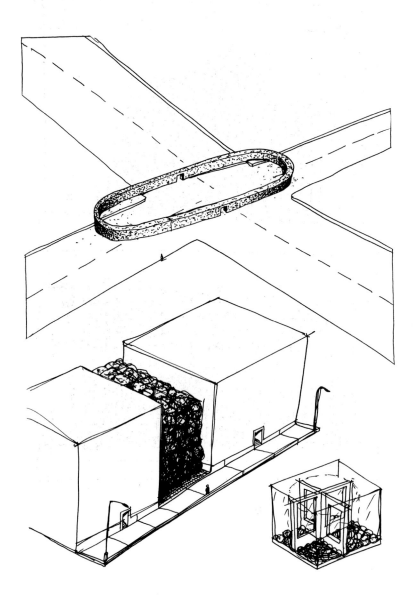

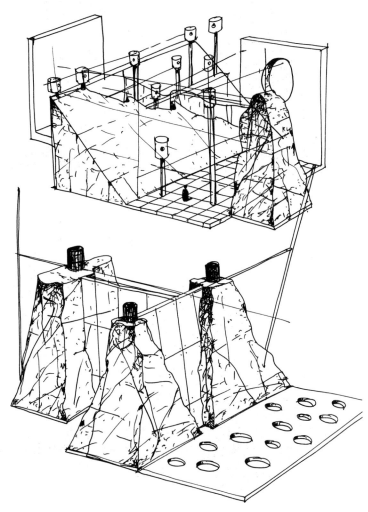

Dann wieder sind die Steine, die Felsen überbaut mit technischem Gerät, mit Antennen oder Solarzellenflügeln zum Beispiel. Steinzeit und Sciencefiction als Stadtplatz-Collage.

Then again the stones, the rocks are built over with technical apparatus, e.g. aerials and solar panels. Stone Age and Science Fiction as city-square collage.

Höhlen- und Grottenhäuser mitten im Verkehr. Darüber die gebaute Zeichnung eines Elektrifizierungsplans. In den gespannten Drähten haben sich Meteore verfangen.

Caves and grotto houses in the middle of the traffic. Above this the constructed design of an electrification plan. Meteors have been caught up in the expanse of wires.

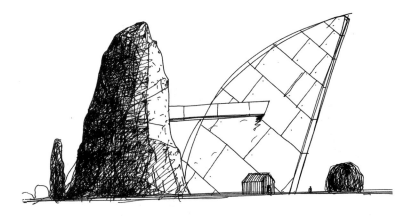

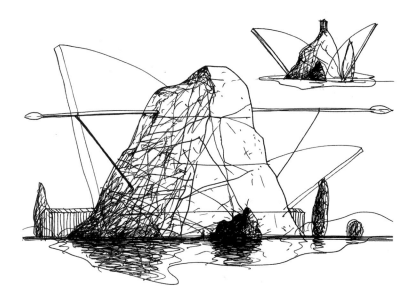

Diese Höhlen und Grotten zu Eingängen in das
Erdinnere umdeuten.

*Reinterpret these caves and grottoes as en-
trances to the interior of the earth.*

Höhleneingangsreihungen.

Series of cave entrances.

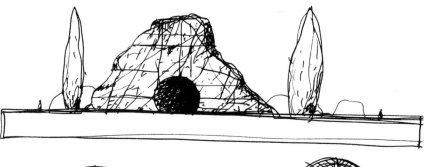

Dringt man ein in das Höhlensystem, führt der Weg über Rolltreppen zu Seen mit dunklen Inseln, leuchtenden Vitrinen-Tempeln, mit Sprungtürmen, mit schwebenden Steinen, Wasserfällen und schwarzen Engeln. Unter Wasser sieht man auf Bildschirmen Direktübertragungen aus dem Weltall.

If you penetrate the cave system the way leads via escalators to lakes with dark islands, glowing showcase temples, with diving platforms, hovering stones, waterfalls and dark angels. Under water you can see direct broadcasts from outer space on screens.

In den Höhlenseitenräumen sieht man versteinerte Bilder von Gärten und Wohnzimmern.

In the side rooms of the caves you can see petrified images of gardens and living rooms.

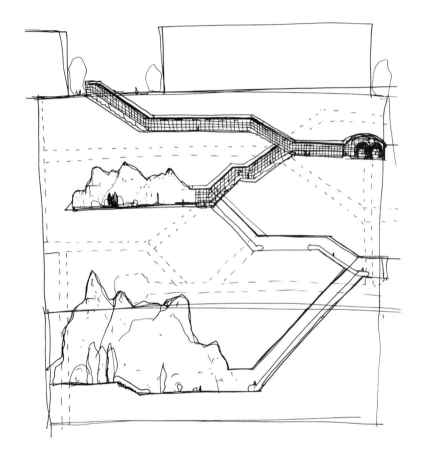

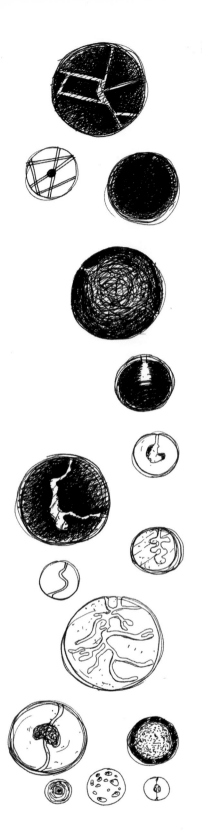

Der Weg führt bis in das Erdinnere, in die
Gedärme, in das Unterbewußtsein der Erde.

*The way leads into the interior of the earth, into
its bowels, into the subconscious of the earth.*

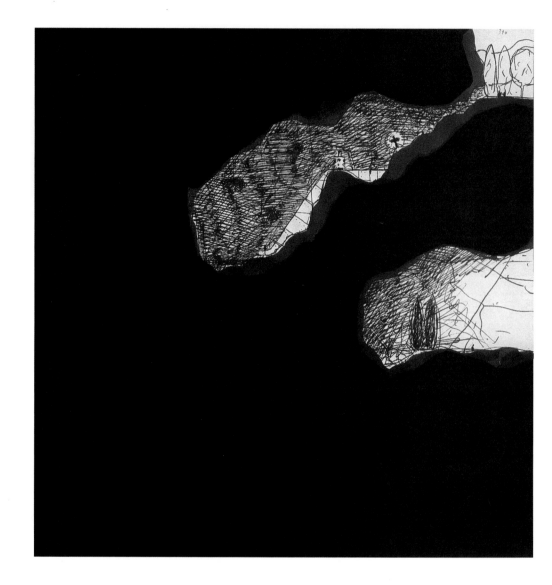

Hier im glühenden Lavakern der Erdkugel ver-
bringen wir vielleicht unsere Nächte, leere, hilf-
lose Hüllen, nahe dem Ursprung und der Dunkel-
kammer des ungeborenen Lebens.

*Here in the glowing lava core of the globe we per-
haps spend our nights, empty, helpless frames
near to the origin and darkroom of unborn life.*

Neue Landschafts- und Gartenarchitektur
Pflanzungen

New landscape and garden architecture
Plantings

Vegetation ist die lebendige Haut der Erdoberfläche, der grüne, millionenblättrige Flaum über der Landschaft, die Landschaft über der Landschaft. Ausdrucksarchitektur des Bodens, die sich im Jahresrhythmus ereignet.
Vegetation als Sauerstofflieferant und Naturschauspiel in einem. Mit der Aussäung, der Pflanzung wird ein Prozeß angeregt, der sich über Jahre, bei Bäumen über Jahrzehnte oder gar Jahrhunderte hinziehen kann. Die Vegetation entwickelt und verändert sich von Jahr zu Jahr. Jeden Sommer ist der Garten, der Park ein anderer.

Vegetation is the living skin of the surface of the earth, a green, million-leafed down over the landscape, landscape laid over the landscape. Expressive architecture of the soil, occurring within the rhythm of the year.
Vegetation as a provider of oxygen and nature's performance in one. With sowing, planting a process is set in motion that can last for years, in the case of trees for decades or even centuries. Vegetation develops and changes from year to year. Every summer the park or garden is a different one.

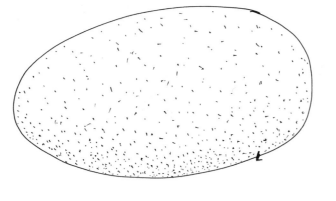

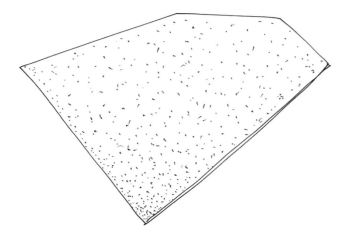

Am Anfang steht die gute, alte Wiese. Eine große, leere, lebendige Fläche, die sich aus einem zart hellgrünen Bild im Frühjahr zu einem bunten, hohen und wilden Wiesenbild im Sommer entwickelt. Jede Begrenzungs-Form ist denkbar: Kreis, Quadrat, Rechteck, unregelmäßige Bruchstücke, Scherben oder gewellte Flecken.

At the beginning is the good old meadow. A large, empty living surface that can develop from a delicate and light green picture in the spring into a colourful, high and wild lawn image in the summer.
Any limiting shape is conceivable: circle, square, rectangle, irregular sections, fragments or wavy patches.

Die Wiese kann sich in der Ebene ausbreiten, sie kann leicht geneigt sein, sich über Schrägen in die Höhe treppen, sie kann gewellt sein, gefaltet, gezackt oder sanft fließend.

The meadow can spread over the surface, it can be slightly sloping, rise in sloping sections like steps, it can be undulating, folded, serrated or gently flowing.

Man kann die Wiese jeden Tag mähen, oder man kann sie wild wachsen lassen. Mischungen sind denkbar: man läßt Blöcke stehen und mäht den Rest flach und glatt. Mähbilder: geometrisch, rhythmisch, in Linien oder in Fleckenform wie Wolkenschatten.

The meadow can be mown every day or it can be allowed to grow wild. Mixtures are conceivable: blocks are allowed to stand and the rest mown flat and smooth. Mowing patters: geometrical, rhythmical, in lines or on patches like shadows of clouds.

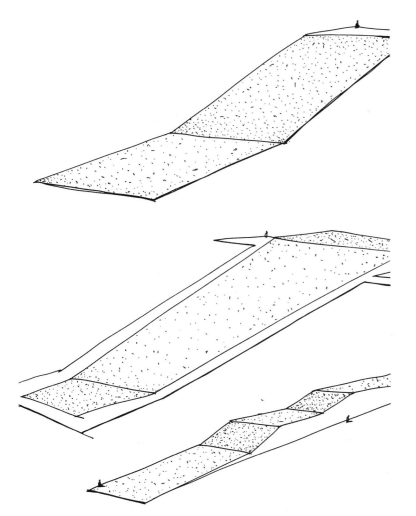

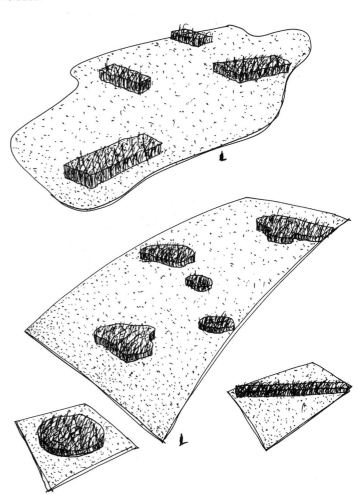

Oder man mäht Linien, Wege und Felder in die hochstehende Wiese.

Or lines, paths and fields can be mown in the long grass.

Oder man bedeckt die Wiese teilweise mit Steinplatten und läßt das Gras nur aus geometrischen Öffnungen wachsen.

Or the lawn is partly covered with stone slabs and the grass is allowed to grow through geometrical openings.

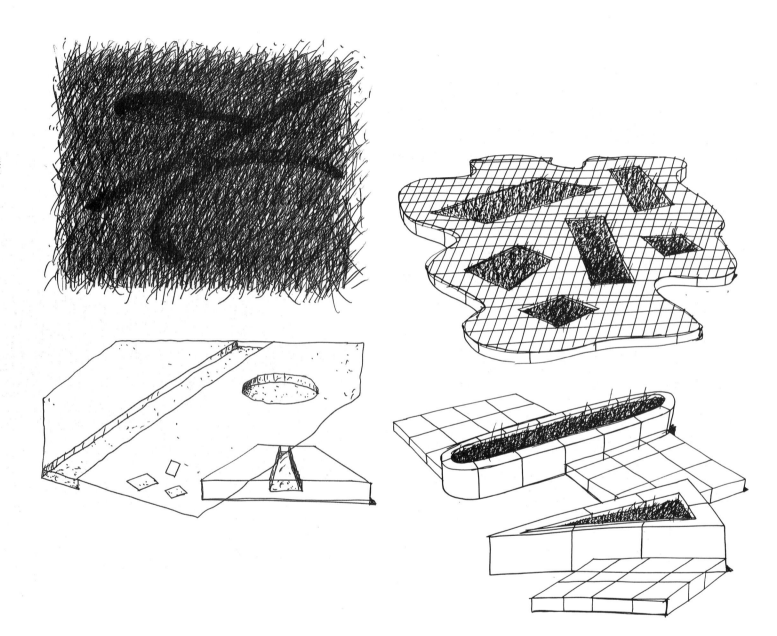

Denkbar sind auch Verformungen des Bodenbereichs, so daß die Wiesenvegetation an manchen Stellen höher, an anderen niedriger wächst. Vorgetäuschte Archäologie.

Or it is also possible to shape the ground so that the lawn grows higher in some places and lower in others. Simulated archaeology.

Die archäologischen Formen werden verstärkt zu markanten Auswölbungen: Wiesen-Architekturen.

The archaeological shapes are reinforced to form striking protrusions: meadow architecture.

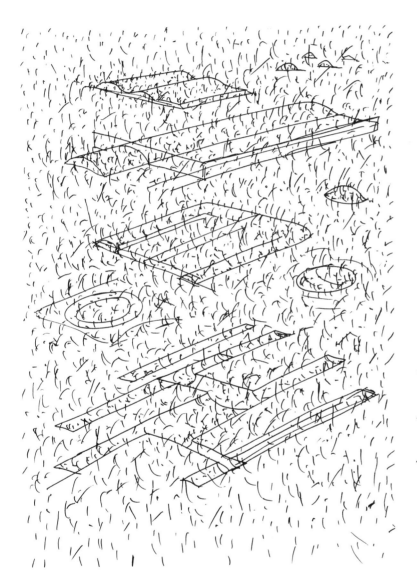

Wiesenlandschaft als Abbild einer versunkenen
Stadt. Das Gehen über die Erhebungen, die
Hügel und bewachsenen Architekturformen wird
zum Gang über eine begrünte Dachlandschaft.

Meadow landscape as copy of a sunken town.
Walking over the raised sections, hills and over-
grown architectural shapes becomes a walk
through a green roof landscape.

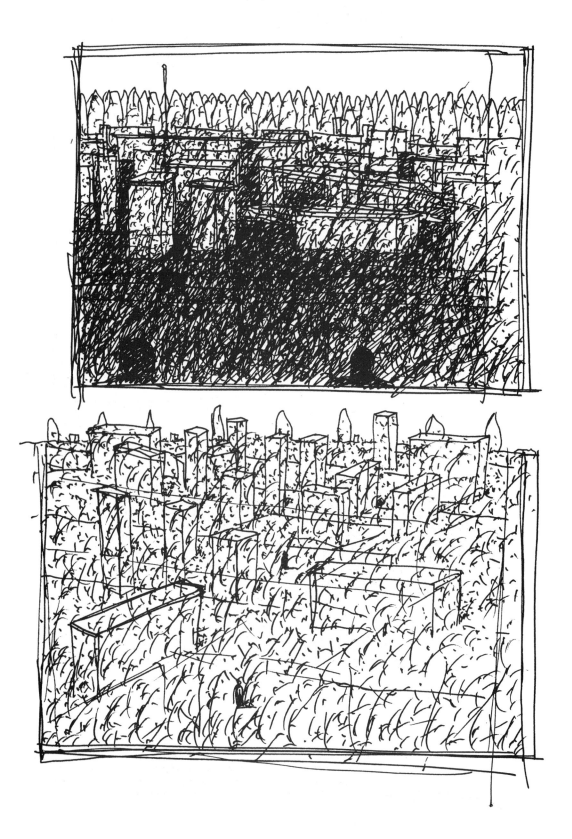

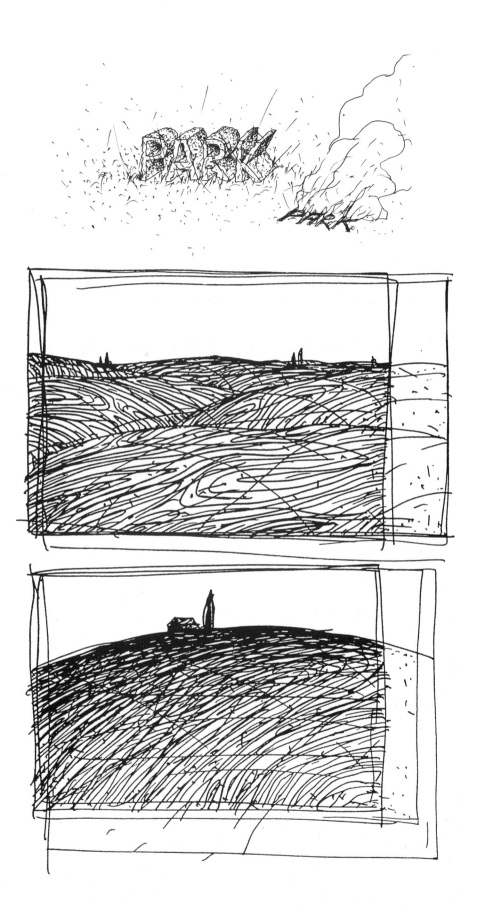

Die Landschaft drückt sich aus in der Vegetation. Zahlen und Buchstaben gibt es in der Natur nicht. Vorstellung: Schriften würden aus der Wiese wachsen, Beschreibungen und Bezeichnungen.

The landscape expresses itself in vegetation. There are no letters and numbers in nature. Imagine: writings growing out of the lawn, descriptions and designations.

Dann wieder die Blumen, das bunte Blütenfeuer-
werk des Frühlings. Sie sind in allen Gärten als
Schmuck- und Ornamentereignis reich vertreten,
in Parks weniger. Ihre Schönheit ist üppig, aber
auch naheliegend. Es ist sicher schwer, neue
Blumen-Ästhetiken zu entwickeln. Vor allem die
Gartenschauen haben alle Möglichkeiten durch-
buchstabiert und die Blumenbilder durch über-
triebenen Einsatz abgedroschen und ausgeleiert.
Die neue Gartenarchitektur sollte Blumen eher
wieder sparsam einsetzen, in monochromen Bildern vielleicht, in zurückhaltenden Linien.

*Then the flowers again, the brightly coloured
blossom fireworks of spring. They are lavishly
represented in all gardens as decoration and
ornament, less so in parks. Their beauty is sump-
tuous, but also obvious. It is certainly difficult to
develop new aesthetics of flowers. Garden
shows in particular have spelled out all the possibilities and created hackneyed and played-out
flower images through exaggerated use. New
garden architecture should start using flowers
sparingly again, perhaps in monochrome images,
in reserved lines.*

Blumenkörbe, Blumentöpfe, Blumenbänke, Blu-
menhäuser, Blumenfelder, Blumenstraßen, Blu-
menflüsse, Blumenmäander, Blumenlava, Blu-
menräder, Blumengläser, Blumenfälle, Blumen-
seen, Blumenbrandung, Blumenparkplätze, Blu-
menläden, Blumenmeere, Blumenrandstreifen,
Blumentheater, Blumendächer, Blumendenk-
mäler, Blumenautos, Blumenschiffe, Blumen-
märkte, Blumenmöbel, Blumenwohnzimmer,
Blumenkirchen, Blumenstaudämme, Blumenge-
birge, Blumenregale, Blumenflure, Blumenfried-
höfe, Blumenstädte, Blumentore, Blumentank-
stellen, Blumenhäfen, Blumentempel, Blumengärten, Blumenfassaden, Blumenhochhäuser,
Blumenbücher, Blumentreppen, Blumendecken,
Blumenunterführungen, Blumenfenster, Blumen-
dialoge, Blumensätze?

*Flower baskets, flower pots, flower benches,
flower houses, flower fields, flower roads, flower
rivers, flower meanders, flower lava, flower
wheels, flower glasses, flower falls, flower lakes,
flower surf, flower parking places, flower shops,
flower seas, flower edging strips, flower theatres,
flower roofs, flower memorials, flower cars, flower
ships, flower markets, flower furniture, flower
living rooms, flower churches, flower dams,
flower mountains, flower shelves, flower corridors, flower cemeteries, flower cities, flower
gates, flower petrol stations, flower harbours,
flower temples, flower gardens, flower façades,
flower skyscrapers, flower books, flower staircases, flower ceilings, flower underpasses,
flower windows, flower dialogues, flower sentences?*

166

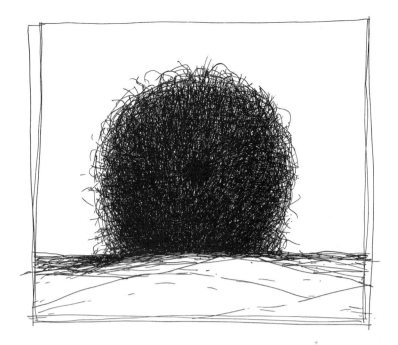

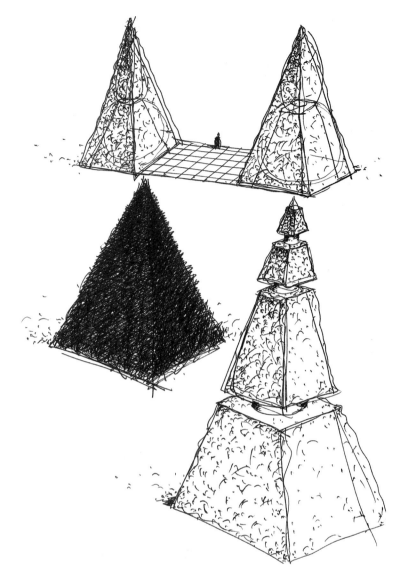

Dann der Busch, die Hecke als Einzelgewächs, als Kugel oder als Gruppe, als Haufen, in Familien, Gesellschaften.

Then the bush, the hedge as a single item, as a sphere or as a group, as an accumulation, in families, societies.

Den Busch, die Hecke frei wachsen lassen oder sie beschneiden, ihnen eine geometrische Form aufzwingen.

Allow the bush, the hedge to grow freely or trim it, force a geometrical shape upon it.

Hecken-Kompositionen. Hecken-Architekturen.
Buchsbaumhäuser. Buchsbaumformen. Buchs-
baumdörfer. Buchsbaumstädte.

Hedge compositions. Hedge architecture.
Box tree houses. Box tree shapes. Box tree vil-
lages. Box tree towns.

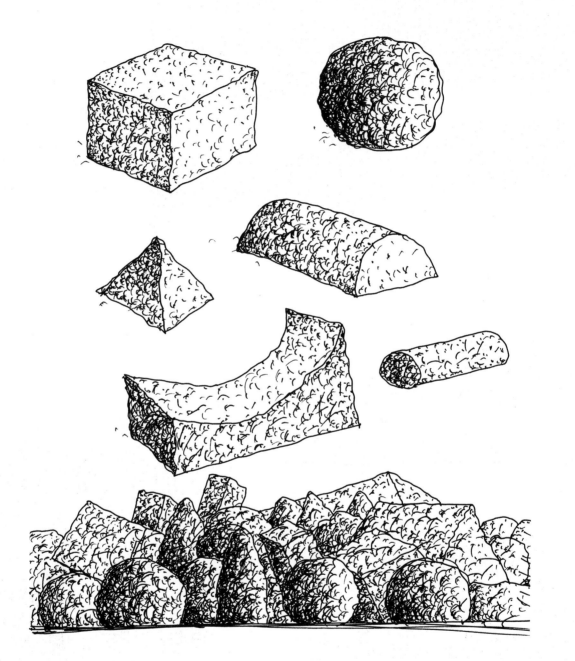

Hecken-Wände, Hecken-Mauern, Hecken-Labyrinthe. Stilisierter Weg ins Innere der Natur: Die Vegetation wird in einen anderen Zustand der Bedeutung überführt.

Stylized way into nature's interior: the vegetation is taken into another condition of meaning.

Hedge screens, hedge walls, hedge labyrinths.

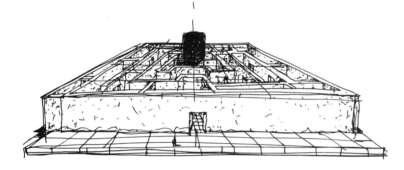

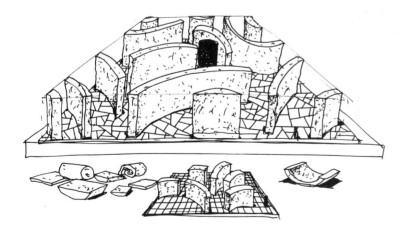

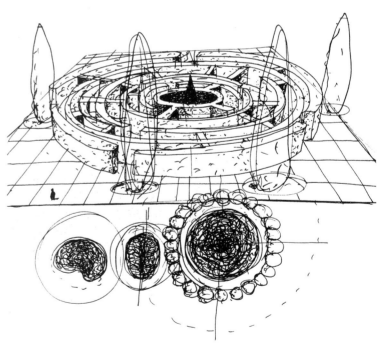

Verbindungen von beschnittenen Hecken und
Architekturteilen (beispielsweise Fenster, Türen,
Wände, Regale usw.).

*Combining trimmed hedges and architectural
items (e.g. windows, doors, walls, shelves etc.).*

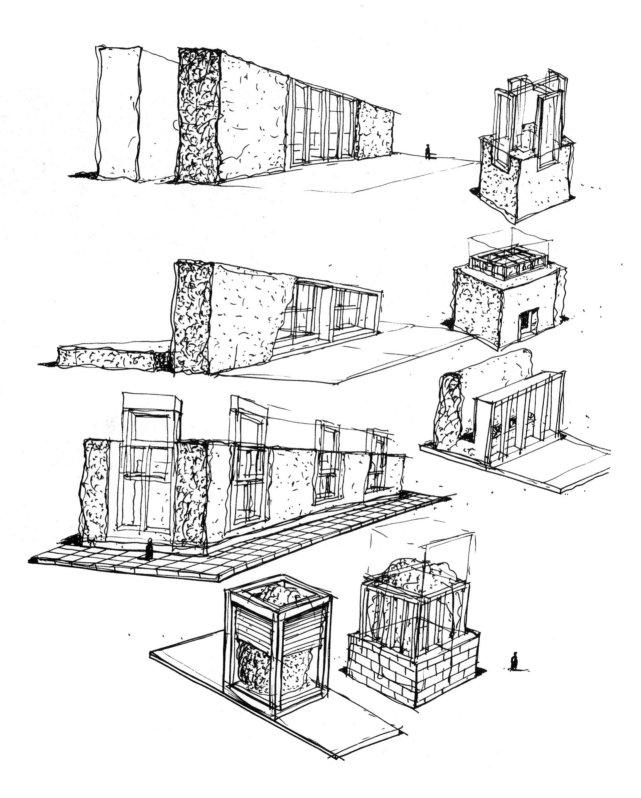

Schließlich die Bäume. Für alle Pflanzen gilt: sie einzukreisen, sie zu beschreiben und sie ihrem Charakter gemäß einzusetzen.

Die steile, gotische Pappel, die helle freundliche Birke, das sichere Dastehen von Buche, Linde, Platane, Kastanie und Esche, die elementare Kraft der Eiche, der sensible Nußbaum, die leidenschaftliche Blutbuche, der knorrige Charme von Obstbäumen, die Düsternis von Fichte und Kiefer und das depressive Hängen der Trauerweidenzweige.

Trauerweiden beispielsweise: Trauerweiden-Kreis, Trauerweiden-Krater, in Friedhöfen oder Gedenkstätten denkbar.
oder Pappeln:
gebogene Pappelreihen, mögliche Pflanzungen in öffentlichen Parks oder in der Nähe von Straßen und Autobahnen als begleitende, das Fließen rhythmisierende Pflanzungen.

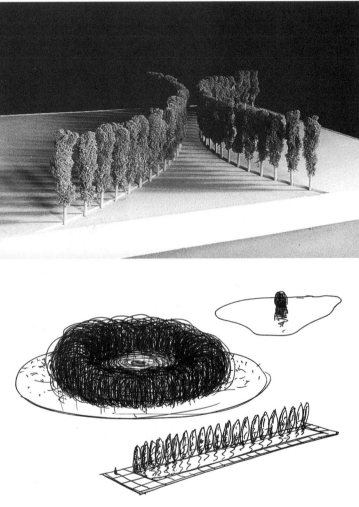

And finally trees. The same is true for all plants: circumscribe their character, define it, and use them according to this.

The upright, Gothic poplar, the bright and friendly birch, the secure stance of beech, lime, plane, chestnut and ash, the elemental force of the oak, the sensitive walnut, the passionate logwood, the gnarled charm of fruit trees, the darkness of spruce and pine and the depressive hang of weeping willow twigs.

Weeping willows for example: circle of weeping willows, crater of weeping willows, conceivable in cemeteries or memorial gardens.

Curving rows of poplars, possible planting for public parks or near roads and motorways as planting to accompany the flow and give it rhythm.

Birkenhaine und Birken-Quadrate, geeignet für heitere Orte wie Kindergärten oder Spielplätze.

Birch groves and birch squares are suitable for cheerful places like kindergartens or playgrounds.

Pappel-Pflanzungen mit Übergängen zur Architektur: Erdwälle, Erddächer, Erdhäuser, darüber Alleen mit Brunnen und Terrassen.

Poplar plantations with transitions to architecture: earth ramparts, earth roofs, earth houses, and above them avenues with fountains and terraces.

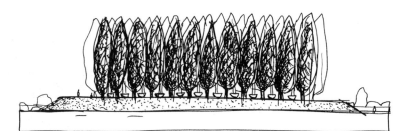

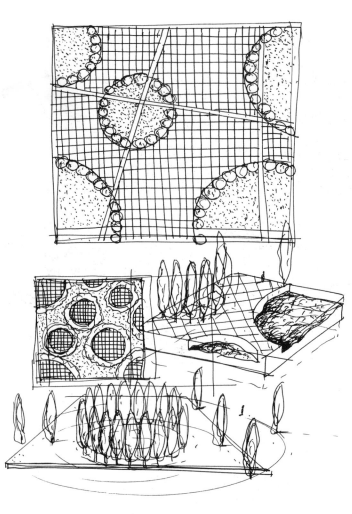

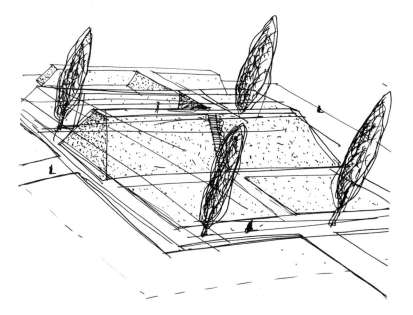

Baumgruppen auf Erdhügeln.

Groups of trees on mounds of earth.

Geflecht aus Wegen, Plätzen, Hainen und Wiesenstücken.
Mischungen von Park- und Stadtbereichen,
bepflanzt mit Linden-Straßen, mit Eichen-Hainen,
mit Pappelquadraten usw. Wichtig ist die Rei-
hung einer Baumsorte.

*Network of paths, squares, groves and pieces
of lawn.*
*Mixtures of park and city areas: planted with rays
of limes, with groves of oak, with squares of
poplar etc. It is important to place one variety of
tree in a row.*

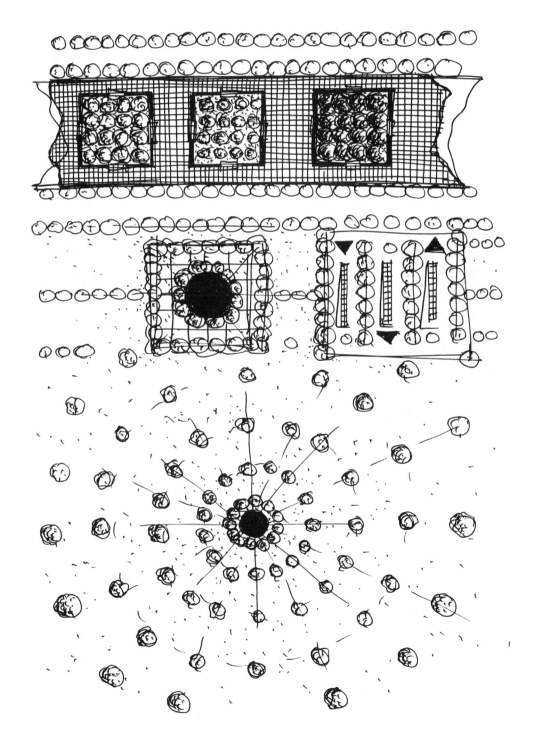

Langsame Verdichtung zu Wäldern. Der Abstand zwischen den gepflanzten Bäumen wird immer geringer. Schließlich stehen die Stämme so dicht, daß man nicht mehr durch die Lücken hindurch kommt. Raumquetschungen, Raumstauchungen, Raumverflechtungen.

A slow increase of density to form woods. The distance between the planted trees becomes less and less. Finally the trunks are so tightly packed that it is no longer possible to pass between them. Space squeezing, space compression, space interlacement.

»Ich muß entschieden zum Vergnügen am Kiefernwald zurückkommen.
Woraus besteht es, dieses Vergnügen? – Hauptsächlich aus dem folgenden: der Kiefernwald ist ein Naturraum, bestehend aus Bäumen, die alle zu einer ganz besonderen Spezies gehören; ein klar abgegrenzter Raum, im allgemeinen ziemlich verlassen, wo man Schutz vor der Sonne findet, vor dem Wind, vor dem Gesehenwerden; jedoch keinen vollständigen Schutz, keine Abgeschiedenheit. Nein! Der Schutz ist relativ. Ein Schutz ohne Heimlichkeit, ein Schutz ohne Kläglichkeit – ein nobler Schutz.
Es ist außerdem ein Ort (und das ist bezeichnend für den Kiefernwald), wo man leicht vorankommt, ohne Unterholz, ohne Zweigwerk in Kopfhöhe, wo man im Trockenen liegen und sich ausstrecken kann, nicht übermäßig weich, doch ziemlich bequem.
Ein jeder Kiefernwald gleicht einem natürlichen Sanatorium, auch einem Musiksalon… einem Zimmer, einer weiträumigen Kathedrale der Besinnung (einer Kathedrale ohne Kanzel, glücklicherweise), geöffnet allen Winden, die aber eintreten durch so viele Pforten, daß es scheint, als seien diese zugleich geschlossen. Denn die Winde stocken dort.
Ist der Wald einigermaßen groß oder dicht, so sieht man, in seinem Herzen stehend, keinen seitlichen Himmel – man muß sich auf den Rand zu bewegen, bis an die Stelle, wo die Schotten sozusagen nicht mehr abgedichtet wirken. Wie wunderbar wäre eine Kathedrale aus einem Wald von Säulen, wo man nach und nach in die völlige Dunkelheit geriete (Krypta).
Und gerade so ist doch, im großen und ganzen, der Wald beschaffen, mag um ihn herum auch keinerlei Mauer stehen: das Monument atmet durch alle seine Poren, in freier Natur, besser als eine Lunge, gleichsam durch Kiemen.
Man könnte sogar sagen, daß gerade dies das Kriterium für Vollkommenheit sein sollte, das Maß für Architektur: den Punkt zu schaffen, wo die totale Dunkelheit herrscht, vorausgesetzt freilich, daß zwischen jeder Säule genug Platz für bequeme Fortbewegung bliebe, usw.« (Francis Ponge)

»I must definitely come back to pleasure in the pine-wood.
Of what does it consist, this pleasure? It is principally as follows: the pine-wood is a natural space, consisting of trees that all belong to a quite particular species; a clearly delineated space, generally fairly deserted, where you can find protection from the sun and wind, and from being seen; but not complete protection, not seclusion. No! The protection is relative. Protection without secrecy, protection without wretchedness – a noble protection.
It is also a place (and this is typical of a pine wood), where it is easy to make progress, without undergrowth, without twigs at head level, where you can lie down and stretch out and be dry, not unduly soft, but fairly comfortable.
Every pine wood is like a natural sanatorium, and also a music salon … like a room, a spacious cathedral for reflection (a cathedral without a pulpit, luckily), open to the winds, but they come in through so many entrances that seem to be they at the same time closed. For the winds come to a standstill there.
If the wood is to a certain extent large or dense then standing at its heart no sky can be seen at the side – you have to move towards the edge, to the place where the doors and windows, as it were, no longer seem to be closed. How wonderful a cathedral would be made up of a forest of columns where you gradually got into complete darkness (crypt).
And that is precisely how it is with the wood, even though there is no wall around it: the monument breathes through all its pores, in free nature, better than a lung, as it were through gills.
One could even say that precisely this should be the criterion of perfection, the standard for architecture: creating the point where there is complete darkness, admittedly with the condition that between every column there was enough room for comfortable progress, etc.« (Francis Ponge)

Neue Landschafts- und Gartenarchitektur
Wasserthema

New landscape and garden architecture
The subject of water

Wasser: im Gegensatz zu Erde, Stein und Vegetation eine schwer faßbare Komponente der Landschaftsarchitektur.

Water: in contrast with earth, stone and vegetation it is a component of landscape architecture that is difficult to grasp.

Das Wasser kreist nicht nur durch Körper und Pflanzen, durch Erde und Himmel, es kreist auch durch Städte und Industriegebiete, durch Rohre und Kanäle, durch Atomkraftwerke und Chemiewerke, durch Kläranlagen und Stadtbäder, durch Autowasch- und Sprinkleranlagen. Es ist in jeder Wohnung anwesend. Wer den Wasserhahn aufdreht, klinkt sich in den Kreislauf ein. Jeder benutzt es, kocht es und trinkt es, jeder spült es über sein Gesicht, seinen Körper und sein Geschirr. Die Bewußtmachung der Wasserkreisläufe ist ein wichtiges Thema der neuen Landschaftsarchitektur.

Water does not only circulate through bodies and plants, through heaven and earth, it also circulates through cities and industrial areas, through pipes and sewers, through nuclear power stations and chemical works, through purification plants and municipal baths, through car-washes and sprinklers. It is present in every residence. Turn on the tap and you're part of the system. Everyone uses it, boils and drinks it, everyone washes his face, body and crockery with it. Revealing the circulation of water is an important subject for new landscape architecture.

Am Anfang steht die Quelle, das alte Brunnen-Thema.

At the beginning is the spring, the old subject of the fountain.

Aus der Dunkelheit der Erde, des Steins, der Mauer, des Rohres tritt das Wasser ans Tageslicht.

From the darkness of the earth, the stone, the wall, the pipe, water comes out into the daylight.

Vorsichtig, zurückhaltend als kleines Rinnsal, als tropfende Spur, als winziger Sprudler, aus Ritzen, Spalten, Löchern oder mit großer Geste, als lärmender Strahl, durch schmale Düsen gepreßt als Fontäne oder als brodelnder Wasserfall über Felswände und Fassaden stürzend in große Wasserbecken auf den Plätzen der Stadt.

Careful and reticent as a tiny trickle, as a dripping trace, as a small bubble from cracks, splits, holes, or as a grand gesture, as a noisy stream, forced through narrow jets as a fountain or crashing as a seething waterfall over rock walls and façades into great pools of water in the city squares.

Das ausfließende Wasser gefaßt in Marmortrögen, in Granitwannen, in Holzrinnen, in Stahlkuben, in künstlichen Seen.

Water is caught as it flows out in marble troughs, in granite tubs, in wooden gutters, in steel cubes, in artificial lakes.

Das Wasser in Tassen geschöpft, in Vasen gegossen, in Flaschen abgefüllt, in Eimern aufgestaut.

Water drawn in cups, poured into vases, filled into bottles, stored in buckets.

Oder inszeniertes Wasserauftreten: als mythologisches Spiel (mit Nymphen), als religiöser Akt (mit Taufe), als Hollywood-Spektakel, nachts, bunt beleuchtet von Scheinwerfern, mit Bade-Ballett und tanzenden Delphinen.

Or water making a staged appearance: as a mythological game (with nymphs), as a religious act (in baptism), as a Hollywood spectacle, at night, brightly lit with spotlights, with bathing ballet and dancing dolphins.

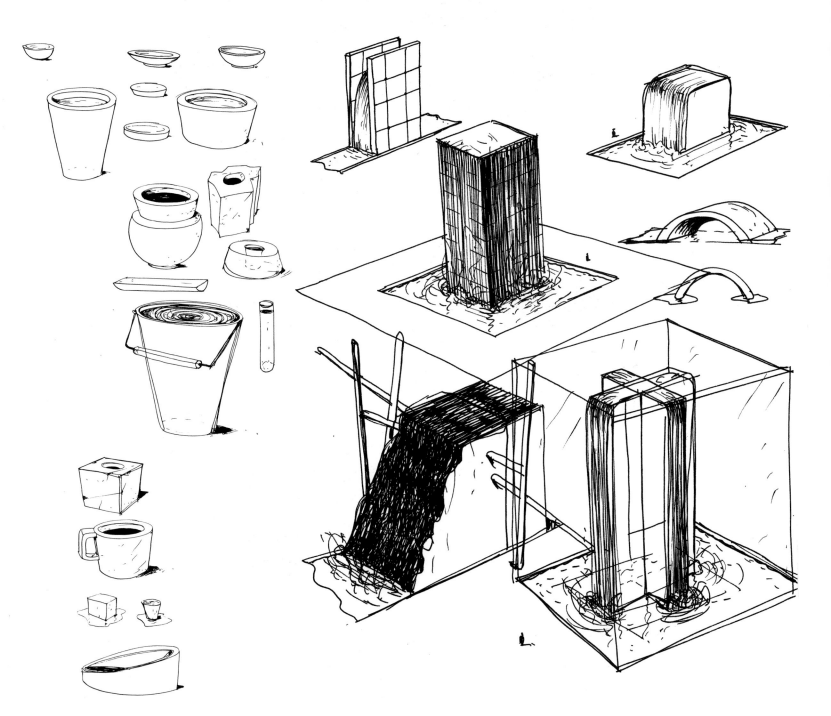

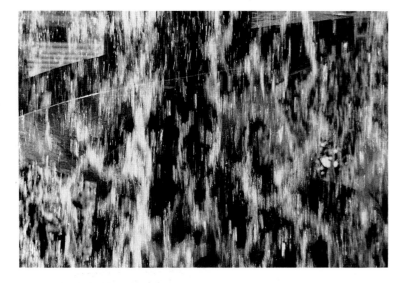

Für die alten und neuen Garten- und Parkanlagen ist das Wasser das edelste und vornehmste Element, es sprudelt – sich ewig selbst erneuernd und reinigend – über Steine und Treppen, läuft durch Wiesenbäche und fängt sich in Seen verschiedener Größe und Form. Die Seenflächen funkeln wie Edelsteine durch die Bäume, in jeder kleinen Welle spiegelt sich die Sonne. Die Wasserfläche sollte die Mitte eines jeden Parks markieren, sie ist der Höhepunkt und der Verbindungspunkt zwischen oben (Himmel) und unten (Tiefe der Erde).

For old and new gardens and parks water is the noblest and most distinguished element, it bubbles – eternally renewing and purifying itself – over stones and steps, runs through grassy streams and is captured in lakes of various shapes and sizes. The lake surfaces sparkle like precious stones through the trees, the sun is reflected in every little wave. The surface of the water should mark the centre of every park, it is the climax and point of connection between above (sky) and below (the depths of the earth).

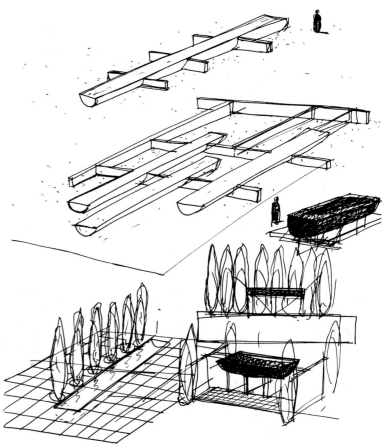

Während die Vegetation einen Zeitrhythmus hat, den man nur über Tage beobachten kann, läßt sich das Wasser auf den Zeitrhythmus des Besuchers einstellen, es scheint mit ihm zu leben, es verändert sich schnell, es reagiert in Sekunden. Und trotzdem strahlt die Wasserfläche Ruhe aus, meditatives Insichruhen.

While vegetation has a time rhythm that can be observed only over a period of days, water can be adjusted to the visitor's time rhythm, it appears to live with him, it changes rapidly and reacts in seconds. And nevertheless the surface of the water radiates calm and the meditative peace that is within it.

Als Inszenierungselement ist das Wasser nicht hoch genug einzuschätzen. Man kann Sprudler-Felder anlegen, Fontänenalleen und -wälder, Wasserfallreihungen und Kaskadenlinien (erinnert sei an die Villa d'Este).

Water cannot be esteemed highly enough as a staging element. Sprayer-fields can be set up, avenues and forests of fountains, sequences of waterfalls and lines of cascades (do not forget the Villa d'Este).

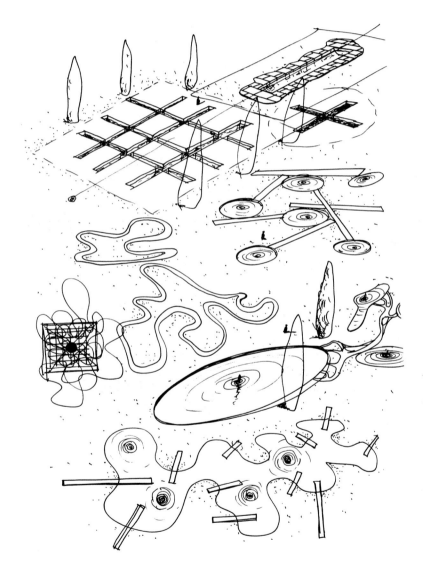

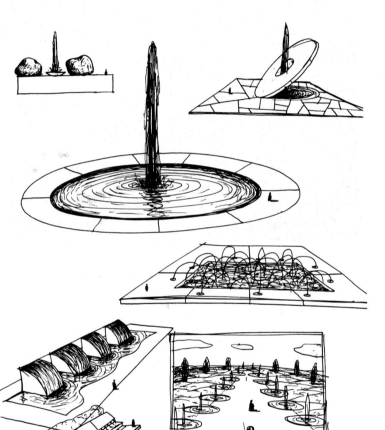

Fontänen-Baustellen, Fontänen-Plantagen usw.

Fountain building sites, fountain plantations etc.

Brunnenplantagen.

Fountain plantations.

Wassergärten zu Schwimmbädern erweitert.

Water gardens extended as swimming pools.

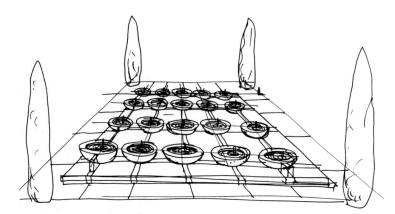

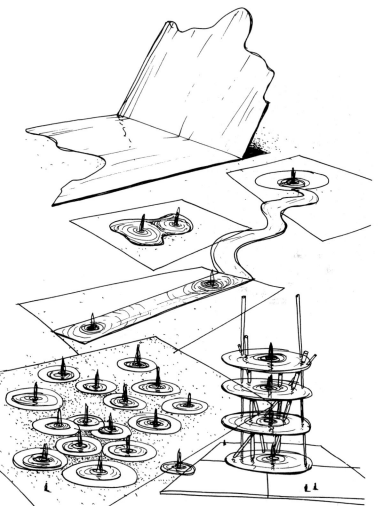

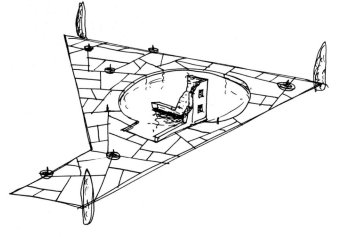

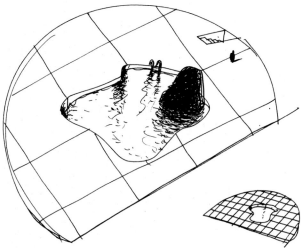

Schwebende Brunnenfelder, schwebende Seenflächen.
Eine Wasserspur zieht sich durch Lichtungen, bis
hin zum Horizont, darüber die Wolken, die sich im
gefangenen Wasser spiegeln.

Floating fountain areas, floating lake areas.
A trail of water runs through clearings to the hori-
zon, above it the clouds, which are reflected in
the captured water.

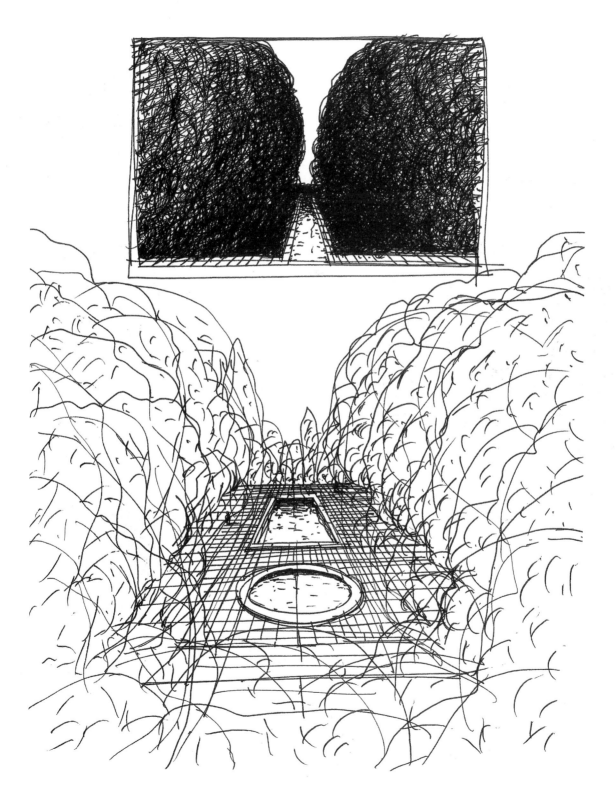

Wasserplätze

Water squares

Plätze mit Brunnenanlagen. Sachliche Anordnungen, sauber beschnitten und begrenzt. Verbunden mit Rinnen, Mauern, Felsen, Bäumen, Blumenfeldern, Flügeln, Masten und Antennen, mit Reklamegestängen und Regalreihen.
Schwarze tiefe Quell-Löcher, mit hallenden, fernen Plätschergeräuschen.
Übertragungen der Grundwasserströme in Ton und Bild auf die öffentlichen Plätze, in die Gärten und Parks.

Squares with fountains. Neutral arrangements, cleanly cut and limited. Connected to small channels, walls, rocks, trees, floral areas, vanes, masts and aerials, with tubular structures for advertising and rows of shelves.
Black, deep spring-holes with echoing, distant splashing sounds.
Transferring ground-water streams in sound and picture to public squares, to parks and gardens.

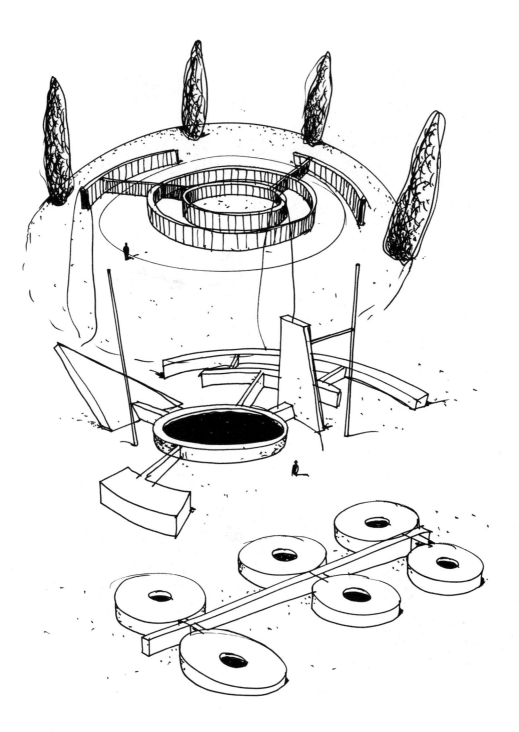

Quellen in Schaufenstern und Telefonzellen.
Blicke in die Kanalisation, in das Zuströmen des
sauberen und das Abströmen des schmutzigen
Wassers.

*Springs in shop windows and telephone boxes.
Glimpses of the sewerage system, of clean water
flowing inwards and dirty water flowing
outwards.*

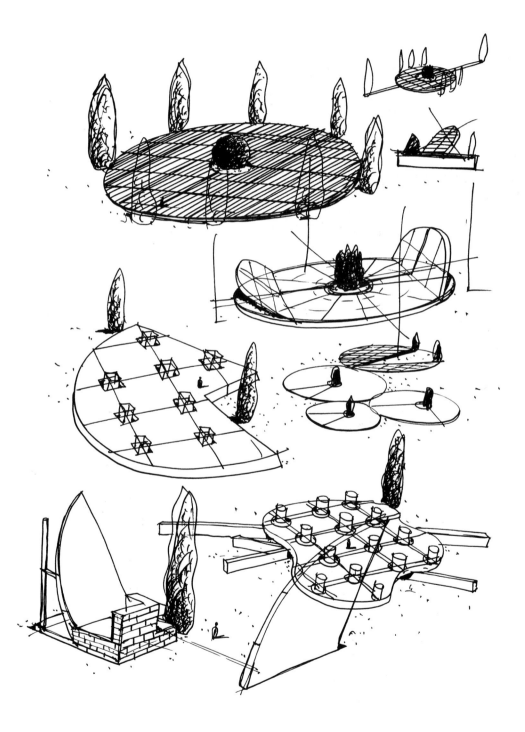

In der Ferne das Meer: Übertragung der Bran-
dungsgeräusche auf jeden Stadtplatz.

*In the distance the sea: bringing the sound of surf
to every city square.*

Über den Plätzen kreisen künstliche Wolken.
Regenplätze.

*Artificial clouds circle above the squares.
Rain squares.*

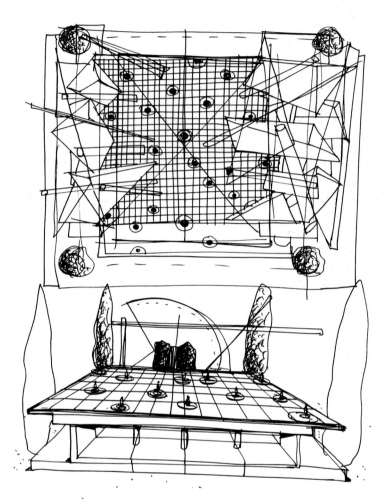

Unterwasser-Bilder: versunkene Blätter, versunkene Häuser, Straßen und Plätze, versunkene Leben. Ruinen: Steine, Scherben.

Pictures under water: sunken leaves, sunken houses, roads and squares, sunken lives. Ruins: stones, shards.

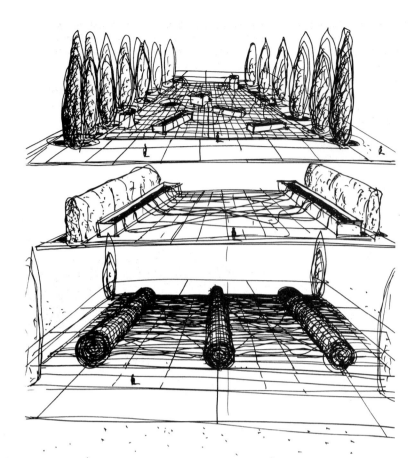

Brunnenanlagen wie Versuchsanordnungen.
Die Verschmutzungen und die Prozeduren der
Reinigung ausstellen. Öffentliche Kläranlagen, die
man sonntags wie Kirchen oder Museen besu-
chen kann.
Das Wasser als Grundlage des Lebens in den
Städten und in den Parkanlagen darstellen. Das
zentrale Gebäude jeder Stadt ist ein Wassersilo.

*Fountain systems like experimental arrange-
ments. Exhibiting the soiled water and the clean-
ing process. Clarification plants that you can visit
on Sundays like churches or museums.
Water to be presented as the basis of life in cities
and parks. The central building is a water silo.*

Abwasser.

Sewage.

Wasserarchitekturen

Water architecture

Brunnenanlagen in Unterführungen, in Kaufhäusern, in Passagen, in Kirchen, in Baustellengruben, in den Baumwipfeln der Stadtparkbäume, in Tankstellen, in Bahnhöfen, auf Kreuzungen, in Bibliotheken, auf Parkplätzen und in Parkhäusern.

Fountains in subways, in department stores, in arcades, in churches, in pits on building sites, in the crowns of trees in the municipal park, in petrol stations, at junctions, in libraries, on car parks and multi-storeys.

Vorstellung: Man fährt nicht mehr mit dem Auto, der Straßenbahn, dem Bus oder dem Fahrrad zum Einkaufen und zur Arbeit, sondern man schwimmt dorthin.

Imagine: no more travelling to work or the shops by car, tram, bus or bicycle, but swimming there.

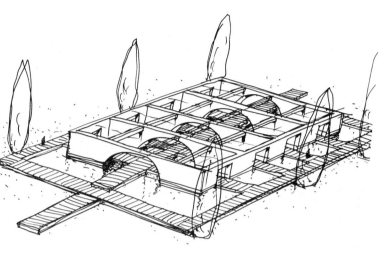

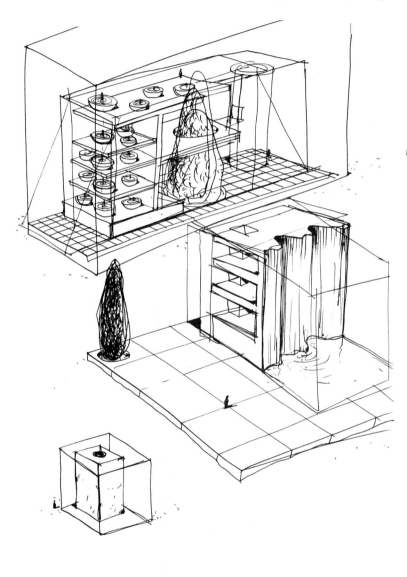

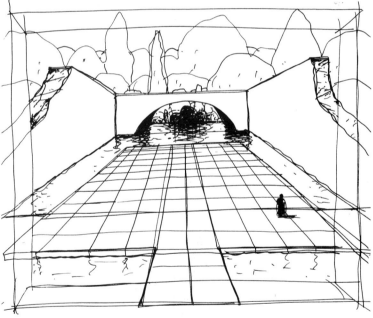

Wasserfälle in Hauszwischenräumen, in aufge-
schlitzten Häusern.
Garten- oder Platzfläche mit Badezimmerfrag-
menten.

Waterfalls in the gaps between buildings, in
buildings that have been slit open.
Garden or square with bathroom fragments.

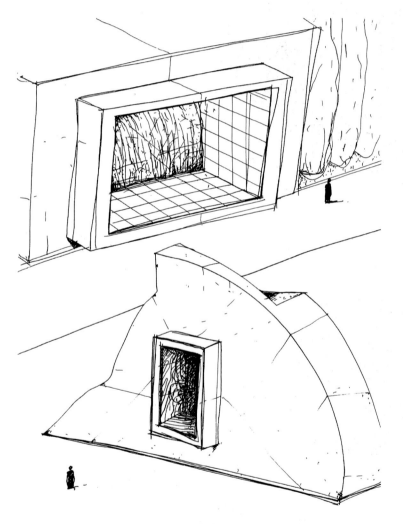

Wasserhäuser.
Wasserfallhäuser.

Water buildings.
Waterfall buildings.

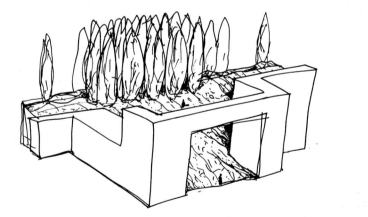

Wasserflächen: Das Wasser steigt

Areas of water: water rising

Steigende Seefläche als Wasserspur durch Städte und Landschaften.
Dinge treiben still über die Wasserflächen. Inseln. Träume und Sehnsüchte.

Rising lake area as a trail of water through cities and landscapes.
Things move silently over the surface of the water. Islands. Dreams and longings.

Vorstellung: Ganze Stadtteile werden unter Wasser gesetzt und überflutet, wenn die Häuser unbewohnbar geworden sind. Nur noch die Dächer erheben sich über den Wasserflächen.
Neue Landschaften.
Neue Landschaftsarchitektur?

Imagine: entire areas of the city flooded and inundated when buildings have become uninhabitable. Only the roofs stick out above the surface of the water. New landscapes.
New landscape architecture?

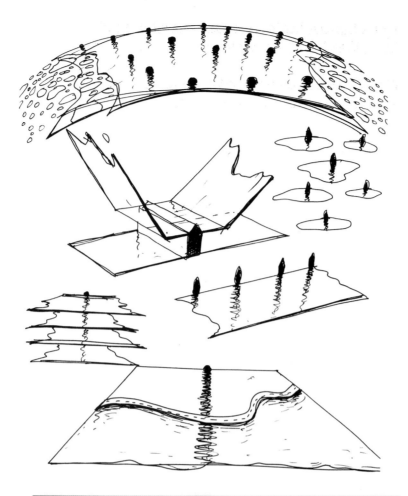

Unter den Dächern, in den Straßenschluchten und in den Wohnungen, in den Passagen und in den Kaufhäusern schwimmen Taucher wie utopische Fische.

Divers swim under the roofs, in the street ravines and in the houses, in the arcades and department stores like utopian fish.

Darüber der Horizont mit vielen untergehenden Sonnen.

Above this the horizon, with many setting suns.

Neue Landschafts- und Gartenarchitektur
Luft-, Wind- und Wolkenthema

New landscape and garden architecture
The subject of air, wind and clouds

Wenn die Erde, der Boden, das Gras, die Steine und das Wasser den Fußboden des Landschaftsraums darstellen und die Bäume, Felsen und Berge die Wände dieses Raums verkörpern, so ist der Himmel die Raumdecke. In diesen Raum hinein ereignet sich die Vegetation, in ihm atmen die Pflanzen, die Tiere und die Menschen.

If earth, grass, stones and water form the floor of the landscape space, and trees, rocks and mountains form the walls of this space, then the sky is the ceiling of the space. Vegetation thrusts up in this space, in it plants, animals and humans breathe.

Wind-Rechen. Wind-Korridor. Wind-Fluß.
Wind-Straße.

Wind grating. Wind corridor. Wind river.
Wind road.

Während die Erde, der Boden, die Vegetation, die
Steine, Felsen und die Architekturen an einem
Ort verharren, bewegt sich die Luft als Wind dar-
über hinweg.

While earth, ground, vegetation, stones, rocks
and architecture stay in the same place, the air
moves over them as wind.

Es ist wie ein surrealer Vorgang: Eine unsichtbare Kraft wirft sich über die Landschaft, über Büsche und Bäume, schüttelt an Stämmen und Blättern, fegt alles in eine Richtung, wirft Zweige hoch und Äste. Ein Rauschen und Tosen, ein Flattern und Fetzenfliegen – und dann wieder Stille, der ruhige Zustand, das schweigende Dastehn als wäre nichts gewesen. Der Wind als immaterielle, für uns nur indirekt sichtbare Kraft.

It is like a surreal happening: an invisible force hurls itself across the landscape, over bushes and trees, shaking trunks and leaves, brushing everything in one direction, throwing twigs and branches into the air. A rushing and roaring, a fluttering and flying of scraps – and then stillness again, as though nothing had happened. Wind as an immaterial force only indirectly visible to us.

Haus-Grundrisse mit Innenhofgärten im ruhigen
Strömen des Windes.

*Ground plans of buildings with courtyard gardens
in the peaceful streaming of the wind.*

Die Windkraft wurde schon in der Vergangenheit eingefangen und von Windmühlen, von den Segeln der Schiffe genutzt. Riesige neue Windräder tauchen am Horizont auf. Geben sie den Städten die notwendige Energie?

The power of the wind has long been used by windmills, harnessed by the sails of ships. Gigantic new windmills are looming on the horizon. Can they provide the necessary energy for our cities?

Wind-Kraftwerke. Wind-Fallen. Wind-Fänge. Wind-Mühlen. Wind-Turbinen. Wind-Maschinen.

Wind power stations. Wind traps. Wind breaks. Windmills. Wind turbines. Wind machines.

Windgärten, Wolkengärten

Wind gardens, cloud gardens.

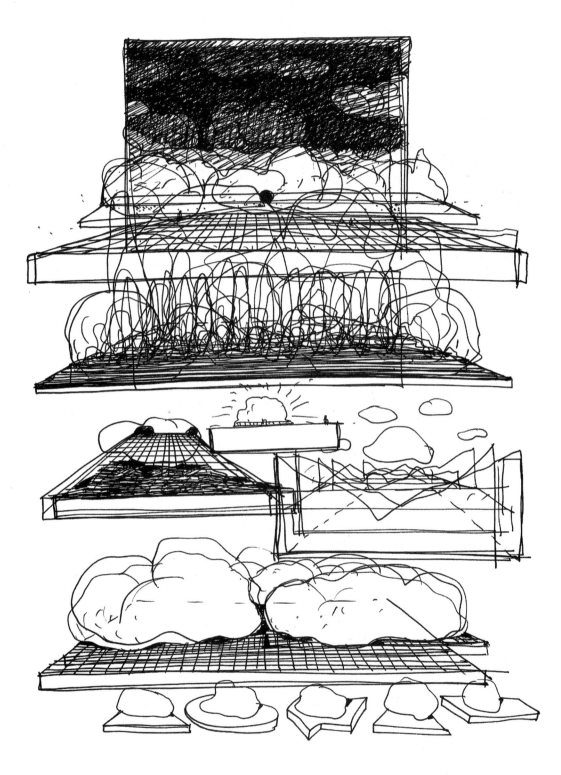

Vorstellung: Der Wind gewinnt die Übermacht
und bläst alle Dinge über den Rand der Welt.

*Imagine: the wind gains the upper hand and
blows everything off the edge of the world.*

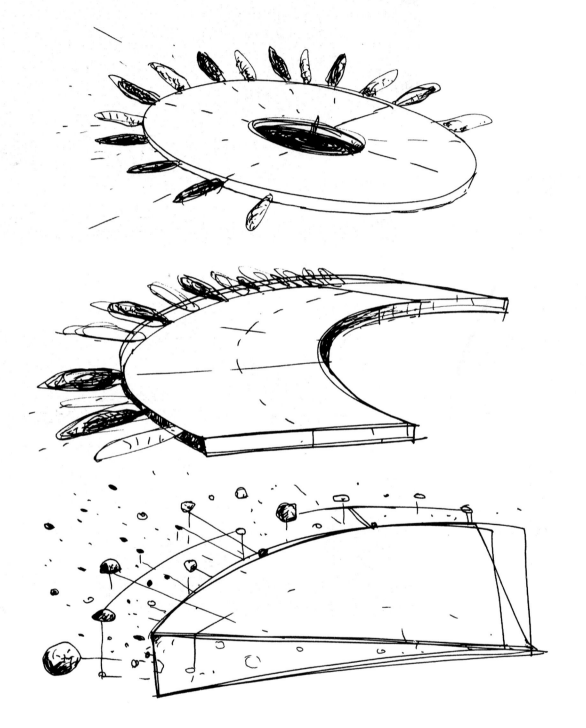

Radfenster, Steinblumen, Windrosen, Windräder und schwarze Architekturfragmente treiben vorbei.

Wheel windows, stone flowers, wind roses, windmills and black fragments of architecture fly past.

Im Zeitalter der Flugzeuge liegt es nahe, auch den Luftraum in die Gestaltungsüberlegungen einzubeziehen. An Ballons oder Flugzeugen hängende Gärten, Terrassen und Hotels auf Wolken, langsam über die Landschaft und über die Meere schwebende Luftschiffe (Zeppeline) mit eingebauten Gärten und Grotten, mit Springbrunnen und Palmenhainen sind vorstellbar. Man könnte auf vorbeiziehende Wolken Bilder und Szenen, Filme und Theaterstücke projizieren oder mit Laserlicht real wirkende Figuren und Landschaften in die Wolken zaubern.

In the age of the aeroplane it seems that we should include airspace in our design considerations as well. It is possible to imagine gardens hanging from balloons or aircraft, terraces and hotels on clouds, airships (Zeppelins) floating slowly over the landscape and the sea, with built-in gardens and grottoes, with fountains and palm groves. It would be possible to project pictures and scenes, films and plays on to passing clouds, or conjure real-looking figures and landscapes on to the clouds with lasers.

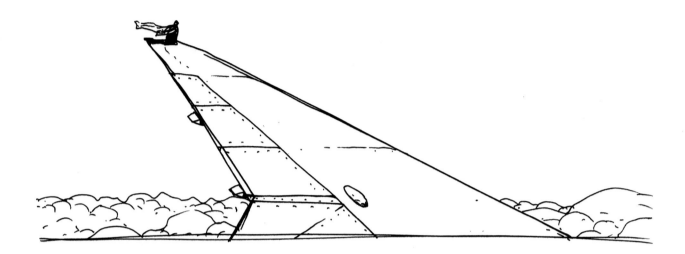

Neue Landschafts- und Gartenarchitektur
Landschaft und Architektur

New landscape and garden architecture
Landscape and architecture

Während wir es bisher mit den Elementen der Landschaft und der Natur, mit möglichen Strukturen, Eingriffen und Umformungen zu tun hatten, kommt mit der Architektur ein fremder und künstlicher Eingriff dazu. Menschliche Architektur kennt keine gewachsenen Gehäuseformen wie die Pflanzen- und Tierwelt.

While hitherto we have been dealing with elements of landscape and nature, with possible structures, intervention and reshaping, architecture brings in an alien and artificial intervention. Human architecture does not have set casing shapes like the plant and animal worlds.

Architektur und Landschaft stehen sich gegenüber wie zwei feindliche Brüder: Landschaft braucht keine Architektur, aber Architektur braucht Landschaft.
Da der Natur-Landschaftsraum der eigentliche Herkunftsbereich des Menschen ist, hat er eine tiefe Sehnsucht danach, in ihr zu sein, in ihr zu wohnen, in ihr zu leben.

Architecture and landscape are juxtaposed like two inimical brothers: landscape does not need architecture, but architecture needs landscape. As natural landscape space is the place from which man actually originates he has a deep longing to be within it, to dwell in it, to live in it.

Der Vorgang des Bauens führt immer zu einer Auslöschung, zur Zerstörung von Natur und Landschaft. Mit Fundamenten wird der Boden verschlossen und versiegelt. Mauern werden gegen Bäume und kalte Winde errichtet, Dächer schützen vor Regen und Sonne. Durch die Architektur wird ein gleichmäßiges Klima innerhalb des Gebäudes hergestellt. Die Architektur umgibt das Leben mit einer Schutzhülle.

The process of building always leads to extinguishing, to destroying nature and landscape. The ground is locked and sealed with foundations. Walls are set to protect against trees and cold winds, roofs protect against clouds, rain and sun. Architecture preserves an even climate within the building. Architecture envelops life with a protective covering.

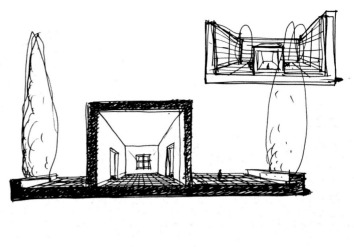

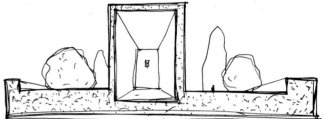

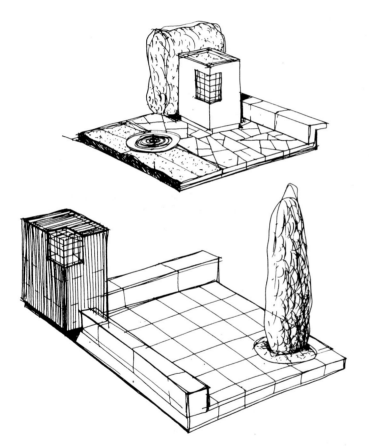

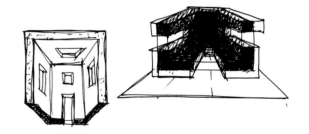

Der Grad der Feindschaft zwischen Architektur und Naturlandschaft wird auch durch die Baumaterialien bestimmt. Am Anfang der Architekturgeschichte stehen Häuser aus Naturbaustoffen, wie Holz, Stein, Rinde, Lehm, Blätter usw., Materialien, die man in der unmittelbaren Umgebung sammelte. Bei Städten überwiegen die künstlichen Baustoffe. Eine gebaute Landschaft überdeckt die Naturlandschaft.

The degree of enmity between architecture and the natural landscape is also determined by building materials. At the beginning of architectural history houses were made of natural building materials, gathered in the immediate surroundings like wood, stone, bark, clay, leaves etc. In cities artificial building materials predominate. The natural landscape is covered with man-made built landscape.

Der alte Traum von einem Haus mit Garten bleibt
bestehen. Aber die Realität der Städte läßt dies
kaum noch zu.
Die kleinen Gartenhäuser bieten Ersatz.

The old dream of a house with a garden lives on.
But the reality of cities scarcely permits this any
more.
Small garden houses offer a substitute.

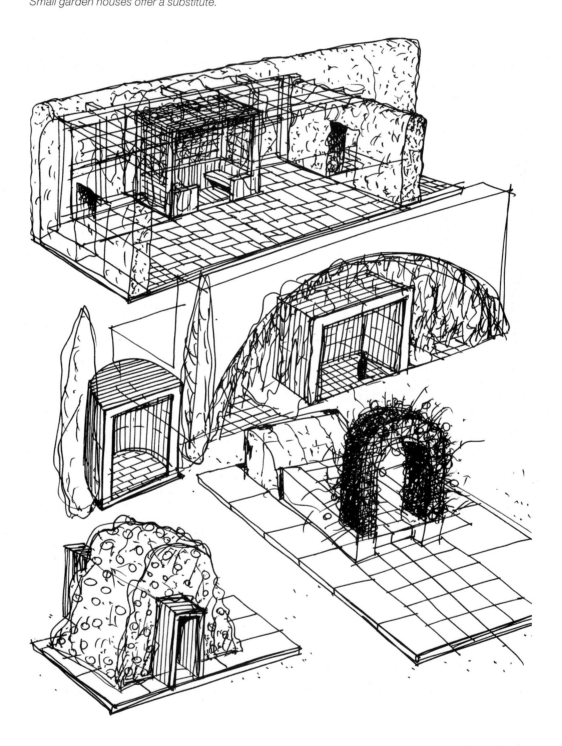

Ein Haus, ganz aus Fenstern gebaut. Glashaus.
Fensterlabyrinth.

A house built entirely of windows. Glasshouse.
Window labyrinth.

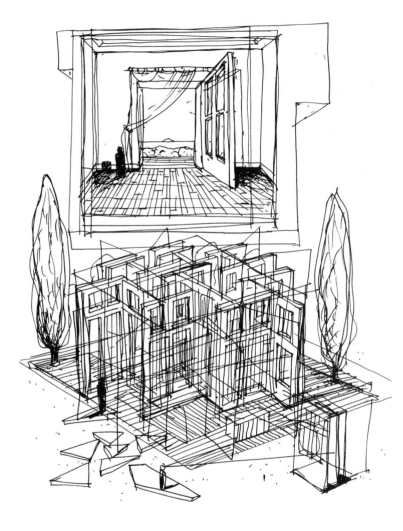

Vielleicht gibt es ein Fenster mit Blick auf einen
Baum. Beruhigende Teilung der Welt. Regen und
Schneefall draußen, Wärme drinnen. Beiden
Räumen angehören: ständiges Pendeln zwischen innen und außen.

Perhaps there is a window with a view of a tree.
Reassuring division of the world. Rain and snow
outside, warmth inside. Belonging to two spaces:
constantly swinging between inside and outside.

Die Wände lösen sich auf, werden transparent
und geben den Blick auf die Natur frei.

The walls dissolve, become transparent and give
way to a view of nature.

Langsame Umkehrungen: Der Außenraum dringt nach innen.
Wiese im Innenraum. Jahreszeiten fließen durch Landschaft und Architektur wie ein sichtbar gewordener Strom.

Slow reversals: the exterior space thrusts its way inside.
Interior lawn. Seasons flow through landscape and architecture like a current that has become visible.

Steinarchitekturen

Stone architecture

Häuser aus Geröll, aus Steinblöcken und Felsbrocken.

*Buildings made of scree, of stone blocks and
lumps of rock.*

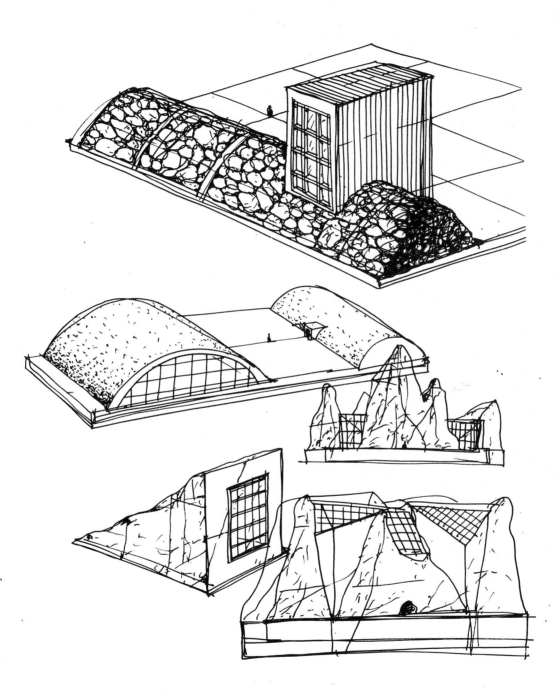

Felswohnungen, Felsbüros, Felsmuseen, Fels-häuser.

Rock dwellings, rock offices, rock museums, rock houses.

Gebirgshäuser. Wohnen an den schönen Land-schaftsstellen der Welt, auf den Gipfeln der Berge, in einem Glashaus mitten im Urwald oder im ewigen Eis der Arktis, auf einem Felsatoll im Meer treibend, von Südseeinsel zu Südseein-sel …

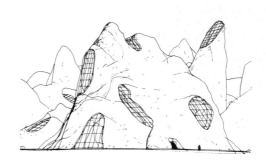

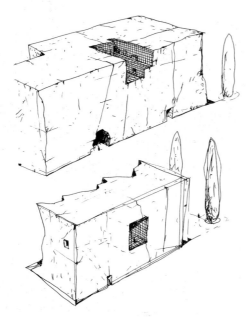

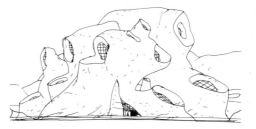

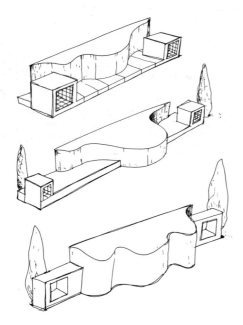

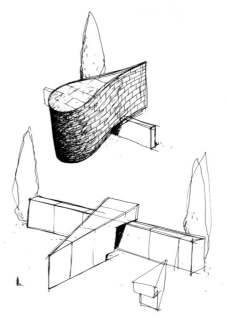

Mountain houses. Living in the world's beautiful places, on mountain tops, in a glass house in the middle of the jungle or in the eternal Arctic ice, on a rocky atoll drifting in the middle of the sea, from South Sea island to South Sea island …

Holzarchitekturen

Wooden architecture

Waldstücke mit Architektur-Einbauten. Wald-Architekturen.

Pieces of woodland with built-in architecture. Wood architecture.

Holzarchitekturen. Wohnen in Holzhäusern. Zersägte Wälder werden zu Kuben verarbeitet, zu Wänden, zu Dächern, zu Türen und Fenstern.

Wooden architecture. Living in wooden buildings. Sawn-up forests are turned into cubes, walls, roofs, doors and windows.

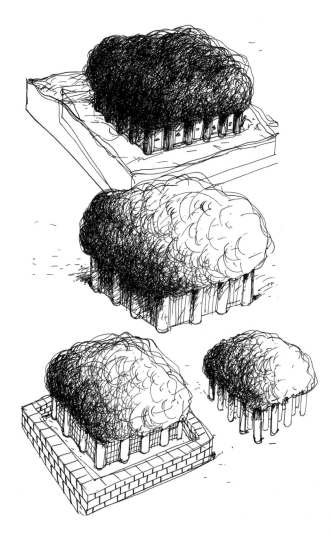

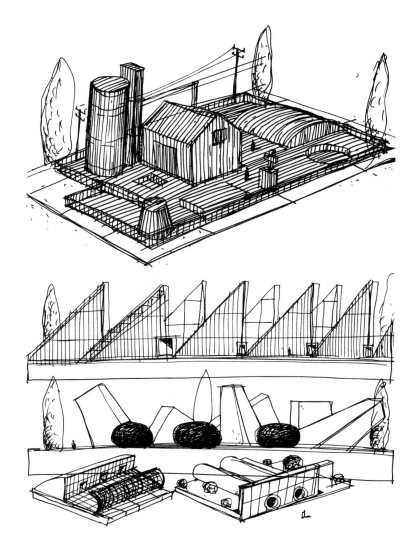

213

Holztürme, Holzkeile, Holzkegel, Holzwände.

*Wooden towers, wooden wedges, wooden
cones, wooden walls.*

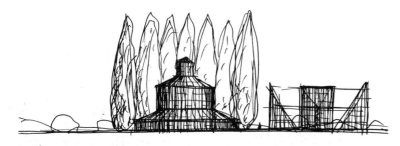

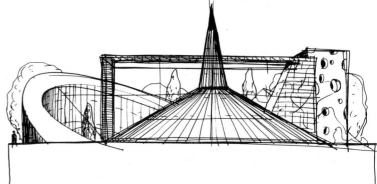

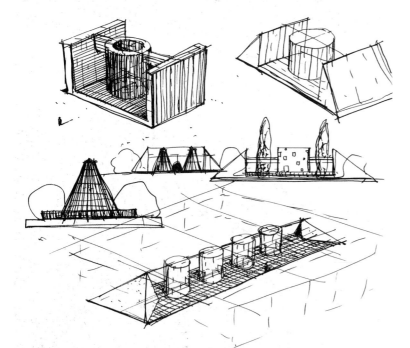

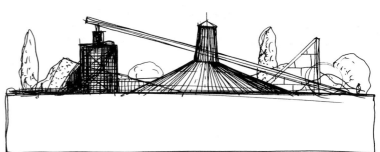

Holz-Flure, Holz-Schiffe, Holz-Flugzeuge, Holz-Züge, Holz-Garagen, Holz-Gedanken.
Holzstädte.

Wooden corridors, wooden ships, wooden aircraft, wooden trains, wooden garages, wooden thoughts.
Wooden cities.

Holzarchitekturen werden langsam zu Holz-Landschaften.

Wooden architecture slowly becomes wooden landscape.

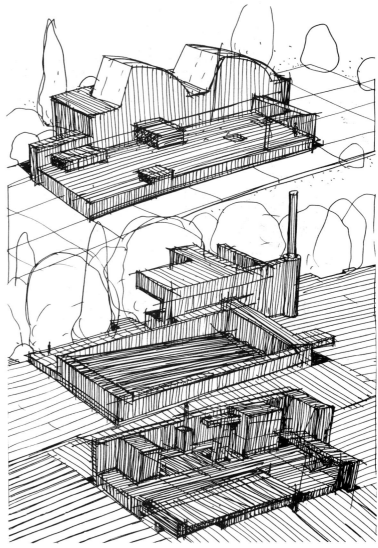

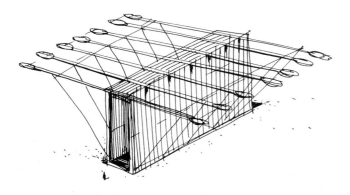

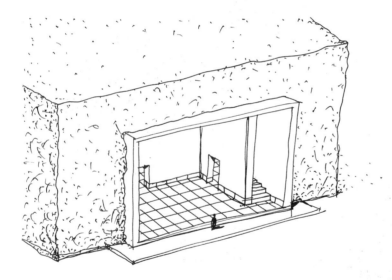

Räume eingebaut in Strohberge, in Strohhaufen.

Rooms built into mountains of straw, into piles of straw.

Strohhaus-Anbauten. Stroh-Architektur-Land-
schaften.

*Straw house extensions. Straw architecture land-
scapes.*

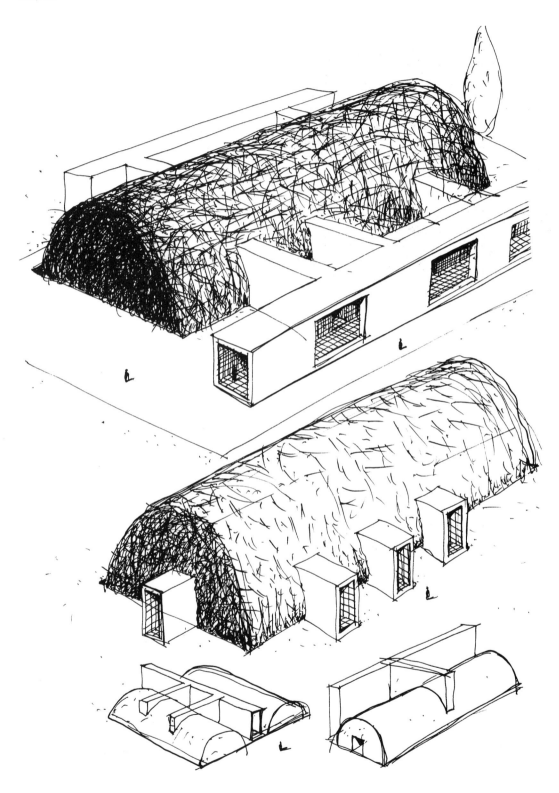

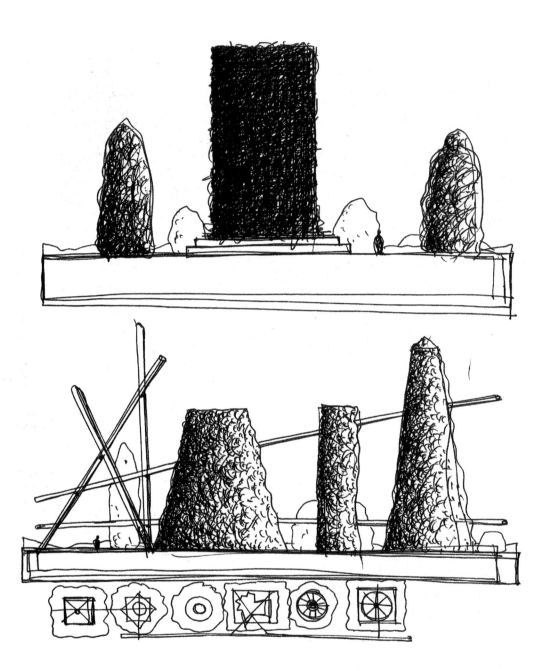

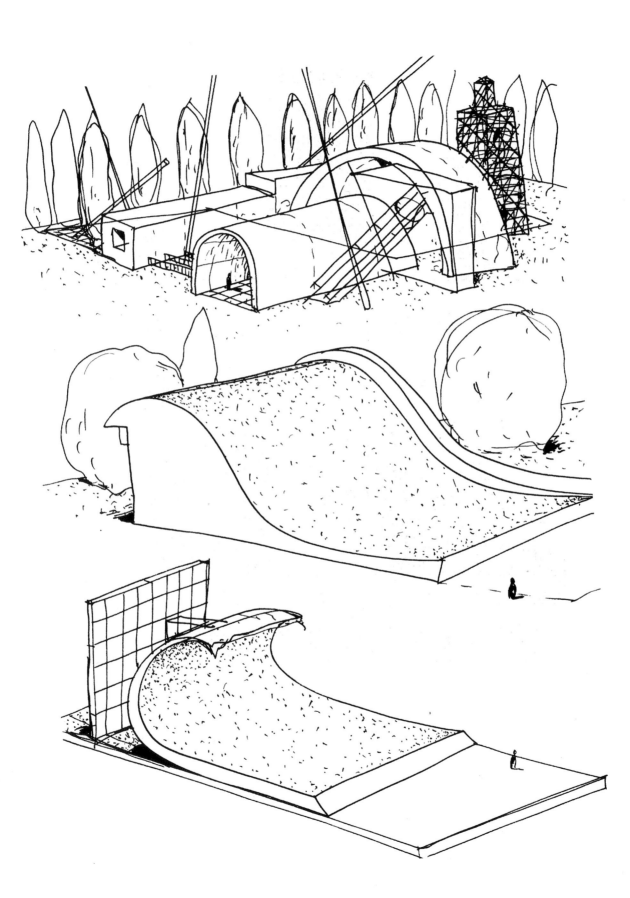

Erdhügelhaus-Städte. Stadt-Gebirge.

Earth-mound house cities. City mountains.

Glashäuser, eingegraben in Wiesen, in Hügeln, versenkt in Erdspalten und Felsmulden.

Glass houses embedded in lawns and mounds, sunk into cracks in the earth and troughs in the rock.

Die Flächen der Glasdächer liegen in einer Wiese wie vereiste Seen.

The surfaces of the glass roofs lie in a meadow like frozen lakes.

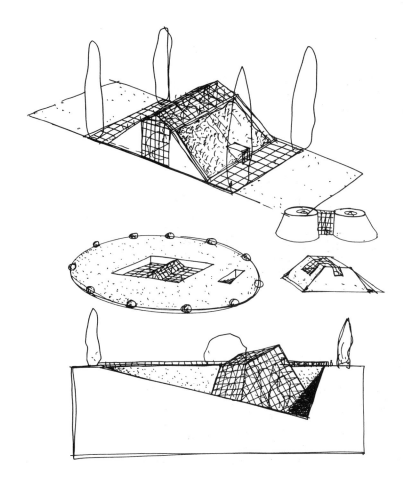

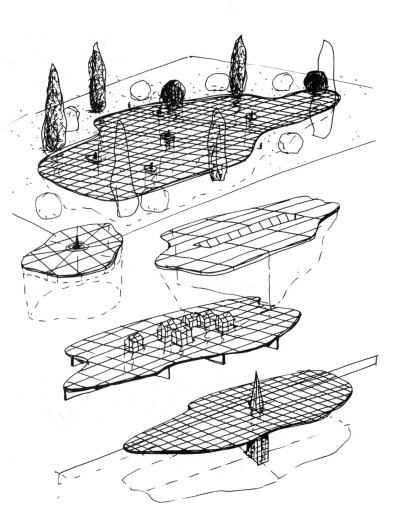

Dachterrassen als öffentliche Gärten und Parks.

Roof terraces as public gardens and parks.

Getarnte Erd-Häuser. Man sieht nur Wiese, alles andere ist im Boden versteckt.
Sich Städte so vorstellen: Nichts wäre zu sehen als eine grüne Landschaft mit Bäumen, Blumen, Seen und darüberschwebenden Wolken.

*Disguised earth houses. All that can be seen is lawn, everything else is hidden in the ground.
Imagine towns like that: nothing to be seen but a green landscape with trees, flowers, lakes and the clouds sailing above them.*

Neue Landschafts- und Gartenarchitektur
Verflechtungen

New landscape and garden architecture
Interconnections

Die Brutalität des architektonischen Eingriffs in die Landschaft kann man als ein Mittel der Konfrontation einsetzen, kann sie aber ebenso durch Anpassung und Tarnung mildern. Eine Möglichkeit, den architektonischen Körper mit der Landschaft zu verbinden, ist die Verflechtung. Dieser Vorgang beinhaltet, daß die Architektur sich an der Grenze zum Naturraum in Strukturen auflöst, die in die Vegetation hineingreifen und im Laufe der Zeit von ihr überwuchert werden.

It is possible to use the brutality of architectural intervention in the landscape as a means of confrontation, but it can also be reduced by methods of adaptation and masking. One possibility of bringing the architectural body into connection with the landscape is interconnection. This process requires the architecture to dissolve into structures on the periphery of natural space that thrust into the vegetation and are overgrown by it in the course of time.

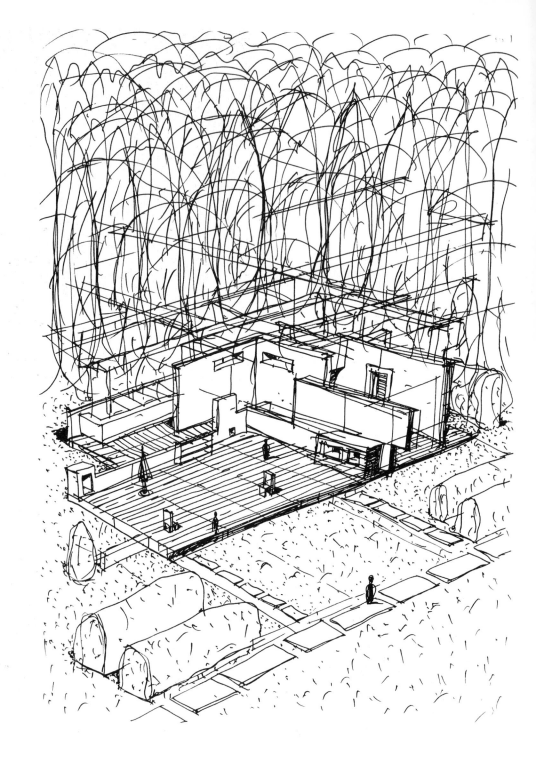

Der Baum als Vorbild: Eine Struktur aus Ästen ist in den Raum hineinverflochten, kahl und leer, dann langsam mit Knospen überzogen und schließlich von Blättern bedeckt.

The tree as model: a branch structure is interwoven with space, bald and empty, then slowly covered over with buds, and finally covered with leaves.

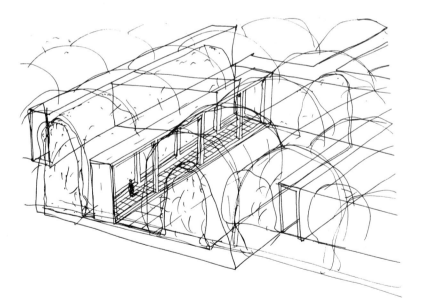

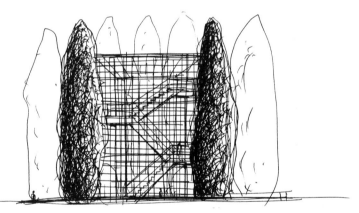

Gebäude, ganz in Linien aufgelöst.
Luft-Fachwerke. Der Wind zieht durch die Architektur als sei sie nicht vorhanden.

Buildings entirely dissolved into lines.
Aerial framework. The wind blows through the
architecture as if it were not there.

Raum-Verflechtung zwischen Zeigen und
Verhüllen.

Space interconnection between showing and
concealing.

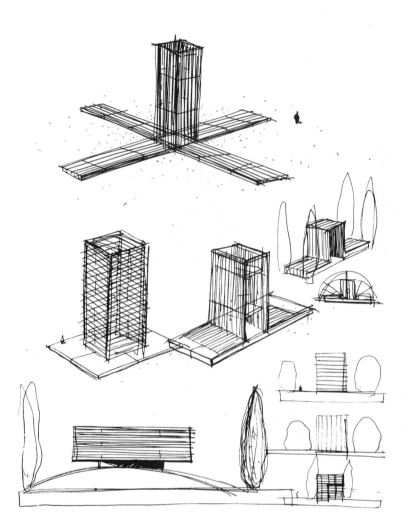

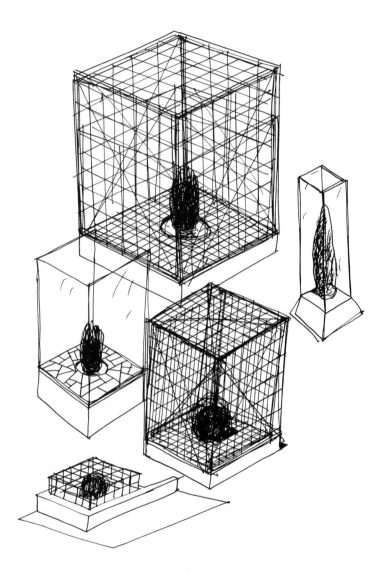

Die Vegetation greift an.

Vegetation attacks.

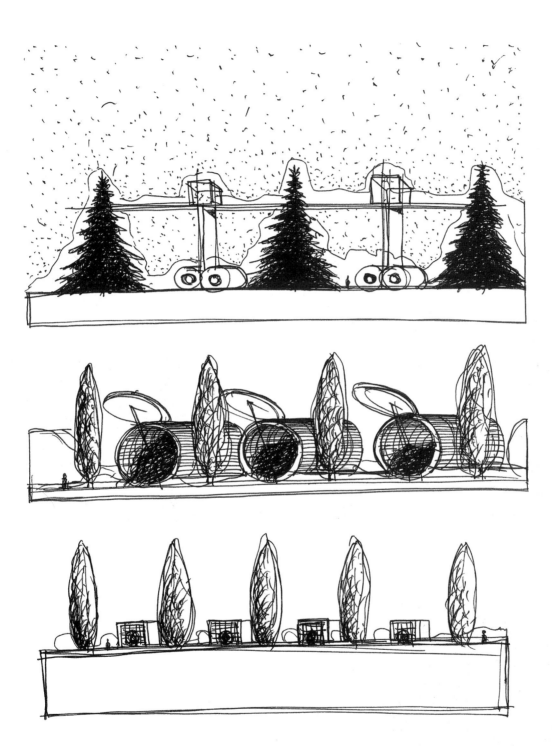

Langsames Einwachsen.

Slowly growing in.

Sommerbild: Die Verflechtung ist vollendet. Die künstliche Struktur, das Gitterwerk, die Linienarchitektur ist eingewachsen und zu einem Teil der Natur geworden.

Summer image: the interconnection is complete. The artificial structure, the grid work, the line-architecture has grown in and become part of nature.

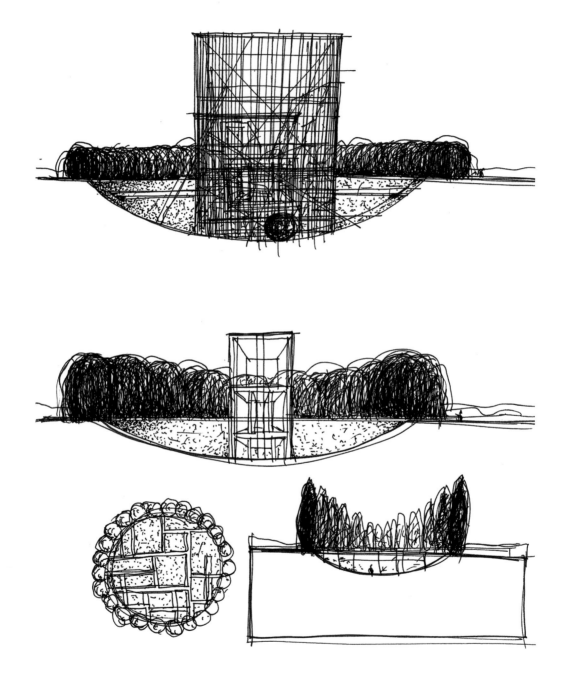

Neue Landschafts- und Gartenarchitektur
Künstliche Landschaften

New landscape and garden architecture
Artificial landscapes

Wo heute die Grenze zwischen »natürlich« und »künstlich« verläuft, ist schwer zu sagen. Bereits der menschliche Blick auf die Landschaft ist im Grunde künstlich, da er nicht die »Wahrheit« vermittelt, sondern nur verschlüsselte Reize aufnimmt, die im Gehirn zu »Abbildern«verarbeitet werden. Die perspektivische Verzerrung, die durch die Konstruktion der Pupille entsteht, führt dazu, daß Täuschung, Fälschung und Fiktion durcheinandergeraten. Ob das geistige Medium der Vorstellung als »künstlich« oder als »natürlich« zu bezeichnen ist, vermag daher niemand mit Bestimmtheit zu sagen.

It is difficult to say today where the boundary between ›natural‹ and ›artificial‹ falls. Even the way in which humans look at the landscape is fundamentally ›artificial‹, as it does not communicate ›truth‹ but perceives only coded stimuli that are processed to form ›copies‹ in the mind. Perspective distortion by the structure of the pupil leads to a confused mixture of deception, falsification, fiction and truth. Nobody can assert positively whether the intellectual and spiritual medium of imagination can be called ›artificial‹ or ›natural‹.

Landschaft ist heute mit vielen künstlichen Häuten überzogen. Mit Häuten aus Stahl, Glas, Aluminium, Asphalt, Beton, Kunststoff, aber auch mit Verkehrshäuten, Kommunikations-, Wellen-, Strahlen-, Medien-Häuten. Die »Nerven« und »Adern« der neuen Landschaften sind nicht mehr gewachsen aus Fleisch und Blut, aus Holz und Wasser, sondern bestehen aus Stahlrohren und Glasfaserkabeln.

Today landscape is covered with many artificial skins. With skins of steel, glass, aluminium, asphalt, concrete, plastic, but also with traffic skin, communication, wave, beam and media skins. The ›nerves‹ and ›veins‹ of the new landscapes are no longer grown from flesh and blood, from wood and water, but made up of steel tubes and fibre-glass cables.

Die nackte Haut der Natur ist mit Kleidung bedeckt.

The naked skin of nature is covered with clothes.

Daß technische Medien, die das Abbilden von Natur-Realität ermöglichen, eher dem Bereich »künstlich« zugeordnet werden, darüber besteht weitgehend Einigkeit. Ein leiser Zweifel bleibt jedoch bestehen.

There is general agreement about the fact that technical media making it possible to copy nature reality should be classed as ›artificial‹. A slight doubt persists.

Die Realität eines Felsens gegen das Foto eines Felsens, gegen das Filmbild eines Felsens, gegen die Video-Übertragung eines Felsens beziehungsweise gegen die Video-Übertragung eines Felsenabbildes.

The reality of a rock against the photograph of a rock, against a film image of a rock, against a video of a rock or against a video of a copy of a rock.

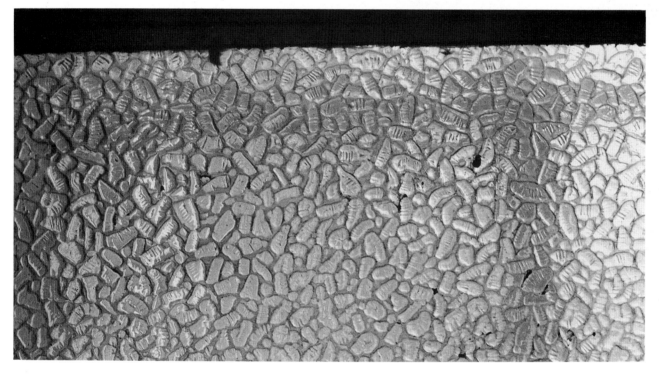

Abgüsse der »natürlichen« Natur. Reproduktionen.

Casts of ›natural‹ nature. Reproductions.

Natur unter der Natur. Natur in der Natur. Natur über der Naturnaturnaturnaturnatur. Abgüsse von Feldern.

Nature under nature. Nature in nature. Nature above naturenaturenaturenaturenature. Casts of fields.

Künstliche Felder.

Artificial fields.

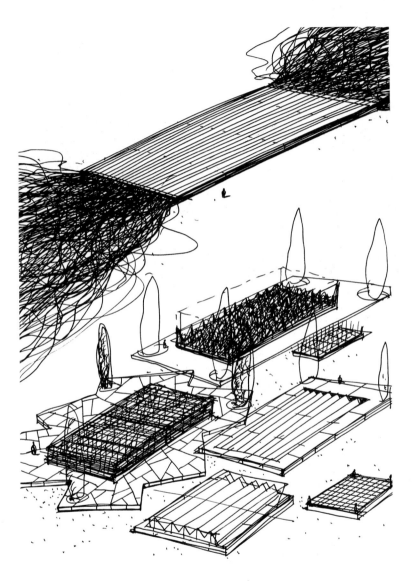

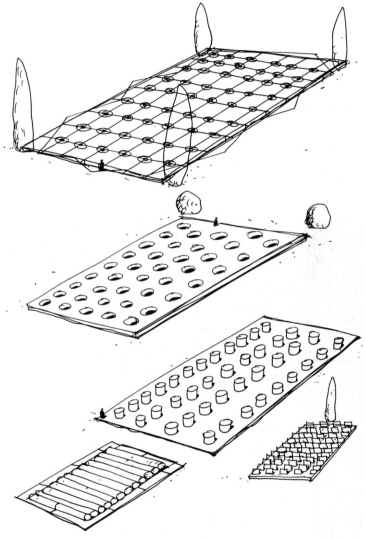

Beschleunigungsfelder, Beziehungsfelder, Kraftfelder, Entwicklungsfelder, Bedeutungsfelder, Lichtfelder, Zahlenfelder, Wasserfelder, Kissenfelder, Blattfelder, Dingfelder, Geldfelder, Treppenfelder, Stuhlfelder, Tischfelder, Brunnenfelder, Energiefelder, Gravitationsfelder, Metallfelder, Duschfelder, Ampelfelder, Nadelfelder, Fotofelder, Kunstfelder, Plastikfelder, Steinfelder, Erdfelder, Magnetfelder, Urnenfelder, Heckenfelder, Nebelfelder, Wolkenfelder, Betonfelder, Asphaltfelder

Acceleration fields, Reference fields, Force fields, Development fields, Meaning fields, Light fields, Number fields, Water fields, Cushion fields , Leaf fields, Thing fields, Money fields, Step fields, Chair fields, Table fields, Fountain fields, Energy fields, Gravitational fields, Metal fields, Shower fields, Traffic light fields, Needle fields, Photographic fields, Art fields, Plastic fields, Stone fields, Earth fields, Magnetic fields, Urn fields, Hedge fields, Fog fields, Cloud fields, Concrete fields, Asphalt fields

Vorgänge in der Natur künstlich reproduziert: das Entstehen einer Wiese etwa, wenn künstliche Gräser sich aus dem Boden schieben, oder das Blühen der Blumen, deren Blüten jetzt zu elektrischen Lampen geworden sind.

Natural processes reproduced artificially: e. g. the growing of a lawn when artificial grass comes out of the ground, or the blossoming of flowers whose blossoms have now become electric lamps.

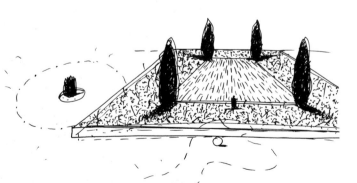

Künstliche Landschaften (zum Beispiel aus
Aluminium) als Gestaltungsmittel eingesetzt.
Übertreibungen.
Natürliche Bäume wachsen aus runden Öffnun-
gen wie fremde Zitate. Neue Ästhetik, neue
Romantik?

*Artificial landscapes (in aluminium, for example)
used as a creative device. Exaggerations.
Natural trees grow out of round openings like
alien quotations. New aesthetics, new Romanticism?*

Künstliche Täler. Metallböschungen, silbern glänzend im Mondlicht.

*Artificial valleys. Metal embankments, gleaming
silver in the moonlight.*

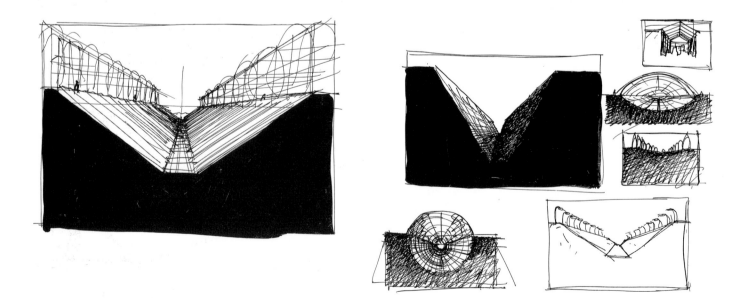

Künstliche Gletscher. Gebaut aus Glas und Stahl, nachts von innen leuchtend.

Artificial glacier. Built of glass and steel, glowing from within at night.

Jahreszeiten, künstlich produziert: Eis im Sommer, Sonnenwärme im Winter. Tropischer Wald in einem Glashaus mitten im arktischen Eis. Gletscherzunge im tropischen Urwald.
Meßstationen. Labors. Versuchsanordnungen. Antennen. Antennenblumen.

Seasons, produced artificially: ice in summer, the heat of the sun in winter. Tropical forest in a glass house, in the middle of the Arctic ice. Glacier tongue in a tropical jungle.
Measuring stations. Experimental arrangements. Aerials. Aerial flowers.

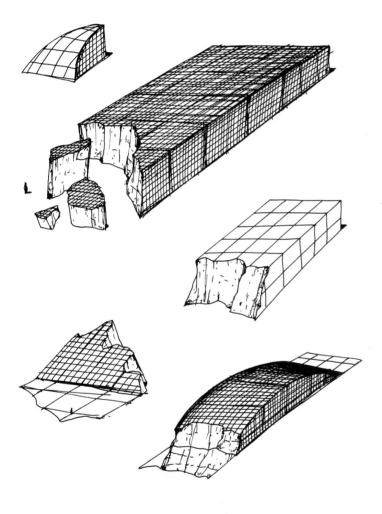

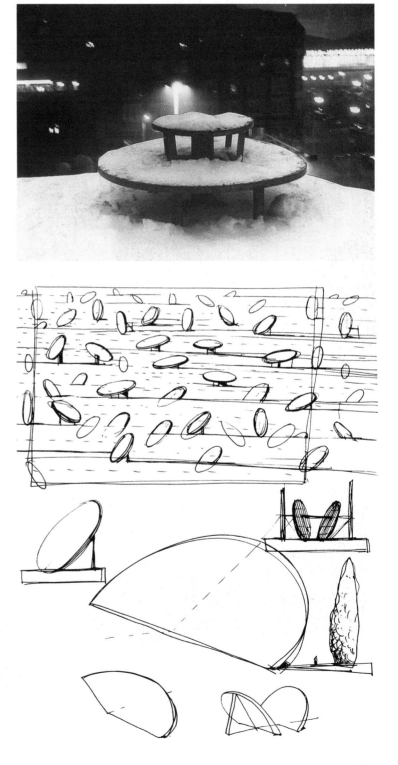

Solar-Felder. Künstliche Landschaften zur Energiegewinnung.

Solar panels. Laboratories. Artificial landscapes to harvest energy.

Solarzellenfelder mit romantischer Seeanlage gemischt.

Solar cells mixed with a romantic lake arrangement.

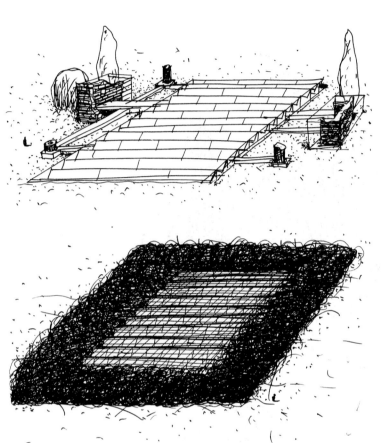

Baustellen der neuen Realität.

Squares with artificial wings. Building sites for the new reality.

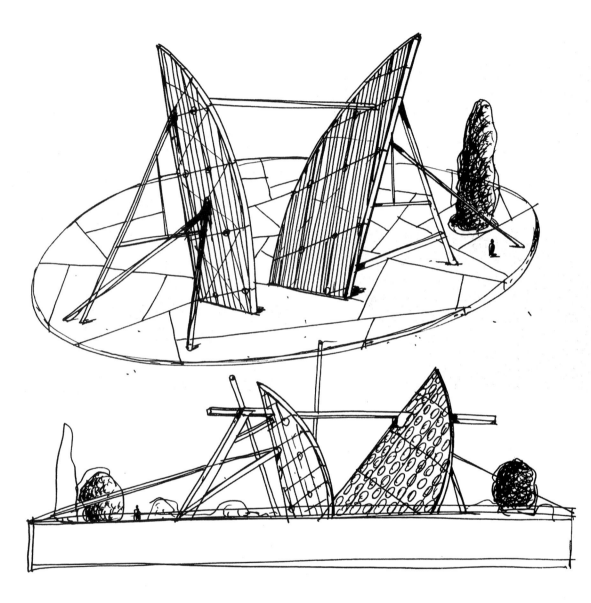

Zwischen Steinzeit und science-fiction: die neue Garten-Architektur als Komposition aus Stadt- und Landschaftsfragmenten, aus Elementen der Technik und der romantischen Gärten.
Nachts flimmert hinter den Ruinen das bläuliche Licht der Fernseher. Auf den Bildschirmen sieht man die Wolken ziehen, die Sonne scheinen, Vögel und Insekten fliegen, kann verfolgen, wie die Zellen wachsen und die Wurzeln arbeiten, sieht die Innenseite der Natur.

Between Stone Age and Science Fiction: new garden architecture as a composition of city and landscape fragments, from elements of technology and romantic gardens.
At night the bluish light of television screens flickers behind the ruins. On the screen you see clouds passing, the sun shining, birds and insects flying, you can follow how roots work and cells grow, see the interior of nature.

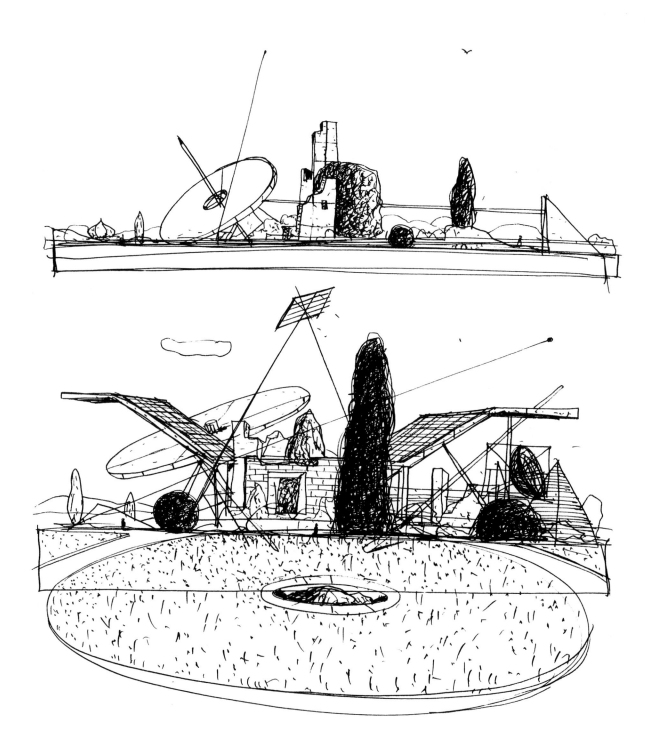

Neue Landschafts- und Gartenarchitektur
Neue Platzgestaltungen

New landscape and garden architecture
New place designs

In den Stadtlandschaften ist die zweite Haut der
künstlichen Natur fast ganz geschlossen. Wie am
Anfang beschrieben, finden hier die Elemente der
Naturlandschaft ihre geometrisierte Entspre-
chung.
Die Stadtlandschaft in ihrer Versteinerung: Gebaute Formen sind aufgetürmt wie Felswände,
wie Gebirge. In den Straßenschluchten lärmt der
Verkehr.

*In urban landscapes the second skin of artificial
nature is almost completely closed. As described
at the beginning elements of the natural landscape find their geometrized counterpart here.
The petrified urban landscape: built shapes are
piled up like rock walls, like mountains. Traffic
roars in the street ravines.*

Straßen und Plätze: Das Strömen der Stadt duldet kein Verweilen. Wer stehen bleibt oder sich
gar auf den Boden legt, begibt sich in Lebensge-
fahr. Plätze sind heute widerwillig geduldete Aus-
buchtungen von Straßenräumen und Fußgängerzonen. Ort für Penner und Fixer. Der eilige Stadt-
besucher meidet sie und hastet mit steinernem
Blick über die Freiflächen.

*Streets and squares: the streaming traffic of the
city will not tolerate any lingering. Anyone who
stands still or perhaps lies down on the ground is
putting himself in great danger. Squares today
are reluctantly tolerated bulges of street space·
and pedestrian areas. A place for drop-outs and
druggies. Visitors who are in a hurry avoid them
and rush across the open spaces with a stony
look.*

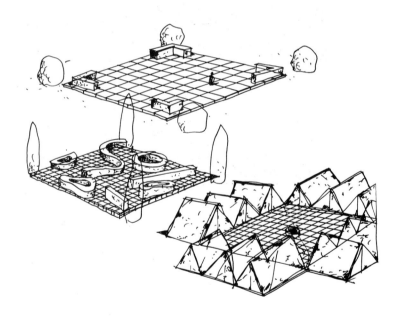

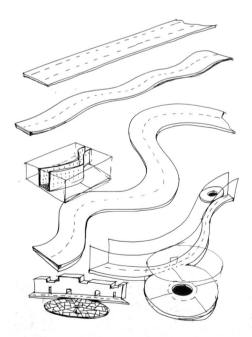

Die Zeit der in sich ruhenden Plätze, der agora,
der piazza, des forums ist vorbei. .

*Peaceful squares, agora, piazza, forum, are a
thing of the past.*

242

Heute sind die Stadtplätze fast alle untergraben von Einkaufszentren, von Straßenbahnhaltestellen und U-Bahn-Schächten, von WC-Anlagen und Bunkern, von Kanalisationsrohren und Fernheizungssystemen.

Today city squares are almost all undermined by shopping centres, tram stops and underground tunnels, public lavatories and bunkers, sewerage systems and district heating.

Fahren, parken, gehen, stehen, sitzen, spielen, reden, schauen, sprechen, kaufen.
Die städtische Öffentlichkeit, die die Stadtplätze in früheren Zeiten belebte, hat sich hinter die Medien (Zeitungen und Fernsehen) zurückgezogen. Auf den Plätzen erfährt man nichts mehr. Es herrscht eine allgemeine Anonymität.
Das eigentliche Stadtgeschehen ereignet sich an anderen Stellen, die tägliche Arbeit wird im Verborgenen verrichtet, das Einkaufen geschieht in den Geschäften und Kaufhäusern, die Versorgung und Entsorgung wird auf Hinterhöfen abgewickelt.
Stadt als Ort des Verbergens. Jede Wand verstellt Einblicke, jeder geschlossene Vorhang verhüllt einen Vorgang. Privat. Öffentlich. Verborgene und offen liegende Szenen.

Driving, parking, walking, standing, sitting, playing, talking, looking, speaking, buying. The public life that used to enliven urban squares has withdrawn behind the cover of the media (newspapers and television.) There is nothing more to be found out in the squares. General anonymity rules.
The actual events of the city take place elsewhere, daily work is carried out behind closed doors, shopping is done in shops and department stores, supply and disposal happen in back yards.
The city as a place for hiding things. Every wall stops you from looking in, every closed curtain hides an incident. Private. Public. Concealed and open scenes.

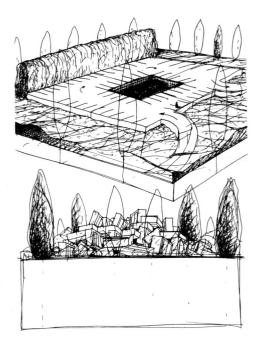

Die Freiflächen sind umstellt von Kaufhäusern und Banken, von Schaufenstern und Vitrinen. Natur kommt selten vor, ab und zu ein Baum, hin und wieder ein Brunnen. Verlogenes Grün. Feigenblätter schamhaft vor die Blöße geklemmt. Denkmäler längst vergessener Personen und Regenten stehen einsam und verloren im Strom der Passanten.

The open spaces are surrounded by department stores and banks, by shop windows and showcases.
Nature is seldom in evidence, a tree from time to time, and perhaps a fountain. Insincere greenery. Fig leaves to cover before nakedness in shame. Memorials to long forgotten people and regents stand lonely and lost in the stream of passers-by.

Die Bewegungen ereignen sich zufällig, chaotisch und flüchtig über dem geometrischen Raster des Platzbelags. Die Korridore der Gehenden entstehen, werden gebildet von Körpern und schließen sich sofort wieder. Nichts bleibt zurück, kein Blick, kein Abdruck. Vorstellung: Alle Bewegungen werden aufgezeichnet und nachts auf Bildschirmen vorgeführt: Tagesschau.

Movement takes place randomly, chaotically and fleetingly on the geometrical grid of the covering of the square. Corridors of people walking come into being, formed by bodies, and immediately closing up again. Nothing remains, not a look, not a print. Imagine: every movement is recorded and presented on screens at night: television news.

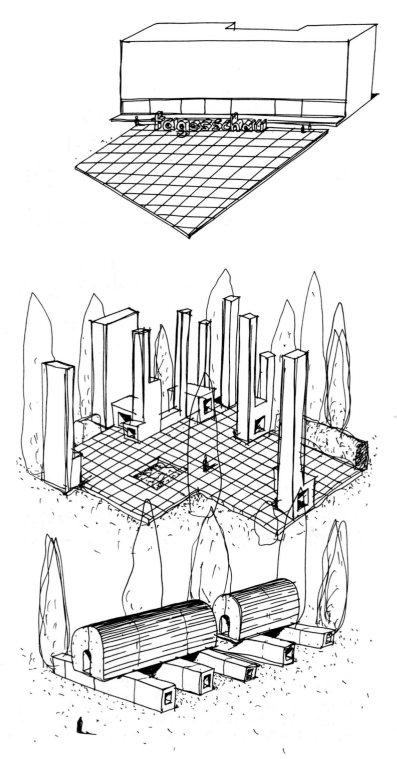

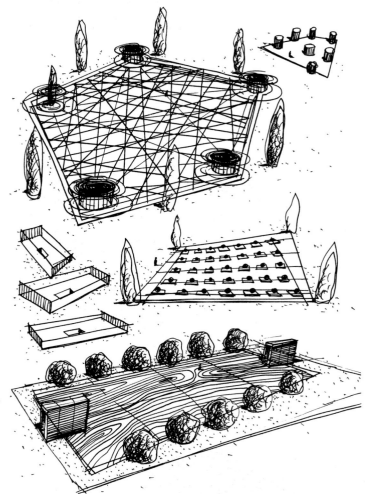

Vorstellung: Platz als öffentliches Wohnzimmer.
Kamine mit brennenden Feuerstellen.
Platzeinbauten wie auf einem Tisch.
Die Teile mobil sehen.
Jeden Morgen eine andere Komposition, ein
anderes Beziehungsgeflecht antreffen.

Imagine: squares as public living rooms. Fire-
places with fires burning in them.
Imagine Objects in the square as if they were on
a table.
See the various parts as mobile.
Every morning you come across a different com-
position, another network of references.
Square landscape with crockery architecture.

Platzlandschaft mit Geschirrarchitektur.

Square landscapes with crockery architecture

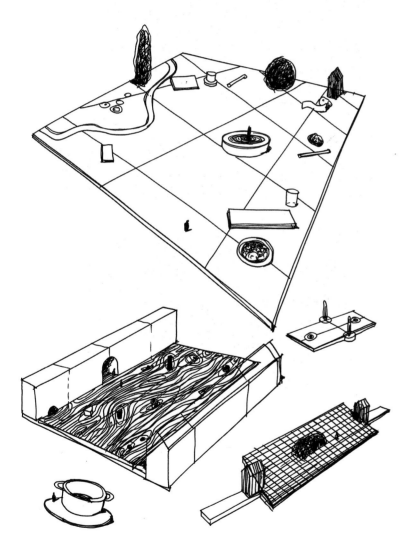

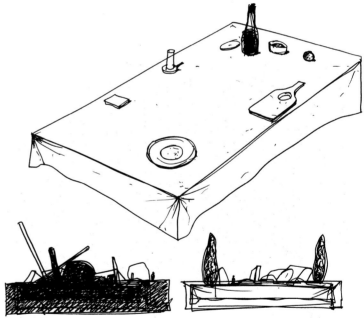

245

Wie könnten Plätze heute aussehen?
Man muß diese Orte wieder als Ereignisflächen des öffentlichen Lebens ernst nehmen. Man darf sie nicht mehr als unnötige Verschwendung, als reine Fußgängerzonen und als getarnte Parkplätze behandeln, sondern muß sie gestalten wie Gebäude, als Gefäße des Lebens, des Handelns und der Kommunikation. Man muß den Augen und dem Geist der Passanten Material in den Weg legen. Dieses Material kann Hindernischarakter oder Schmuckcharakter haben, es kann sowohl das Spielerische betonen als auch ernste Würde ausstrahlen. Wichtig ist es, die Leere zu durchbrechen, die Flächen aus ihrer Unpersönlichkeit, ihrer indifferenten Anonymität herauszuholen.

How could squares look today?
These places should be taken seriously again as areas for events in public life. They should no longer be treated as an unnecessary extravagance, merely as pedestrian areas and masked car parks, they must be designed as buildings are designed, as vessels for life, activity and communication instead. Material has to be put in the path of the minds and spirits of passers-by. This material can be obstacle or ornament, it can choose to emphasize the playful or radiate solemn dignity. The important thing is to break through the vacuum, to strip areas of their impersonal quality, their indifferent anonymity.

Plätze als liegende, begehbare Bilder. Hier kreuzen sich die Wege und die Blicke. Transparenz der Gleichzeitigkeit. Überlagerungen.
Das Strömen der Stadt, ihre Unruhe, ihre unsichtbaren Kräfte sichtbar machen.

Die Demokratie duldet keine Denkmäler, jeder Passant ist gleich wichtig. In dem Moment, in dem er den Platz überquert, ist er das Denkmal, ist er der Mittelpunkt der Stadt.

Squares as horizontal pictures in which it is possible to walk. Here paths and looks cross. The transparency of simultaneity. Superimpositions.
Making visible the streaming life of the city, its unrest, its invisible forces.
Making visible the streaming life of the city, its unrest, its invisible forces.

Democracy can tolerate no memorials, every passer-by is equally important. At the moment when he crosses the square he, too, is the memorial, he is the centre of the city.

Platz mit Tresorberg.

Square with safe-mountain.

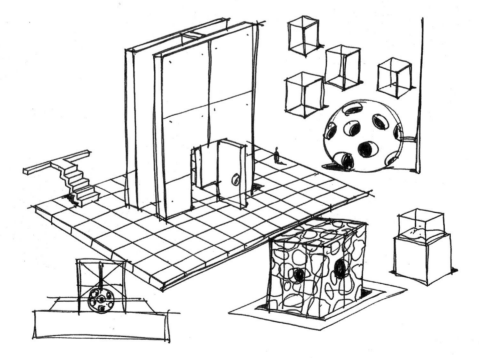

Helle Plätze, dunkle Plätze. Steinplätze, Grünplätze. Laute Plätze, stille Plätze. Plätze als Sackgassen.

Steinplätze, Asphaltplätze, Wiesenplätze, Wasserplätze, Eisplätze, Schwimmbadplätze, Museumsplätze, Denkmalsplätze, Turmplätze, Pappelplätze, Brunnenplätze …

Marktplätze, Ruheplätze, Spielplätze, Tourismusplätze, Ruinenplätze, Theaterplätze, Vergnügungsplätze, Jahrmarktsplätze, Treppenplätze, Filmstudioplätze, Zeitungsplätze, Übungsplätze, Gesprächsplätze, Gedankenplätze, Kunstplätze, Bibliotheksplätze, Palmenplätze, Lichtplätze …

Market squares, quiet squares, play squares, tourist squares, ruin squares, theatre squares, pleasure squares, fair squares, step squares, film studio squares, newspaper squares, exercise squares, conversation squares, thinking squares, art squares, library squares, palm squares, light squares …

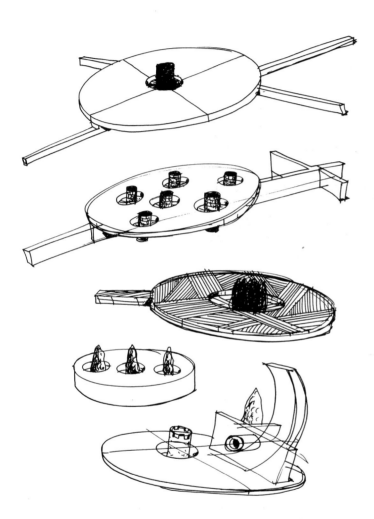

Bright squares, dark squares. Stone squares, green squares.
Noisy squares, quiet squares.
Squares as culs-de-sac.

Stone squares, asphalt squares, grassy squares, water squares, ice squares, swimming-pool squares and museum squares, memorial squares, tower squares, poplar squares, fountain squares…

Antennenplätze.

Aerial squares.

Plätze mit, Energie-Quellen, Kraft-Quellen, Licht-Quellen, Lärm-Quellen, Musik-Quellen, Lebens-Quellen, Wärme-Quellen, Hitze-Quellen, Geld-Quellen, Wasser-Quellen.

*Squares with
energy sources power sources, light sources,
sound sources, music sources, life sources,
warmth sources, heat sources, money sources,
water sources.*

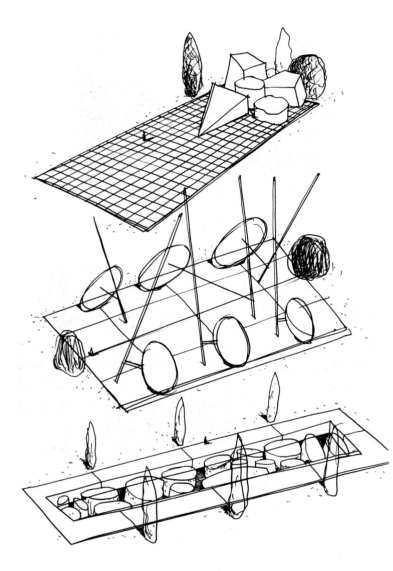

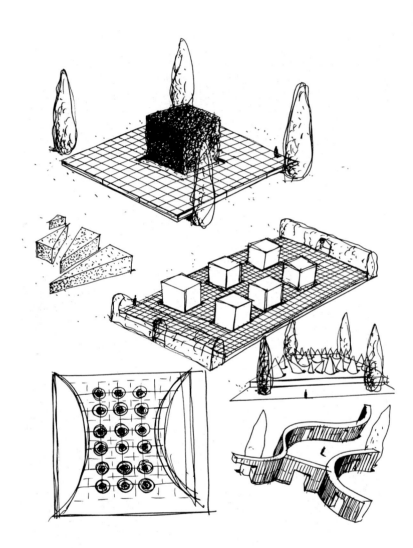

Platzbaustellen.

Squares as building sites.

Baugruben, Baugerüste als permanente Einrich-
tungen. Versteinert.
Im künstlichen Geäst, in der Drahtverspannung
hängen Türme, Hausfragmente, Treppen, Türen,
Fenster, Antennen, Kugeln, Steinfiguren, Brunnen, Spiegel, Naturbilder, Bildschirme, Bäume,
Büsche und Blumenteppiche …

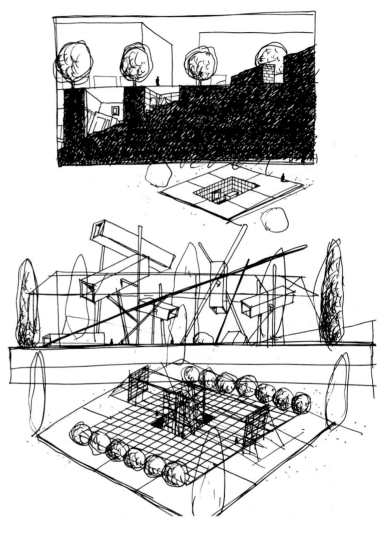

*Building excavations and scaffolding as perma-
nent fixtures. Petrified.*
*In the artificial branches, the network of wires are
hanging towers, fragments of buildings, steps,
doors, windows, aerials, spheres, stone statues,
fountains, mirrors, natural pictures, screens,
trees, bushes and carpets of flowers …*

251

Vitrinenplätze, Schaufensterplätze. Plätze mit
großen Segeln, mit Leitern, Zelten und Kugeln.
Plätze mit gemalten Bildern usw.

Showcase squares. Shop-window squares.
Squares with large sails, with ladders, tents and
spheres. Squares with painted pictures etc.

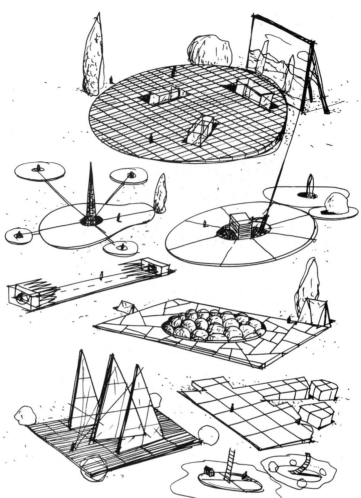

Kreisender Platz, kippender Platz, schaukelnder
Platz. Platz wie eine Schallplatte, wie eine CD-
Scheibe. Eingeätzt sind die Geschehnisse des
Platzes, seine Geschichte. Konservierte Zeit.

Circling square, tipping square, rocking square.
Square like a gramophone record, like a CD.
Etched in are the events of the square, its history.
Time preserved.

Platz-Vervielfältigung.

Square multiplication.

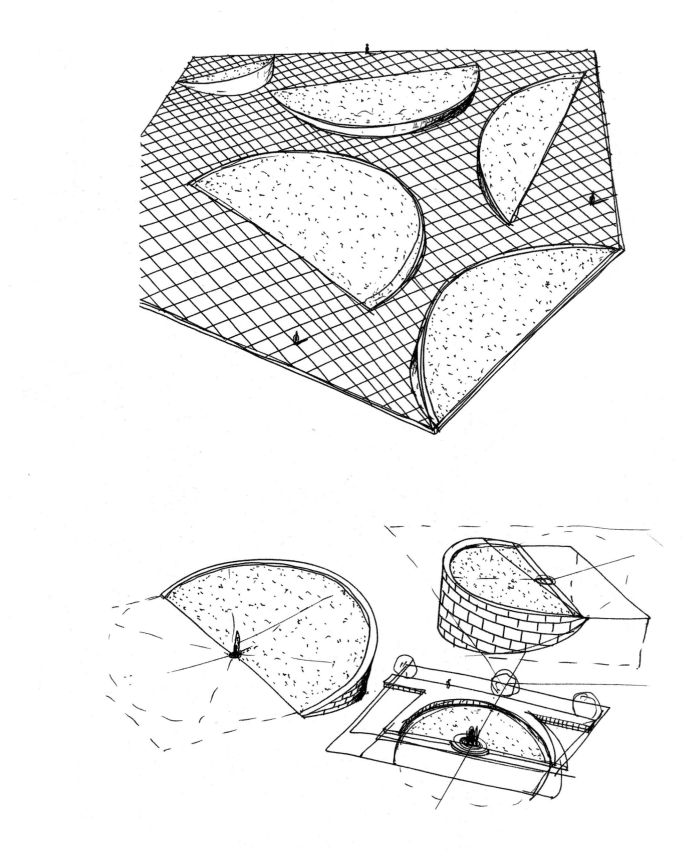

Plätze mit Wiesenkorridoren. Das Strömen der Stadt gegen das Strömen der Natur.

Squares with lawn corridors. The streaming of the city as opposed to the streaming of nature.

Rasenhügel wellen sich durch Städte und über Plätze wie grüne Raupen.

Small lawn hills are rolling across cities and squares like green caterpillars.

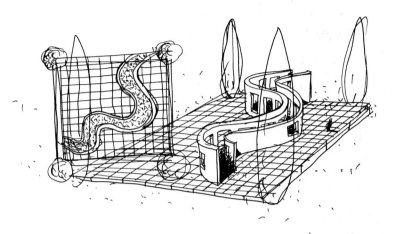

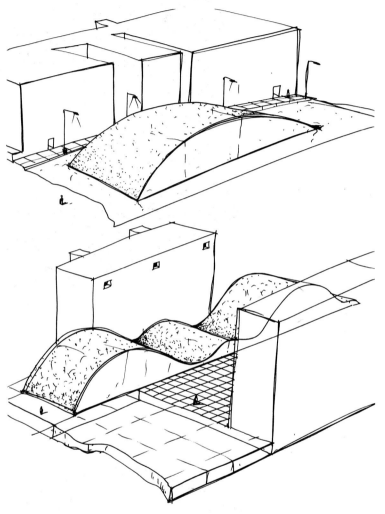

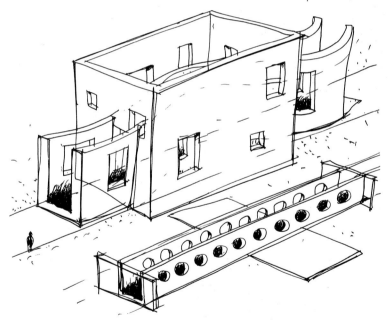

Holzstapelplätze, Rindenplätze, Schneeplätze, Erdplätze, Rasenplätze, Nebelplätze, Metallplätze, Tagplätze, Nachtplätze, weiße Plätze, schwarze Plätze, Blumenplätze, Eßplätze, Kissenplätze, Sommerplätze, Herbstplätze, betrunkene Plätze, nüchterne Plätze …

Wood stacking squares, bark squares, snow squares, earth squares, lawn squares, fog squares, metal squares, day squares, night squares, white squares, black squares, flower squares, eating squares, cushion squares, summer squares, autumn squares, drunken squares, sober squares . . .

Wellen- und Wogenmotiv.

Wave and billow motif.

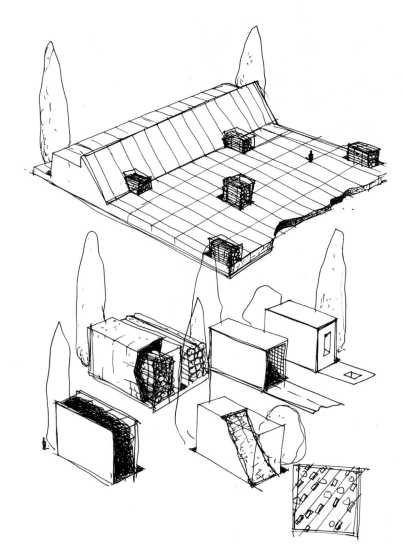

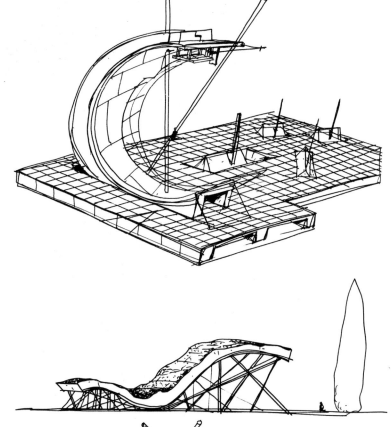

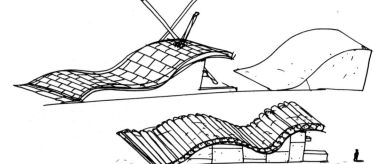

Plätze mit Steinbruchfragmenten.

Squares with quarry fragments.

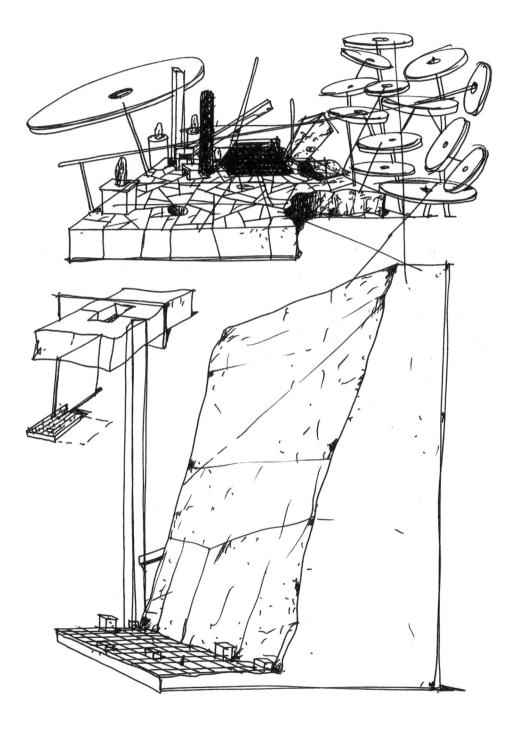

Plätze mit künstlichen Gletschern.

Squares with artificial glaciers.

Platzauslöschung: Er ist bedeckt mit Blättern und Ästen, mit Steinen und Stämmen, mit Rinde und Sand.

Eradicating the square: it is covered with leaves and branches, with stones and trunks, with bark and sand.

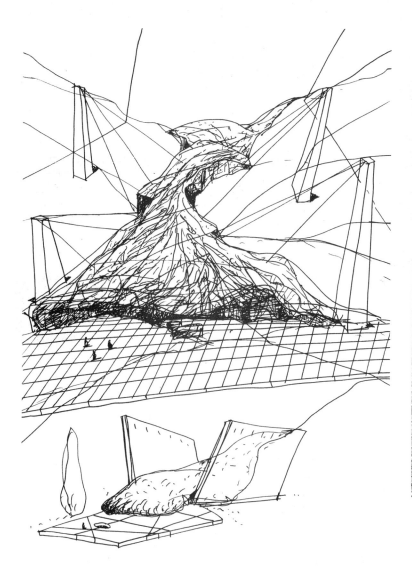

Platzfläche als Ort der Verdrängung und des Aufbrechens

The square as a place of repression and of breaking up.

Jede Platzfläche bedeutet auch Verdrängung, Verhinderung. Natur bleibt unter der Steinfläche verschlossen und begraben. Die Härte des Platzes gegen die Weichheit des Himmels.

Every square also implies repression, prevention. Nature remains locked and buried under the stone surface. The hardness of the square compared with the softness of the sky.

Vorstellung: Unter dem Platz liegen nicht nur die zum Verfaulen verurteilten Samen der Natur, sondern auch die verdrängten Gefühle, die Emotionen, das Unterbewußtsein. Darüber das freundliche Gehen der Passanten, das unverbindliche Lächeln der Gesichter, unter dem Platz die Katakomben des Hasses, der Wut, der Empörung, der Aggression und des Todes.

Imagine: under the square are not only the seeds of nature condemned to rot, but also suppressed feelings, emotions, the subconscious. Above this is the amiable walking of the passers-by, the impersonally smiling faces, under the square are the catacombs of hatred, rage, indignation, aggression and death.

259

Das Brodeln der Lava, das Leuchten der Hölle ...

The seething of lava, the glow of hell ...

Der gläserne Moment.

The glazed moment.

Dann bricht aus Ritzen und Gräben die Natur wie wilde Emotion hervor.

Then nature breaks out of the cracks and holes like raw emotion.

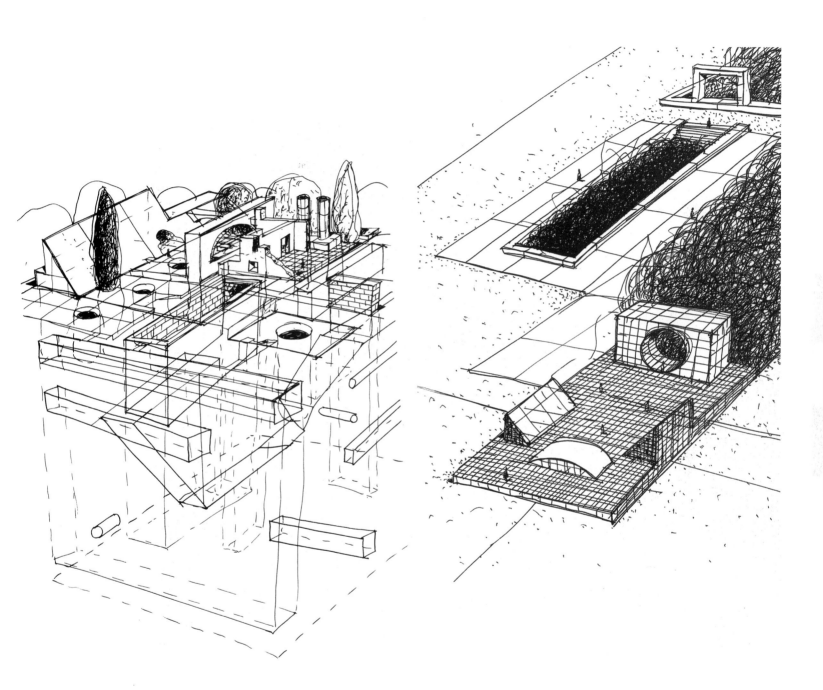

Platzlandschaft als Ort der Inszenierung

The square as a place for staging things

Wenn man heute neue Plätze anlegt oder alte Stadtplätze in ihrer Funktion überdenkt und sie einer neuen Lebensform zuführen will, muß man sie als Ort der Inszenierung verstehen, als öffentliche Bühne mit Handlungsangeboten.
Man könnte Platzintendanten berufen, die Programme entwickeln, Spielzeiten entwerfen, wie das in Theatern üblich ist.
Neue Spielformen, die das tägliche Drama spiegeln.

Plätze als Fernseh-Studio: Baustellen der neuen Stadtrealität.

Zwischen die Mauern schieben sich Szenen aus Opern, aus Theaterstücken, aus Gemälden.

Plätze mit Schiffen und Flugzeugen, mit Zwiebeltürmen und Aufzugsschächten, Plätze mit Käfigen und goldenen Kugeln, Plätze mit Maschinen und Seilbahnen, Plätze mit Kurvenfragmenten und Show-Treppen, Plätze mit Kleiderschränken und Beichtstühlen, Plätze mit Schwimmbecken und Kulissenbauten.

Today, when new squares are laid out or the function of old city squares is being rethought with the intention of giving them a new life-form, they have to be seen as places where things are staged, as a public stage with various available plots. Artistic directors could be appointed for squares to develop programmes, design seasons, as is usual in theatres. New varieties that reflect the daily drama.

Squares as television studios: building sites for a new urban reality.

Scenes from operas are thrust between the walls, from plays, from paintings.

Squares with ships and aeroplanes, with onion towers and lift shafts, squares with cages and golden balls, squares with machines and cableways, squares with curve fragments and show steps, squares with wardrobes and confessionals, squares with swimming pools and scenery.

Plätze mit Stahlzelten und blitzenden Kabinen.

Squares with steel tents and flashing cabins.

Erotische Plätze.

Erotic squares.

Plätze mit surrealen Aufbauten. Baustellen der Phantasie.

Squares with surreal structures. Building sites of the imagination.

Realitätsschaukeln. Schaukelnde Formen. Annäherungen an die neue Stadtrealität. Bühnenbildplatz: ein Stück Gletscher mit Brunnen (Brunnen vor dem Tore). Die Dorflinde ist versunken in die Tiefgarage. Gestänge verzweigt sich über dem Loch: Baustelle mit wechselnden Inhalten. Suche nach Mitte, kreisend ums Zentrum wie ein Karussell.

Reality rockers. Rocking shapes.
Approaches to the new urban reality.
Stage-set square: a piece of a glacier with fountain (the fountain outside the city gate of the old song). The village lime tree is sunken in the underground car-park, and metal rods interweave above the hole: a building site with changing content. Search for a core, circling around the centre like a roundabout.

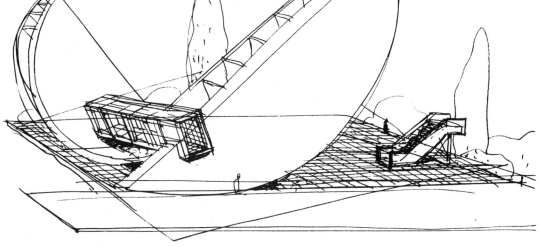

Vergangenes. Orte der Transzendenz.

Things of the past. Transcendent places.

Wie mit dem Kopf in einer anderen Welt.
Durch die Decke hindurch.
Im Formenwirbel.
In der Klarheit.
Momente metaphysischer Überhöhung.
Die Haare im Wind aus Wörtern.
Wirbel der Fragen.
Erstarrung in Schwärze.

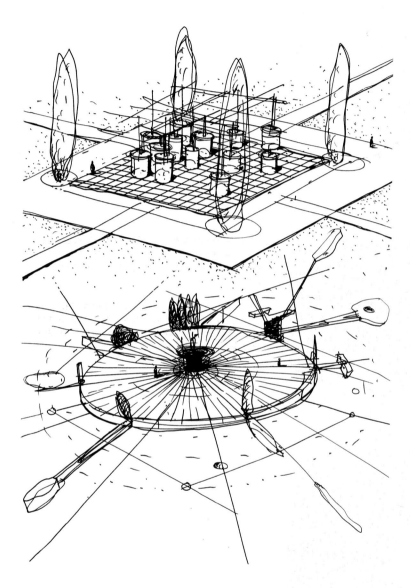

As if with your head in another world.
Through the ceiling.
In the whirlpool of shapes.
In clarity.
Moments of metaphysical excess.
Your hair in the wind of words.
Whirlpool of questions.
Paralysis in blackness.

Langsames Auflösen der Plätze, langsames Zerfallen.

Gradual dissolution of the squares, slow decay.

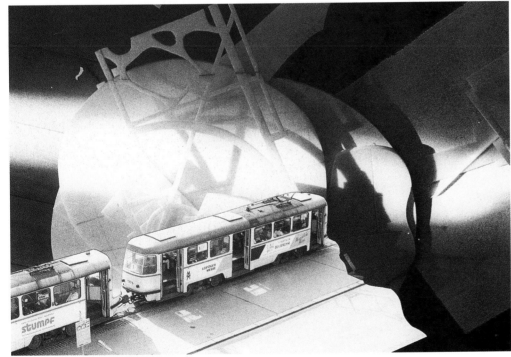

Dann das Verlassen der Plätze, der Straßen, der Städte. Abends vielleicht, im Dämmerlicht – geheimnisvoller Pendler zwischen Traum und Wirklichkeit.

Then the abandonment of the squares, the streets, the cities. In the evening perhaps, at twilight as a mysterious commuter between dream and reality.

Übergang zum öffentlichen Park,
zur Landschaft

Transition to a public park, to landscape

Die Platzfläche schiebt sich wie ein Schiff über
die Häuser hinweg, hinaus in die freie Landschaft.

*The area of the square thrusts away over the
buildings like a ship, out into the open country.*

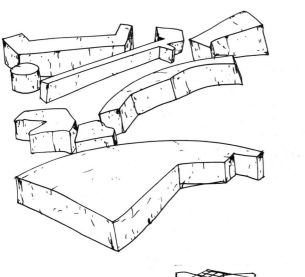

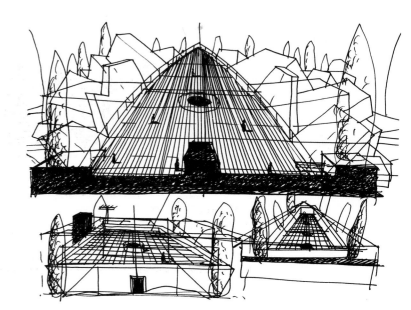

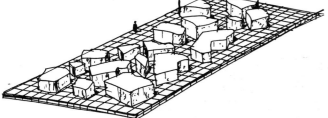

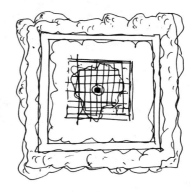

Vorstellung: Die Platzflächen liegen leer und funktionslos in der freien Landschaft herum. Gras und Bäume wachsen durch Lücken, Löcher und Zwischenräume.

Imagine: squares lying empty and functionless in the open countryside. Grass and trees grow through gaps, holes and spaces.

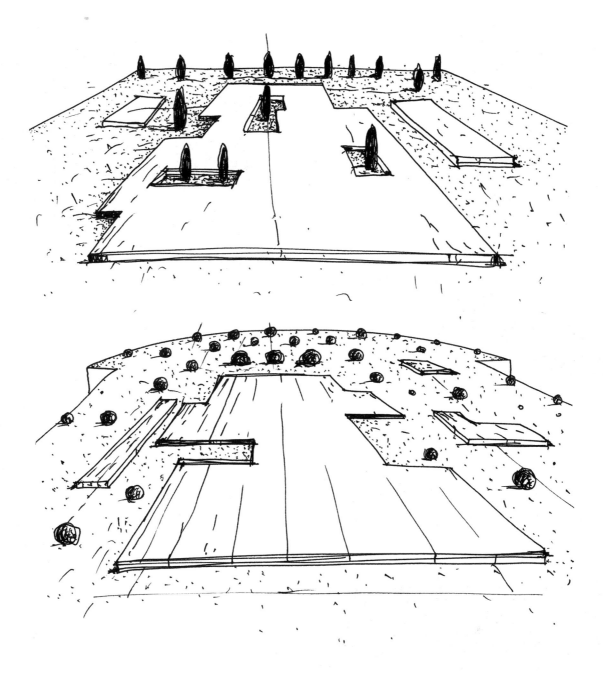

Pappelinseln tauchen wieder auf.
Dann der Horizont, die Sommerwiese, das im
Wind wogende Weizenfeld, die jubilierende Ler-
che, Grillen, Sonne, Wärme und der alles über-
wölbende tiefblaue Himmel mit den großen,
weißen, langsam dahinschwebenden Wolken.

Islands of poplars crop up again.
The horizon, the summer meadow, the field of
wheat waving in the wind, jubilant larks, grass-
hoppers, sun, warmth and the deep blue sky
arching over everything with its great white,
slowly floating clouds.

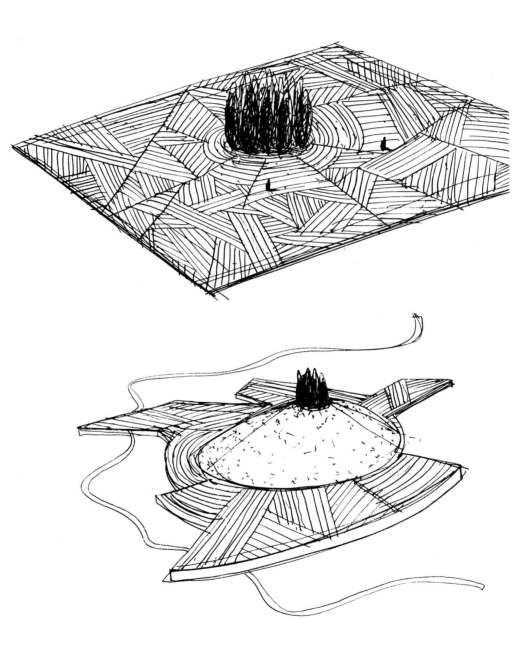

Neue Landschafts- und Gartenarchitektur
Ruinen und Archäologie

New landscape and garden architecture
Ruins and archaelogy

Der Aufbau von Realität, von künstlicher und natürlicher, von Haus und Stadt, von Straße und Platz, von Garten und Park, ist ein Thema, ein anderes ist der Zerfall des Aufgebauten, das Absterben des Gepflanzten, das Verwesen und der Tod.
Architektur und Landschaft befinden sich in einem permanenten Zerfallszustand: Gebirge zerfallen, alle Steine zerfallen, Bäume sterben ab und zerfallen, Häuser verwesen, Städte verschwinden.
Die Zerfallsarbeit ist auch eine Arbeit des Öffnens: Langsam wird die innere Struktur der Architekturen und der Landschaft sichtbar.

Building up reality, artificial and natural, house and town, road and square, garden and park is one topic, another is the decay of what has been built up, the dying of what has been planted, decomposition and death.
Architecture and landscape are in a permanent state of decay: mountains disintegrate, all stone decays, trees die off and rot, buildings decompose, cities disappear.
The work of decay is also work related to opening: the inner structure of architecture and landscape slowly becomes visible.

Zerfall durch Alterung, langsam und unaufhaltsam. Oder abrupter Zerfall durch ein Unglück, eine Katastrophe (Brand, Erdbeben, Attentat, Krieg).

Decay through ageing, slow and inexorable. Or abrupt decay as a result of an accident, a disaster (fire, earthquake, assassination, war).

Im Zerfall verwandelt sich das Haus in Landschaft.

In decay buildings transform themselves into landscape.

Ruinen haben die Menschen schon immer fasziniert. Sie gehören zum Bereich der Romantik, sind Symbole der Vergänglichkeit auf dem Weg zum Verschwinden, zur Auslöschung. Die machtvolle Geste des Aufbauens ist zerbrochen, Natur und Wetter gewinnen die Oberhand.

People have always been fascinated by ruins. They are part of the realm of the Romantic, they are symbols of transience, on their way to disappearing, extinction. The powerful gesture of building up is broken, nature and weather are gaining the upper hand.

Alte und neue Ruinenromantik. Künstliche Ruinen der Zukunft: Wohnzimmerfragmente treiben als von innen beleuchtete Inseln auf lauschigen Seen. In Parks tauchen efeuumrankte Ruinen von Bibliotheken und Schwimmbädern auf. Verlassene Büros mit blinkenden Computer-Terminals hängen in den Bäumen.

Old and new romanticism of ruins.
Artificial ruins of the future: fragments of living-rooms drift as islands lit from within on secluded lakes. Ivy-clad ruins of libraries and swimming pools are found in parks. Abandoned offices with flashing computer terminals hang in the trees.

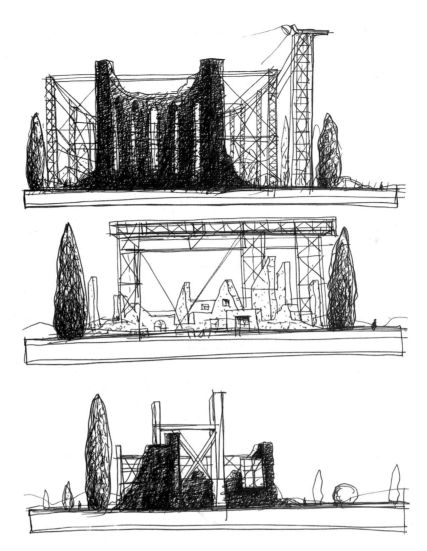

Vorstellung: Ganze Fabrikanlagen zerfallen und werden von Efeu und wildem Wein umrankt. Fließbänder liegen auf dem Grund von Seen. Regale und Schränke stehen untätig vor schwarz verbrannten Wänden.

Imagine: entire factories decay and are entwined in ivy and wild vines. Conveyor belts lie at the bottom of lakes. Shelves and cupboards stand inactive in front of walls that have been burned black.

Maschinen im Dickicht sehen aus wie vernarbte Wunden der Natur, wie die abgenagten Knochen unbekannter Saurierarten, wie surreale Blumen.

Machines in the thicket look like healed wounds of nature, like the gnawed-off bones of unknown species of dinosaur, like surreal flowers.

275

Seltsame Vermehrung der Ruinen. Scherben fallen über Felder her und dringen in die Wälder vor. Makabre Romantik. Schauerlich, tödlich. Die Wahrheit ist eine Trümmerlandschaft, die Wahrheit ist der Tod.

Strange increase of ruins. Shards attack fields and force their way into woods.
Macabre romanticism. Horrifying, deadly. Truth is a ruined landscape, truth is death.

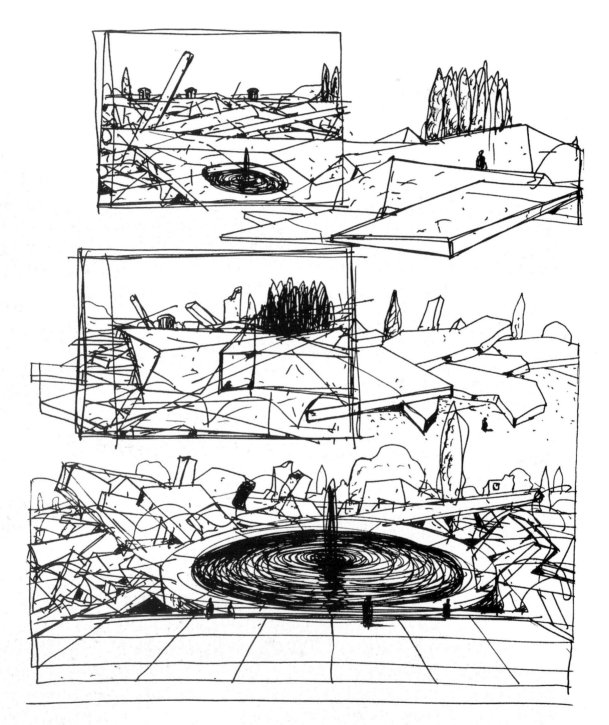

Archäologien

Archaeology

Später, in den nächsten Jahrhunderten und Jahrtausenden werden sie die Erde wieder aufgraben, werden die Spuren unseres Lebens, unserer Städte, unserer Straßen und Plätze, unserer Taten und Katastrophen finden.

Later, in the next centuries and millennia they will dig the earth up again, will find the traces of our life, of our cities, of our streets and squares, of our deeds, our disasters.

In der Tiefe der Erde liegt die Zeit begraben.
Fragmente von Badezimmern und Garagen, von
Autos und Flugzeugen, von Zeitungen und Post-
karten, von Akten und Video-Kassetten, von
Müllplätzen und Fußgängerzonen.

*Time lies buried deep in the earth. Fragments of
bathrooms and garages, of cars and aeroplanes,
of newspapers and postcards, of documents and
video cassettes, of rubbish dumps and pedestrian areas.*

Späte Gärten.

Late gardens.

Auf den Bildschirmen der zukünften Archäologen
erscheinen die Steingötter der Vergangenheit,
leicht verwest, aber noch gut erkennbar.
Im Hintergrund flimmern die Erinnerungen an
Städte, Straßen, Plätze, an für immer verschwun-
dene Gärten.

*The stone gods of the past appear on the future
archaeologists‹ screens, slightly decomposed
but still easily recognizable.
In the background are flickering memories of
cities, of roads, of squares, of gardens that have
disappeared for ever.*

Neue Landschafts- und Gartenarchitektur
Friedhöfe

New landscape and garden architecture
Cemeteries

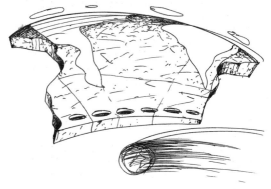

Die Welt: Ein Ort zum Leben, ein Ort zum Sterben. Friedhöfe sind dem Tod geweihte Landschaften. Orte des Verlassens der Welt, Orte der Transzendenz und Orte der Erinnerung.

The world: a place to live, a place to die. Cemeteries are landscapes dedicated to death. Places concerned with leaving the world, places of transcendence and places to remember people who have gone away for ever.

Heute wird der zentrale Aspekt des Sterbens weitgehend verdrängt. Beerdigungen sind lästige Rituale, und immer mehr Friedhöfe sehen aus wie alltägliche Stadtparks. Im Zeitalter von Leichenschauhaus, Anatomie und Organspende ist der Abschied von der Welt sachlich, bürokratisch und unromantisch geworden. Die Kosten dafür würde man am liebsten sparen. Und die Grabpflege ist auch nicht billig. Dabei ist das Totenreich allmächtig und unermeßlich groß: Wenn man sich alle bisher gestorbenen Menschen vergegenwärtigt, verwandelt sich die Erde in einen riesigen Friedhof …

Today the central aspect of dying is largely suppressed. Burials are irksome rituals and more and more cemeteries look like ordinary municipal parks. In the age of the morgue, of anatomy and organ donation our farewell to the world has become neutral, bureaucratic and unromantic. People would prefer to avoid the expense. And caring for graves is not cheap either. And yet the realm of the dead is all-powerful and immeasurably large: if one recalls all the people who have died so far the earth is transformed into a gigantic cemetery …

Die Phantasien über das Verschwinden für immer
reichen von einer gespiegelten Welt hinter der
Welt, einem Jenseits, einem Reich der Abge-
schiedenen, einem Schattenreich, bis zu der Vorstellung, daß hinter der Grenze nichts mehr zu
finden sei. Ein ewiges Noch-nicht-sein vor dem
Leben und ein ewiges Nicht-mehr-sein nach dem
Leben.

*Imagining disappearing for ever extends from a
reflected world beyond the world, a hereafter, a
kingdom of the departed, a shadow kingdom to
the idea that there is nothing to be found beyond
the border. An eternal not-yet existence before
life and an eternal no-more existence after life.*

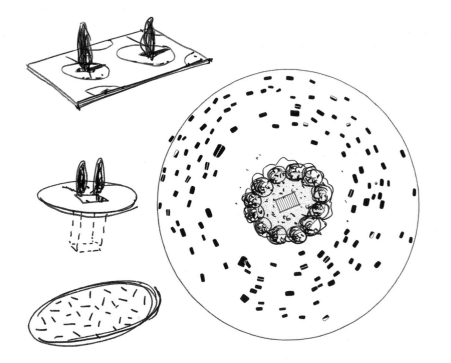

Die Erinnerung der Lebenden an die Toten ist das, was wirklich bleibt.

Our memories of the dead are what really remains.

Um das Verschwinden der Körper zu überspielen, wurden zu allen Zeiten Totensteine errichtet, Totendenkmäler, Totengedenksteine, Grabsteine, Steinfiguren.

To cover up the disappearance of the body stones for the dead have been put up at all times, memorials of the dead, memorials and commemorative stones for the dead, tombstones, stone statues.

Gräber als Stellen des endgültigen Übergebens der Körper an die Erde, an den Boden.

Tombs as places for the transition of the body to the earth, to the soil.

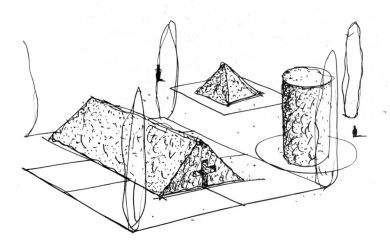

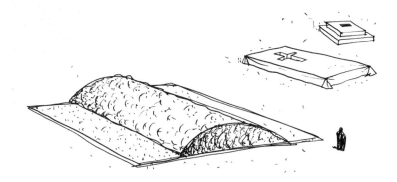

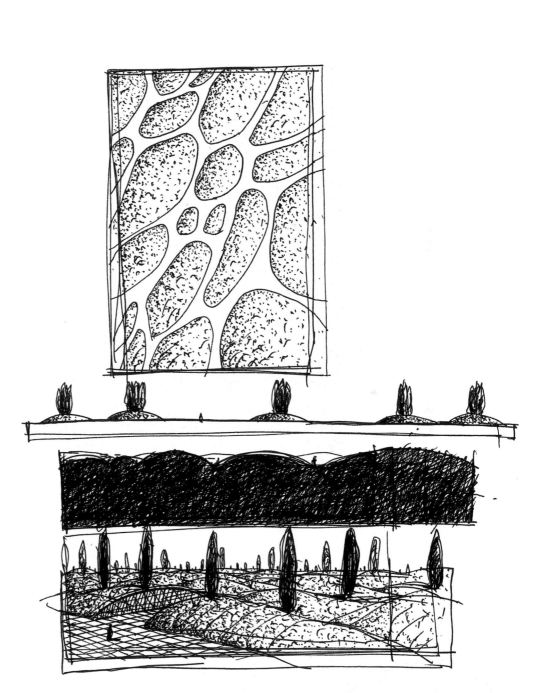

Friedhöfe der Vergangenheit. Friedhöfe des Heute. Friedhöfe der Zukunft.

Cemeteries of the past. Cemeteries of today. Cemeteries of the future.

Der Tod bedeutet zwar in jedem Kulturkreis, in jeder Religion etwas anderes, in Wirklichkeit ist er aber für alle Menschen gleich. Was die Natur hervorgebracht hat, nimmt sie hiermit wieder zurück. So gesehen gehört jeder Tod vor allem zur Landschaft: Totenlandschaft aus sanften Wiesenhügeln, von flachen Wegadern durchzogen.

Death may mean something different in every culture, in every religion, but in reality it is the same for all people. With it nature takes back what it has produced. Seen in this way every death belongs above all to the landscape: a landscape of the dead made up of gentle grassy hills, shot through with paths as shallow veins.

283

Leere Totenlandschaft oder Landschaften mit
Urnen-Gefäßen.

*Empty landscape of the dead or landscape
with urns.*

Totenlandschaften mit schwarzen Toren. Der Vorgang der Beerdigung als schwarze Prozession,
als Kahnfahrt, als Autofahrt, abends in der Dämmerung oder nachts bei künstlicher Beleuchtung.

*Landscapes of the dead with black gates. The
process of burial as a black procession, as a
barge journey, a car journey, in the evening, at
twilight or at night with artificial lighting.*

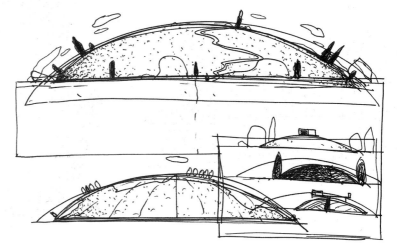

Totenwiesen, Totenfelder, Totenmulden,
Totenfurchen, Totengräben …

Haine.

Meadows of the dead, fields of the dead, hollows
of the dead, furrows of the dead, tombs of the
dead …

Groves

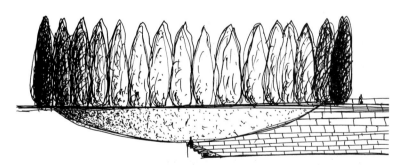

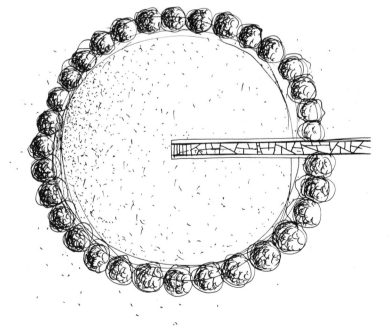

Getreppte Anlagen, in den Wänden die Gräber und Urnenfächer.

Stepped areas, with tombs and places for urns in the walls.

Versenkte Grabanlagen in freier Landschaft.

Sunken tombs in the open air.

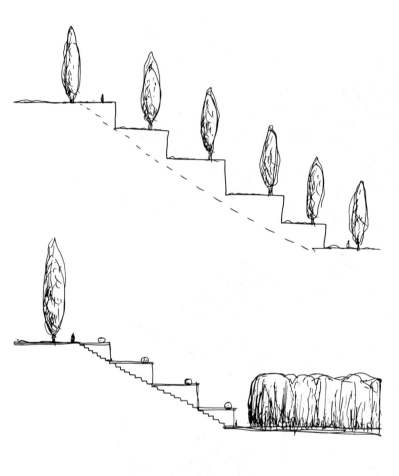

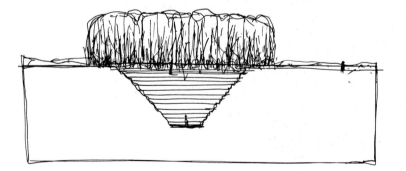

Die alten Motive wieder aufgreifen: Pyramiden
aus Stein, aus Erde und Gras.

*Taking up ancient motifs again: pyramids of
stone, earth and grass.*

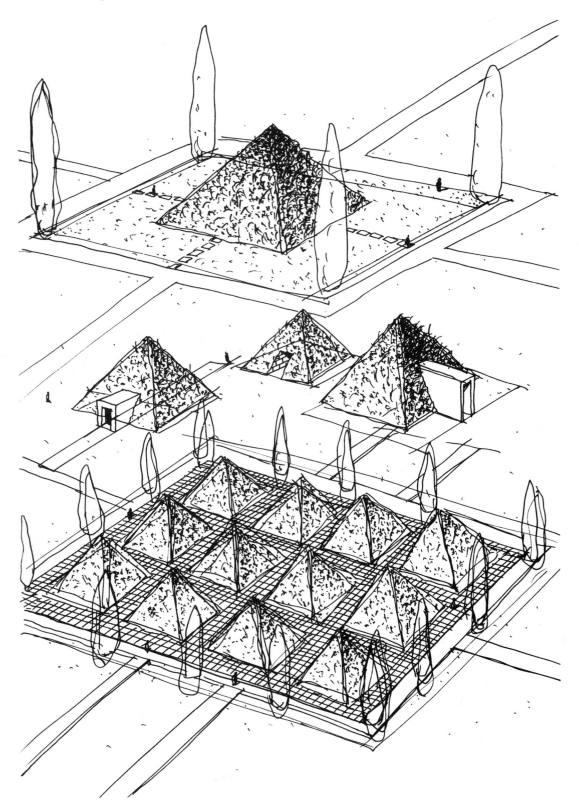

Totenwälder. Vorstellung. Die Wälder rings um die Städte werden in Totenwälder verwandelt. Jeder Tote bekommt einen Baum zugewiesen. Der Name des Verstorbenen wird in die Rinde eingeritzt, seine Asche ist im Wurzelbereich vergraben.

Forests of the dead. Imagine: the forests all around the cities are transformed into forests of the dead. Each dead person is allotted a tree. The name of the deceased is scratched into the bark, his ashes are strewn round the roots.

Korridore des Todes im Wald.

Corridors of the dead in the forests.

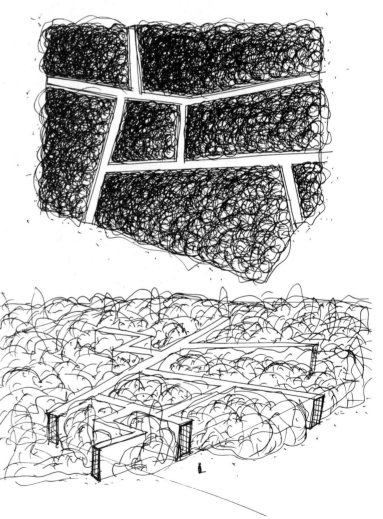

Oder: Wälder mit gebauten Gräbern zwischen
den Stämmen, in den Lichtungen.

*Or: forests with built tombs, between the trees, in
the clearings.*

Friedhofs-Seen. Toteninseln.
Rousseaus Pappelinsel taucht wieder auf.

Cemetery lakes. Islands of the dead.
Rousseau's island with poplars comes back
again.

Totenschiffe. Totenflugzeuge, Toten-Raumschiffe.
Der Mond als Friedhof der Zukunft?

*Ships of the dead. Aeroplanes, space ships of
the dead. The moon as the cemetery of the
future?*

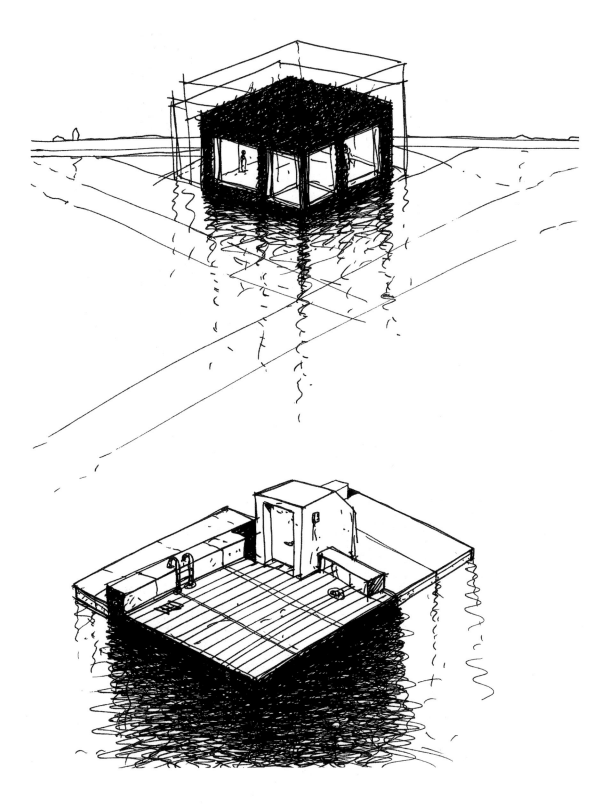

Totentäler.

Valleys of the dead.

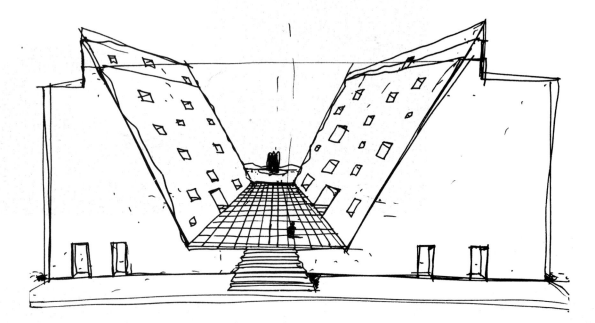

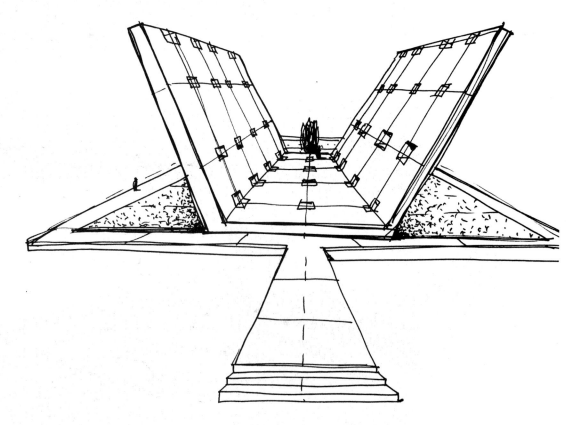

Friedhofsanlagen im Gebirge. Ganze Berge als Totenbereiche. Aussegnungshallen in den Gipfelstationen?

Cemeteries as recumbent façades: the coffins and urns are sunken in windows and doors.

Friedhöfe als liegende Fassaden: In den Fenstervertiefungen und in den Türöffnungen sind die Särge und Urnen versenkt.

Cemeteries in the mountains. Entire mountains as areas for the dead. Halls for administering the last rites in summit stations?

Totenwege. Totenstraßen.
Totenhäuser. Totendörfer. Toten-Gehöfte. Toten-
türme. Friedhofsruinen. Ruinenfriedhöfe.

Paths of the dead. Roads of the dead.
Houses of the dead. Villages of the dead. Farms
of the dead. Towers of the dead. Cemetery ruins.
Ruined cemeteries.

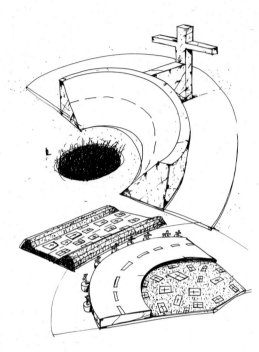

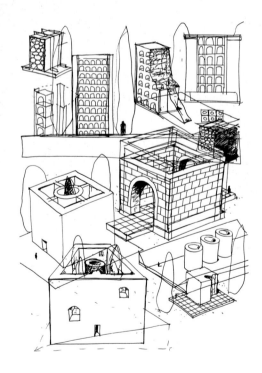

Toten-Plätze, nachts.

Squares of the dead, at night.

Totenstädte. Vorstellung: Eine ganze Großstadt wird leergeräumt und nur noch von Toten »bewohnt«, alle Beerdigungen des Landes finden dort statt.

Cities of the dead. Imagine: an entire city is emptied and ›inhabited‹ only by the dead, all the country's burials take place there.

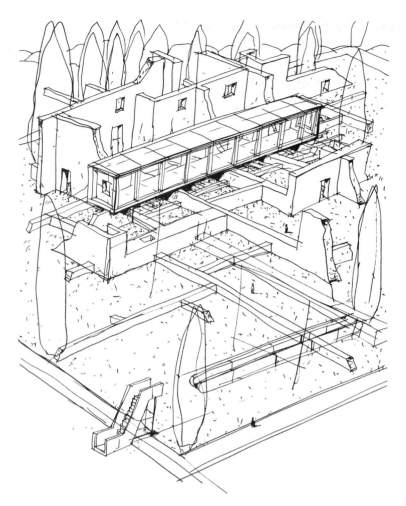

Toten-Unterführungen. Toten-Passagen. Toten-Flure. Toten-Treppenhäuser. Toten-Züge ...

Underpasses of the dead. Arcades of the dead. Corridors of the dead. Staircases of the dead. Trains of the dead ...

Bahnhöfe als Aussegnungshallen und die Bahnsteige als Orte des Abschieds für immer und ewig.

Stations as halls for the administration of the last rites and platforms as places of farewell for ever and ever.

Neue Landschafts- und Gartenarchitektur
Inszenierte Situationen

New landscape and garden architecture
Stage situations

Die Landschaft ist auch Ursprungsort von Mythos und Theater. Sich vorstellen, daß alle Gedanken und Handlungen, alle Figuren und Bilder aus Mythologie und Theater in ihr enthalten sind, als verpuppte Gedanken gewissermaßen, als Klänge und Spuren.

The landscape is also the place where myth and theatre originate. It is possible to imagine that all thoughts and actions, all figures and images from mythology and theatre are contained in it as pupated thoughts, as sounds and traces.

Die Gedanken werden sichtbar, die Figuren treten hervor.

Thoughts become visible, figures emerge.

Steinerne Krieger tauchen auf, kriechen aus Erdfurchen und verstecken sich hinter Stämmen,
Büschen und dunklen Häusern.

*Stone warriors appear, crawl out of furrows in the
earth and hide behind tree-trunks, bushes and
dark buildings.*

Seltsame Nymphen tauchen auf, locken die Passanten mit erotischen Versprechungen. Dann
aber schlagen sie zu, mit Stöcken und Peitschen.
Sie wollen Blut sehen und Schmerzensschreie
hören. Kein liebliches Cythera mehr mit tändeln-
den Schäferstunden, sondern ein pervertiertes
Arkadien, aggressiv und gefährlich.

*Strange nymphs appear, luring the passers-by
with erotic promises. But then they start to beat
people, with sticks and whips. They want to see
blood and hear cries of pain. No more lovely
Cythera with hours of pastoral dalliance, but a
perverted Arcady, aggressive and dangerous.*

Landschaft ist das Urbühnenbild. Der Fernblick als Tangente an jede Handlung, der Himmel mit seiner blauen Unendlichkeit als alles überwölbender Rundhorizont.

Landscape is the primeval stage set. The distant view as a tangent to every action, the sky with its blue infinity as a round horizon vaulting over everything.

Szenen aus der eigenen Innenwelt: Erlebtes, Gesehenes, Gehörtes, Befürchtetes, Ersehntes in die Landschaft projiziert. Denkraum, Gefühlsraum. Spiegelkabinett. Spielort. Die Gedanken von Anfang und Ende, von Zeugung und Verwesung. Die Gedanken von Innen und Außen, von Landschafts-Innenseite und Landschafts-Außenseite. Blicke auf die eigene Nacktheit, auf fremde Nacktheit. Blicke in die Nähe, Blicke in die Ferne. Kamerafahrten. Tahiti-Projektion und arktische Spiegelungen. Dann wieder der bloße Stein, das kleine Stonehenge. Szenen. Szenen von Szenen. Aufzeichnungen von Szenen. Mögliche Szenen.

Scenes from our own interior world: that which is experienced, seen, heard, feared, longed for projected into the landscape. Thinking space. Feeling space. Hall of mirrors. A place to play. Thoughts of beginning and end, procreation and decay. Thoughts of inside and outside, of the inside and outside of the landscape. Looking at our own nakedness, at other people's nakedness. Looking nearby, looking into the distance. Camera journeys. Tahiti projection and Arctic reflections. Then again the naked stone, the little Stonehenge. Scenes. Scenes of scenes. Records of scenes. Possible scenes.

Die Landschaft als Handlungsraum zurücker-
obern. Szenen parallel zu den Alltagshandlungen
erfinden, entlang der Ausfallstraßen, der Autobahnen, auf Brücken und Telegrafenmasten, an
Autobahnraststätten und Stadträndern. Führun-
gen durch die Landschaft veranstalten, die Wälder erklären, die Wiesen und Seen. Das darstellen, was war. Das vermuten, was sein wird. Den
Schmerz der Natur zeigen, ihr Leben, ihr Aufblühen, ihr Strömen, ihr Absterben, ihr Verwesen.
Die Innenseiten nach außen stülpen. Konzentration, Blicke, Sätze, Bilder.

Winning back the landscape as a space for ac-
tion. Inventing scenes parallel with everyday
actions, along main roads out of town, along
motorways, on bridges and telegraph poles, at
motorway service stations and on the edge of
cities. Arranging guided tours of the landscape,
explaining the woods, the meadows and lakes.
Presenting things that have been. Imagine things
that are to be. Show the pain of nature, nature's
life, blossoming, streaming, dying, rotting. Turn
the inside outside. Concentration, looks, senten-
ces, images.

Reflexionen über Liebe, Gewalt, Haß und Tod, über Rausch und Verklärung, über Dionysos und Apollo.

Reflections on love, violence, hatred and death, about intoxication and transfiguration, about Apollo and Dionysus.

Tatorte.

Places where something happened.

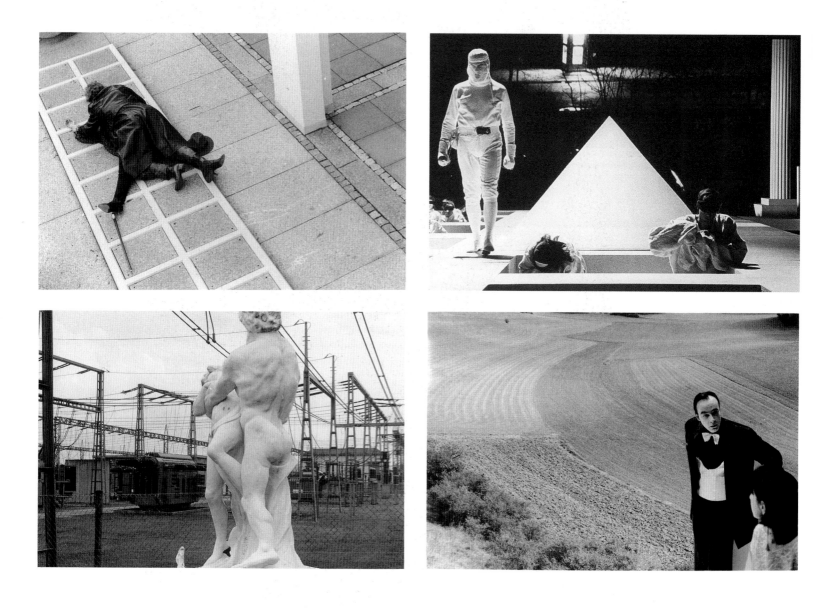

Spuren.

Traces.

Spuren von Kämpfen.

Traces of struggles.

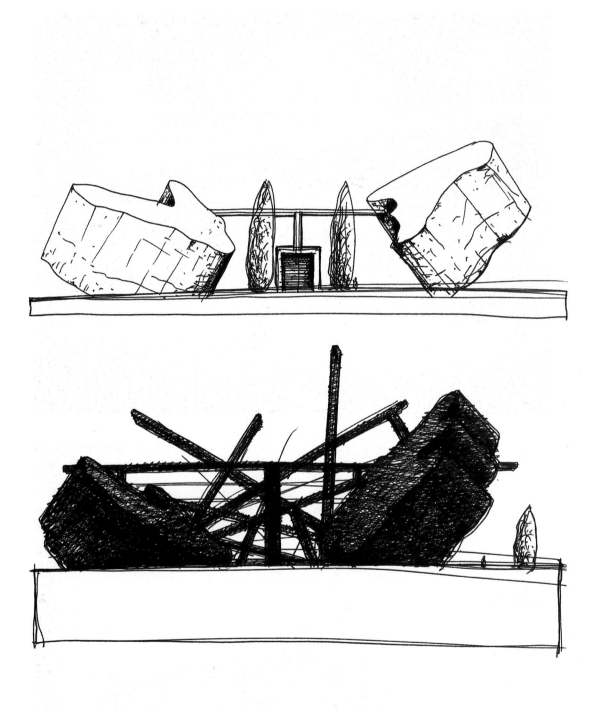

Traumbilder. Traumszenen.

Dream images. Dream scenes.

Ein Waldstück als neues Gartentheater. Waldeingänge mit leuchtenden Versprechungen.

Part of a wood as a new garden theatre. Entrances to woods, glowing with promises.

Inszenierung von Waldgedanken. Angst und Romantik, Schauer und Bedrohung, Jagd und versteckte Leidenschaft, Mord und Flucht, Eifersucht und Liebe.

Staging woodland thoughts. Fear and romance, horror and threat, hunting and concealed passion, murder and flight, jealousy and love.

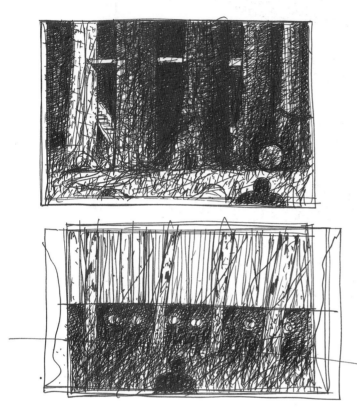

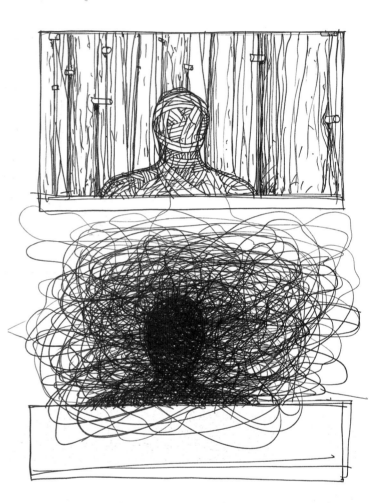

Szenen in Lichtungen.

Scenes in clearings.

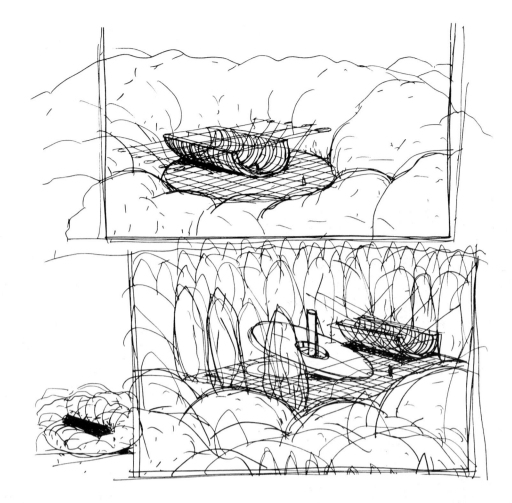

Zwischen den Stämmen sitzen Figuren mit Tonbandgeräten und Schreibmaschinen: Sie zeichnen die Geräusche der Natur auf, das Rauschen der Blätter, das Fallen der Tannennadeln, das Zwitschern der Vögel, das Atmen der Bäume, den Herzschlag der Erde.

Figures with tape recorders and typewriters sit between the tree-trunks: they are recording nature's sounds, rustling leaves, falling pine needles, twittering birds, breathing trees, the heartbeat of the earth.

Neue Landschafts- und Gartenarchitektur
Literarische Themen

New landscape and garden architecture
Literary subjects

Literarische Themen und Texte wurden schon in der Vergangenheit als Garten-Programme verwendet, die Odyssee etwa oder die Metamorphosen von Ovid. Garten- und Parkanlagen nach Texten von Goethe, Hölderlin, Novalis, Flaubert, Michelet, Renard, Roussel, Hesse, Kafka, Pessoa, Michaux, Aragon, Ponge, Pavese, Miller, Plath, Aichinger, Beckett, Cioran oder Handke sind denkbar.

Even in the past literary subjects were used for garden programmes, the Odyssey, for instance, or Ovid's Metamorphoses. Gardens and parks based on texts by Goethe, Hölderlin, Novalis, Flaubert, Michelet, Renard, Roussel, Hesse, Kafka, Pessoa, Michaux, Aragon, Ponge, Pavese, Miller, Plath, Aichinger, Becket, Cioran or Handke are conceivable.

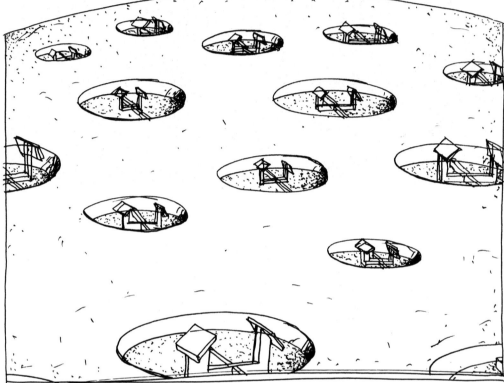

Am Anfang könnte die Darstellung des biblischen Garten-Urtextes stehen.

The starting-point could be the Bible's original garden text.

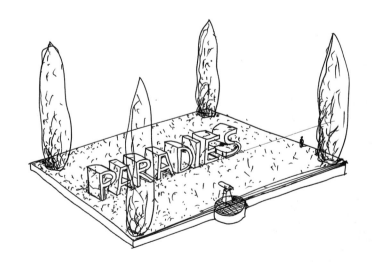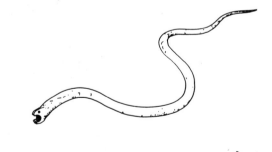

310

Mythologische Spuren, Sätze, Bilder.
Bruchstücke von Marmorgöttern und Marmor-
göttinnen.

*Mythological traces, sentences, images. Frag-
ments of marble gods and goddesses.*

Landschaft mit Fragmenten aus Daphnes
Wohnung.

*Landscape with fragments from Daphne's
dwelling.*

Eine Landschaft für Orpheus. »Die stumme Landschaft, in die die Stimmen dringen.«
(Ilse Aichinger)

A landscape for Orpheus. »The silent language into which the voices force their way.«
(Ilse Aichinger)

Eine Garten-Landschaft für Novalis: Seine Fragmente hängen als Texte zwischen den Blättern der Bäume, Büsche und Blumen:
»Alles ist Samenkorn.
Sollten die Weltkörper Versteinerungen sein? Vielleicht von Engeln …
Kristallisationen: akustische Figuren chemischer Schwingungen (chemischer Sinn.)
Es sind vergangene, geschichtliche Wesen. Die Natur ist eine versteinerte Zauberstadt.
Über die Natur als einen geschlossenen Körper – als einen Baum – woran wir die Blütenknospen sind.« (Novalis)

A garden landscape for Novalis: his fragments hang as texts among the leaves of the trees, bushes and flowers:
»Everything is seed corn.
Could the words be petrifications? Perhaps of angels …
Crystallization: acoustic figures of chemical oscillations (chemical sense).
They are creatures of the past, of history. Nature is a petrified enchanted city.
About nature as a closed body – as a tree – on which we are the flower buds.« (Novalis)

»Alles Absonderliche des Menschen und das, was von einem Vagabunden und von einem Verirrten in ihm ist, könnte er gut und gern in diese beiden Silben fassen: Garten. Nie, und schmückte er sich gleich mit Diamanten oder blies ins Blech, war ihm ein seltsamerer Einfall, eine abwegigere Idee gekommen als damals, als er die Gärten erfand. Ein Bild der Muße bettet sich auf den Rasen zu Füßen der Bäume. Es ist, als befände der Mensch sich da mit seinen zauberischen Wasserspielen und kleinen Kieseln wieder im legendären Paradies, das er keineswegs völlig vergessen hat. Gärten, mit euren Kurven, mit eurer Traulichkeit, mit der Wölbung eures Busens und der Weichheit eurer Locken seid ihr die Frauen des Geistes, oft töricht und schlecht, aber ganz Trunkenheit, ganz Illusion. Innerhalb eurer Umfriedung aus Spindelbäumen, zwischen euren Buchsbaumreihen wird der Mensch gelöst und findet zurück zu einer Sprache der Liebkosungen, zu dem kindlichen Wesen einer Gießkanne. Er selber ist die Gießkanne in der Sonne mit ihrem frischen Haar. Er ist der Rechen und die Schaufel. Er ist der Felsbrocken. Gärten, ihr erinnert an Muffe aus Fischotter, an Spitzentaschentücher, an Pralinen. Manchmal hängt ihr mit euren Lippen an den Balkons; ihr bedeckt die Dächer wie Tiere und miaut in der Tiefe der Innenhöfe. Ich habe in euren Pirogen geschlafen: mein Arm war ausgebreitet und auf der Erde flüchteten kleine Ameisen. Am Himmel standen die Blumen dichtgedrängt. —« (Louis Aragon)

»Pécuchet zeichnete mehrere Grundrisse, wobei er sich seines Reißzeugs bediente. Bouvard gab ihm Ratschläge. Zu einem befriedigenden Resultat kamen sie jedoch nicht. Glücklicherweise fanden sie in ihrer Bibliothek das Werk von Boitard, betitelt *Der Gartenarchitekt*.
Der Autor teilt die Gärten in eine endlose Zahl von Arten ein. Da gibt es zunächst einmal das melancholische und romantische Genre, das gekennzeichnet wird durch Immortellen, Ruinen, Grabmäler und ein der Jungfrau Maria geweihtes Votivbild, welches die Stelle anzeigt, an der ein hoher Herr dem Stahl eines Mörders zum Opfer fiel. Das schreckliche Genre wird mit Hilfe überhängender Felsen, zerschmetterter Bäume, ausgebrannter Hütten dargestellt; die exotische Gattung, indem man peruanische Fackeldisteln pflanzt, um in einem Farmer oder einem Reisenden Erinnerungen zu wecken. Das ernste Genre muß, wie Ermenonville, einen Tempel der Philosophie aufweisen. Obelisken und Triumphbögen charakterisieren das majestätische Genre, Moos und Grotten das mysteriöse, ein See das träumerische Genre. Es gibt sogar die phantastische Gartenform, deren schönstes Beispiel man unlängst in einem Park in Württemberg bewundern konnte – denn hier sah man nacheinander ein Wildschwein, einen Eremiten, mehrere Grabmäler und eine Barke, die von selbst vom Ufer abstieß, um den Besucher in ein Boudoir zu führen, wo ihn Wasserstrahlen naß spritzten, wenn er sich aufs Sofa setzte.
Vor diesem Horizont von Wundern standen Bouvard und Pécuchet wie geblendet. Das phantastische Genre schien ihnen Fürstlichkeiten vorbehalten. Der Tempel der Philosophie würde zuviel Raum einnehmen. Das Votivbild der Madonna hätte keine Beziehung angesichts der nicht vor-

handenen Mörder, und die amerikanischen Pflanzen würden – zum Bedauern der Farmer und Reisenden – zu teuer sein. Aber die Felsen lagen im Bereich der Möglichkeit, ebenso die zerschmetterten Bäume, die Immortellen und das Moos – und in steigender Begeisterung, nach vielem Herumtasten, bastelten sie sich mit Hilfe eines einzigen Knechts und für eine winzige Summe eine Residenz zusammen, die im ganzen Departement nicht ihresgleichen hatte.
Der hier und da durchbrochene Laubengang ließ den Blick auf den Hain fallen, dessen Wege sich wie in einem Labyrinth schlängelten. In der Spaliermauer hatten sie ein Bogengewölbe anbringen wollen, durch das man in die Ferne blicken sollte. Da die Wölbung sich nicht in der Schwebe halten wollte, war eine riesige Bresche entstanden, deren Trümmer an der Erde herumlagen. Sie hatten die Spargelbeete geopfert, um darauf ein etruskisches Grabmal zu bauen, das heißt einen Würfel aus schwarzem Gips, der sechs Fuß hoch war und aussah wie eine Hundehütte. Vier Tannen an den Ecken flankierten das Monument, das noch von einer Urne überragt und durch eine Inschrift bereichert werden sollte.
Auf der andern Seite des Gemüsegartens überbrückte eine Art Rialto einen Teich, dessen Rand mit Muscheln ausgelegt war. Die Erde schluckte das Wasser. Ganz egal; es würde sich schon eine Tonkruste bilden, die es halten sollte.
Der Geräteschuppen war mit Hilfe farbiger Glasscheiben in eine ländliche Kate verwandelt worden.« (Gustave Flaubert)

»Everything strange in man, and the qualities within him of a vagabond or lost soul he could well put in these two syllables: garden. Never, even if he immediately adorned himself with diamonds or blew into brass did he have a stranger notion, a more outlandish idea than at the time he invented gardens. An image of idleness lies on the lawn at the foot of the trees. It is as though man is here in that legendary paradise again, with his magical water-games and little pebbles, a paradise that he has never completely forgotten. Gardens, with your curves, with your intimacy, with the swelling of your bosom and the softness of your tresses, you are the women of the spirit, often foolish and bad, but all drunkenness, all illusion. Inside your enclosure of spindle trees, between your box-tree rows man is released and finds his way back to a language of caresses, to the child-like nature of a watering-can. He himself is the watering-can in the sun, with its fresh hair. He is the rake and the spade. He is the piece of rock. Gardens; you remind me of otter-skin muffs, of lace handkerchiefs, of chocolates. Sometimes you hang on to balconies with your lips; you cover roofs like animals and mew deep down in the courtyard. I have slept in your pirogues: my arm was stretched out and little ants were running away on the ground. In the sky the flowers were close together . . . « (Louis Aragon)

»Pécuchet drew several ground plans, using his drawing equipment. Bouvard made suggestions to him. But they did not achieve a satisfactory result. Fortunately they found in their library a book by Boitard called *Der Gartenarchitekt*.
The author divides gardens into an endless number of types. First of all there is the melancholy

and romantic genre, with characteristic immortals, ruins, tombs and ›a votive image dedicated to the Virgin Mary showing the place at which a great man fell victim to a murderer's steel.‹ The horrific genre is presented with the assistance of overhanging rocks, smashed trees and burnt-out huts; the exotic genre involves the planting of Peruvian torch thistles ›to awaken reminiscences in a farmer or a traveller.‹ The serious genre must have a Temple of Philosophy, like Ermenonville. Obelisks and triumphal arches are characteristic of the majestic genre, moss and grottoes of the mysterious genre and a lake of the dream-like genre. There is even the fantastic garden form, the most beautiful example of which could recently be admired in a park in Württemberg – for here one saw one after the other a wild boar, a hermit, several tombs and a barge that set off from the bank itself to take the visitor into a boudoir where he was sprayed with jets of water when he sat down on the sofa.
Bouvard and Pécuchet stood as if dazzled before this horizon of miracles. The fantastic genre seemed to them to be reserved for princes. The Temple of Philosophy would take up too much room. The votive image of the Madonna would have no meaning as no murderer was available, and the American plants – to the regret of travellers and farmers – would be too expensive. But the rocks were within the bounds of the possible, and so were the smashed trees, the immortals and the moss – and with mounting enthusiasm, after many tentative approaches, with the help of a single servant and for a tiny sum of money, they put together a residence that did not have an equal throughout the Département.
The arbour, broken here and there, afforded a glimpse of the grove, with its paths snaking as if in a labyrinth. They had intended to put an arched vault into the espalier wall to afford a view into the distance. But as the vault would not remain suspended an enormous breech had come into being, and ruins lay all over the ground.
They had sacrificed the asparagus beds to build an Etruscan tomb upon them, in other words a cube of black plaster that was six feet high and looked like a dog kennel. Four fir trees flanked the monument at the corners, which was to be further enriched with an inscription and an urn towering above it.
On the other side of the vegetable garden a kind of Rialto formed a bridge over a pool, the edge of which was lined with shells. The earth swallowed up the water. Never mind; it would soon form a clay crust to hold it properly.
The toolshed had been transformed into a rustic cottage with the assistance of coloured panes of glass.« (Gustave Flaubert)

Ein Garten für Pessoa: Man hört seine leise
Stimme durch die Äste und Blätter sprechen.

*A garden for Pessoa: you can hear his soft voice
speaking through the branches and leaves.*

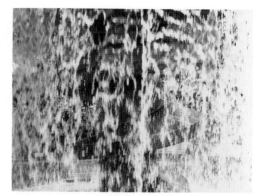

»Wenn ich zuweilen sage, die Blumen lächeln,
und wenn ich sage, die Flüsse singen,
so nicht, weil ich meinte, es gäbe lächelnde Blumen
und singend strömende Flüsse …
Vielmehr, weil ich so den verlogenen Menschen
das wirkliche Wesen der Blumen und Flüsse
zeige.

Weil ich schreibe, damit sie mich lesen, bring ich
zuweilen
der Unzulänglichkeit ihrer Sinne mich zum
Opfer …
ich tue es ungern, doch ich spreche mich frei,
denn im Grunde bin ich nur dies: ein Dolmetscher
der Natur,
weil es Menschen gibt, die ihre Sprache nicht
fassen,
weil ihre Sprache keine ist.«

(Fernando Pessoa)

*»And if I sometimes say the flowers are smiling,
and if I say the rivers sing,
it is not because I thought there were smiling
flowers
and singing flowing rivers …
Rather, because it is a way of showing menda-
cious man
The real nature of flowers and rivers.*

*As I write so that they will read me, I sometimes
sacrifice myself to the inadequacy of their senses
…
I do it unwillingly, but I exonerate myself
because ultimately I am only this: an interpreter
for nature,
because there are people who cannot understand its language,
because it is not a language.«*

(Fernando Pessoa)

Ein Garten für Pavese: Seine Tagebuchblätter sind auf dem Waldboden verteilt und an die Stämme geheftet. Jeder Stamm ist ein Tag.

A garden for Pavese: the pages of his diary are spread on the floor of the wood and fastened to the tree-trunks. Each trunk is a day.

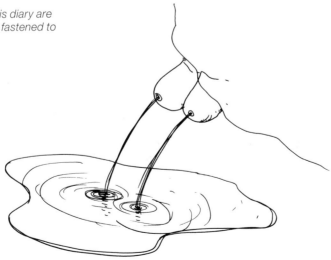

»9. Januar

Die maßlose Leidenschaft für die natürliche Magie, für das Wilde, für die dämonische Wahrheit von Bäumen, Wassern, Felsen und Landstrichen ist ein Zeichen von Furchtsamkeit, von Flucht vor den Pflichten und Verpflichtungen der Welt der Menschen.

Da der mythische Anspruch, die Wirklichkeit der Dinge zu empfinden, fest bleibt, braucht es Mut, mit denselben Augen die Menschen und ihre Leidenschaften zu betrachten. Aber es ist schwierig, es ist unbequem – die Menschen haben nicht die Festigkeit der Natur, ihre weite Deutbarkeit, ihr Schweigen. Die Menschen kommen uns entgegen, wobei sie sich aufdrängen, sich bewegen, sich ausdrücken. Du hast auf mannigfaltige Arten versucht, sie zu Stein zu machen – indem du sie in ihren natürlichsten Momenten isoliertest, sie in die Natur eintauchtest, sie auf Schicksal beschränktest. Und doch reden und reden deine Menschen – in ihnen kämpft der Geist, taucht an die Oberfläche. Dies ist deine Spannung. Aber du erträgst diesen Geist, du möchtest ihn nie von dir aus finden. Du strebst nach der natürlichen Unbeweglichkeit, nach dem Schweigen, dem Tode. Aus ihnen hochwertige Mythen machen, ewige, unberührbare, die doch einen Zauber auf die historische Wirklichkeit werfen und ihr einen Sinn geben könnten, einen Wert.«
(Cesare Pavese)

»9th January

A boundless passion for the magic of nature, for wildness, for the demonic truth of trees, water, rocks and landscape is a sign of timidity, of flight from the duties and obligations of the world of man.

As the mythical claim to feel the reality of things remains firm it needs courage to view human beings and their passions with the same eyes. But it is difficult, it is uncomfortable – people do not have the steadfastness of nature, its breadth of interpretability, its silence. People co-operate with us, by pushing themselves forward, moving, expressing themselves. You have tried all manner of ways of turning them to stone – by isolating them in their most natural moments, plunging them into nature, limiting them to fate. And yet your people talk and talk – the spirit is struggling within them, coming to the surface. This is your excitement. But you tolerate this spirit, you would never want to find it of your own accord. You strive for natural immobility, for silence, for death. Making high-value myths of them, eternal and intangible, that could still cast a spell on historical reality and give some meaning, some value.«
(Cesare Pavese)

Ein Garten für Borges.

A garden for Borges.

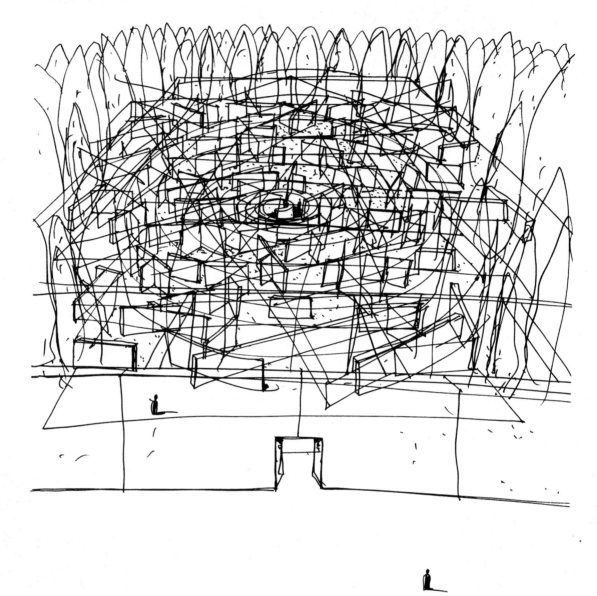

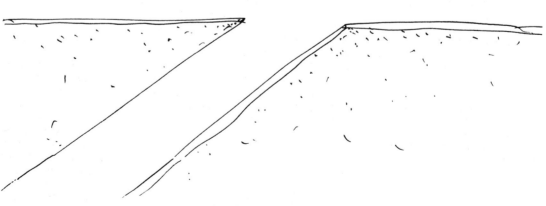

Garten der Romantiker. Versammlung aller romantischen Gartenbilder auf einem Gartenfloß.

The romantic's garden. Collection of all romantic garden images on a garden raft.

»Die Eltern lagen schon und schliefen, die Wanduhr schlug ihren einförmigen Takt, vor den klappernden Fenstern sauste der Wind; abwechselnd wurde die Stube hell von dem Schimmer des Mondes. Der Jüngling lag unruhig auf seinem Lager und gedachte des Fremden und seiner Erzählungen. Nicht die Schätze sind es, die ein so unaussprechliches Verlangen in mir geweckt haben, sagte er zu sich selbst; fern ab liegt mir alle Habsucht: aber die blaue Blume sehn' ich mich zu erblicken. Sie liegt mir unaufhörlich im Sinn, und ich kann nichts anders dichten und denken. So ist mir noch nie zu mute gewesen: es ist, als hätt' ich vorhin geträumt, oder ich wäre in eine andere Welt hinübergeschlummert; denn in der Welt, in der ich sonst lebte, wer hätte da sich um Blumen bekümmert, und gar von einer so seltsamen Leidenschaft für eine Blume hab' ich damals nie gehört. Wo eigentlich nur der Fremde herkam? Keiner von uns hat je einen ähnlichen Menschen gesehn; doch weiß ich nicht, warum nur ich von seinen Reden so ergriffen worden bin; die Andern haben ja das Nämliche gehört, und Keinem ist so etwas begegnet. Daß ich auch nicht einmal von meinem wunderlichen Zustande reden kann! Es ist mir oft so entzückend wohl, und nur dann, wenn ich die Blume nicht recht gegenwärtig habe, befällt mich so ein tiefes, inniges Treiben: das kann und wird Keiner verstehn. Ich glaubte, ich wäre wahnsinnig, wenn ich nicht so klar und hell sähe und dächte, mir ist seitdem alles viel bekannter. Ich hörte einst von alten Zeiten reden; wie da die Tiere und Bäume und Felsen mit den Menschen gesprochen hätten. Mir ist gerade so, als wollten sie allaugenblicklich anfangen, und als könnte ich es ihnen ansehen, was sie mir sagen wollten. Es muß noch viel Worte geben, die ich nicht weiß: wüßte ich mehr, so könnte ich viel besser alles begreifen. Sonst tanzte ich gern; jetzt denke ich lieber nach der Musik. Der Jüngling verlor sich allmählich in süßen Fantasien und entschlummerte. Da träumte ihm erst von unabsehlichen Fernen, und wilden, unbekannten Gegenden. Er wanderte über Meere mit unbegreiflicher Leichtigkeit; wunderliche Thiere sah er; er lebte mit mannichfaltigen Menschen, bald im Kriege, in wildem Getümmel, in stillen Hütten …« (Novalis)

»His parents were already in bed and asleep, the wall clock ticked in its monotonous rhythm, the wind howled outside the rattling windows; sometimes the room was lit by the shimmer of the moon. The youth lay uneasily on his couch and thought of the stranger and his stories. It is not the treasure that has awakened such inexpressible longing in me, he said to himself; all greed is very far from me: but I long to see the blue flower. It is ceaselessly in my mind, and I cannot compose and think anything else. I have never felt like this before: it is as though previously I had dreamed, or as if I had slumbered over into another world; for in the world where else I lived, who would have concerned himself with flowers there, and there I never heard anything of so strange a passion for a flower. Where can the stranger actually have come from? None of us has ever seen a man like that; but I do not know why it is only I who was so moved by what he said; the others heard the same thing, and nothing like this happened to any of them. And I cannot even talk of my strange condition! I often feel so rapturously well, and it is only when I do not have the flower quite present that I am overcome by such deep and fervent longings: no-one can or will understand that. I would think that I was mad if I could not see so clearly and brightly and did not think that everything is so much more familiar to me since then. I once heard tell of the old days; how then the animals and trees and rocks were said to have talked to people. I feel just as though they wanted to start at any moment, and as though I could see what they wanted to tell me from the way they looked. There must still be a lot of words that I do not know: if I knew more I could understand everything so much better. I used to enjoy dancing; now I prefer to think in terms of music. The youth gradually lost himself in sweet imaginings, and fell asleep. Then he dreamed of unimaginable distances, and wild and unknown places. He crossed the oceans with incredible ease; he saw strange creatures; he lived with all manner of people, sometimes at war, in wild tumult, in silent homesteads . . . « (Novalis)*

»Die Strände, Gestade und Steilfelsen zeigen die See unter drei jeweils unverzichtbaren Aspekten. Sie erklären sie und übertragen sie in unsere Sprache; sie setzen diese auf den ersten Blick wilde, aber im Grunde göttliche und demnach befreundete große Macht zu uns in Beziehung. Der Vorteil bei den Steilfelsen liegt darin, daß man am Fuß dieser hohen Wände viel deutlicher noch als sonst die Ebbe und die Flut, die Atmung oder gar (warum nicht?) den Puls des Meeres verspürt. Wenn er beim Mittelmeer kaum wahrzunehmen ist, so ist er beim Ozean dagegen stark ausgeprägt. Der Ozean atmet wie ich selbst, er ist im Einklang mit meiner inneren Bewegung und mit der des Himmels. Er verpflichtet mich, unablässig mit ihm zu rechnen, die Tage und Stunden zu überschlagen und auf den Himmel aufzumerken. Er ruft mich zu mir selbst und zur Welt zurück …« (Jules Michelet)

»The beaches, shores and cliffs show the sea in three aspects, each of which is indispensable. They explain them and translate them into our language; they place this power, wild at a first glance, but fundamentally divine and thus amicable, in some relationship with us.
The advantage of the cliffs is that at the foot of these great walls one can feel more clearly than at other times the ebb and flow, the breathing or even (why not?) the pulse of the sea. Even if it is scarcely perceptible in the Mediterranean it is most marked in the case of the ocean. The ocean breathes as I do myself, it is in harmony with my inner movement and with that of the sky. It obliges me to reckon with it ceaselessly, to count the days and hours and pay attention to the sky. It calls me to myself and back into the world . . . «
(Jules Michelet)

»Und schließlich, da ich unvorsichtig wurde, nahm sie mich wieder gefangen, diese fürchterliche Unordnung, das Labyrinth des Gartens, diese Verwirrung aller Sinne. Wieder schritt ich sämtliche Wege ab, verirrte mich in Sackgassen, täuschte mich in der Richtung. Aber das Labyrinth, das war diesmal keine Architektur von Dädalus, wie zu Theseus' Zeiten; keine hohen, grauen Mauern, in deren sorgsam verschachtelter Mitte der Minotaurus lauerte. Vergebens suchte ich nach diesen Mauern, nach dem Roten Faden oder dem leuchtenden Kranz der Ariadne, der mich durch das Labyrinth hätte führen können.« (Martin Dean)

»And finally, as I became careless, it captured me again, this terrible lack of order, the labyrinth of the garden, this confusion of all my senses. Once more I walked down all the paths, got lost in culs-de-sac, was mistaken about the direction. But the labyrinth this time was not architecture by Daedalus, as in Theseus' times; no high, grey walls in the carefully encapsulated centre of which the Minotaur lurked. I looked in vain for these walls, for the Red Thread or the gleaming garland of Ariadne that could have led me through this labyrinth.« (Martin Dean)

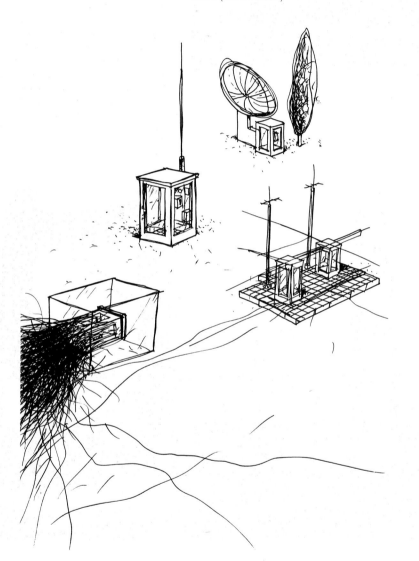

Garten der Idealisten, der Realisten, der Lyriker, der Dramatiker, der Expressionisten, der Philosophen, der Journalisten …

Garden of the idealists, realists, lyric poets, dramatists, Expressionists, philosophers, journalists …

»An diesem Donnerstag, Anfang April, hatte mich mein gelehrter Freund, Meister Martial Canterel, zusammen mit einigen anderen Vertrauten eingeladen, den ausgedehnten Park zu besichtigen, der seine schöne Villa in Montmorency umgibt. Locus Solus – so heißt die Besitzung – ist ein stiller Zufluchtsort, auf dem Canterel seine vielfältigen und fruchtbringenden Arbeiten in völliger Ungestörtheit des Geistes zu verrichten pflegt. An diesem einsamen Ort ist er vor den Aufregungen von Paris hinreichend geschützt – und kann doch in einer Viertelstunde die Hauptstadt erreichen, wenn seine Forschungen den Aufenthalt in einer Spezialbibliothek erfordern oder wenn der Augenblick gekommen ist, der wissenschaftlichen Welt in einem außerordentlich gut besuchten Vortrag irgendeine sensationelle Mitteilung zu machen.

In Locus Solus verbringt Canterel fast das ganze Jahr, umgeben von Schülern, die ihn voll leidenschaftlicher Bewunderung für seine fortwährenden Entdeckungen begeistert bei der Vollendung seines Werkes unterstützen. Die Villa birgt mehrere Räume, die mit großem Aufwand als Musterlaboratorien eingerichtet sind; zahlreiche Gehilfen sind hier tätig, und der Meister widmet sein ganzes Leben der Wissenschaft, wobei er, als Junggeselle ohne Verpflichtungen, mit seinem großen Vermögen alle materiellen Schwierigkeiten spielend aus dem Wege räumt, die sich im Laufe seiner hartnäckigen Arbeit aus den verschiedenen festgesetzten Zielen ergeben.

Eben hatte es drei Uhr geschlagen. Es war ein schöner Tag, die Sonne funkelte an einem fast gleichmäßig klaren Himmel. Canterel hatte uns unweit seiner Villa im Freien unter alten Bäumen begrüßt, deren Schatten eine Reihe bequemer Korbsessel umfing.« (Raymond Roussel)

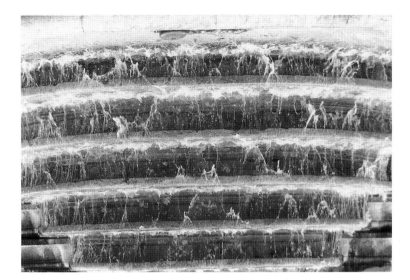

Garten der Erinnerungsbilder:

Garden of the images of memory:

»OCEAN 1212-W.
Die Landschaft meiner Kindheit war nicht Land, sondern das Ende vom Land – die kalten, salzigen, rollenden Hügel des Atlantik. Manchmal denke ich, daß mein Bild vom Meer das Klarste ist, was ich besitze. Ich trage es in mir, verbannt, wie ich bin, wie die purpurnen weißumrandeten Glückssteine oder die blauschaligen Muscheln, deren Inneres regenbogenfarben schimmert wie die Fingernägel von Engeln; und in einer Welle der Erinnerung werden die Farben tiefer und glänzend, die frühe Welt holt Atem …« (Sylvia Plath)

»OCEAN 1212-W
The landscape of my childhood was not land, but the end of the land – the cold, salty rolling hills of the Atlantic. I sometimes think that my image of the sea is the clearest that I possess. I carry it within me, exiled as I am, like the purple, white-edged lucky stones or the blue-shelled mussels whose interior shimmers in all the colours of the rainbow like angels' fingers; and in a wave of memory the colours become deeper and shining, the early world takes a breath … «
(Sylvia Plath)

»On this Thursday, in early April, my learned friend Maître Martial Canterel invited me and some other close friends to visit the extensive park that surrounds his beautiful villa in Montmorency.
Locus Solus – that is the name of the property – is a quiet place of refuge in which Canterel produces his diverse and fruitful work with a spirit absolutely untroubled by interruption. In this lonely place he is adequately protected from the excitements of Paris – and yet can be at the capital within a quarter of an hour if his research requires a visit to a specialized library or when the moment has come to make some sensational revelation to the academic world in an extraordinarily well-attended lecture.
Canterel spends almost the entire year at Locus Solus, surrounded by pupils who support him enthusiastically as he completes his work, full of passionate admiration for his continuing discoveries. The villa contains several rooms that have been equipped as model laboratories at great expense; numerous assistants work here, and the master devotes his whole life to science, and, as a bachelor without obligations effortlessly clears aside all material difficulties that occur in the course of his tenacious work because of the various goals that are set, because of his great fortune.
It had just struck three. It was a beautiful day, the sun was sparkling in an almost uniformly clear sky. Canterel had greeted us not far from his villa in the open air under old trees whose shadows contained a series of comfortable basket chairs.«
(Raymond Roussel)

»Stille ringsum: Meine Landschaft liegt auf dem Grund des Meeres.« (Jules Renard)

»Silence all around: my landscape lies at the bottom of the sea.« (Jules Renard)

»Metaphysik der Orte, du bist es, die die Kinder in den Schlaf wiegt, du bist es, wovon sie träumen. Unser ganzes geistiges Gut säumt diese Ufer des Unbekannten und des Schauders. Ich kann keinen Schritt in die Vergangenheit tun, ohne daß mich wieder dieses Gefühl des Fremdartigen überkommt, das mich ergriff, als ich noch das Staunen selbst war, in einer Umgebung, wo mir zum erstenmal ein dunkler Zusammenhang bewußt wurde, der in meinem Innern Widerhall fand.

Die ganze Fauna der Phantasie samt ihrer Meeresvegetation stirbt dahin wie ein nächtlicher Kometenschweif und lebt fort in den schlecht beleuchteten Bereichen menschlicher Tätigkeit. Dort tauchen die großen geistigen Leuchttürme auf, die in ihrem Aussehen an weniger reine Zeichen gemahnen. Eine menschliche Schwäche stößt die Tür zum Geheimnis auf und schon befinden wir uns in den Reichen des Schattens. Ein Stolpern, ein Stottern verraten das Denken eines Menschen. Im Dämmer der Orte gibt es solche Türen zum Unendlichen, die schlecht schließen. Dort, wo die Lebenden ihrer höchst zweifelhaften Tätigkeit nachgehen, nimmt das

Unbeseelte manchmal einen Abglanz ihrer geheimsten Beweggründe an: unsere Städte sind so von unerkannten Sphinxen bevölkert, die den nachdenklichen Passanten so lange nicht anhalten, als er seine schweifenden Gedanken nicht auf sie richtet. Sie geben ihm keine todbringenden Rätsel auf. Doch wenn er, dieser Weise, sie zu lösen versteht, so möge er sie ruhig befragen, es sind immer nur seine eigenen Abgründe, die er dank dieser ungestalten Ungeheuer neu auslotet. Das Licht, das das Ungewöhnliche heute erhellt, aber wird ihn fortan davon abhalten …« (Louis Aragon)

»Metaphysics of places, it is you who rocks children in their sleep, and it is you of whom they dream. All our mental and spiritual belongings line this bank of the unknown and of shudders. I cannot take a step into the past without being overcome again by this feeling of strangeness that seized me when I was still astonishment itself, in surroundings where I first became aware of a dark connection that found an echo within me. All the fauna of imagination and its ocean vegetation pass away like a nocturnal comet's tail

and live on in the poorly illuminated realms of human activity. There the great spiritual light-houses appear, with their appearance reminiscent of less pure symbols. Human weakness pushes open the door of the secret and we are already in the realms of shadow. Stumbling and stuttering reveal the thinking of a human being. In the twilight of places there are such doors to the infinite that are hard to close. In the place where the living pursue their extremely dubious activities the soulless sometimes take on a reflection of their most secret motives: in this way our cities are populated with unrecognized sphinxes who do not detain the nocturnal passer-by for as long as he does not direct his wandering thoughts at them. They do not set him any death-bringing riddles. But if he, this wise man, knows how to solve them, then he should be happy to ask them, it is only his own dark depths that he is plumbing anew, thanks to these shapeless monsters. But the light that illuminates the unusual today will keep him away from it in future …« (Louis Aragon)

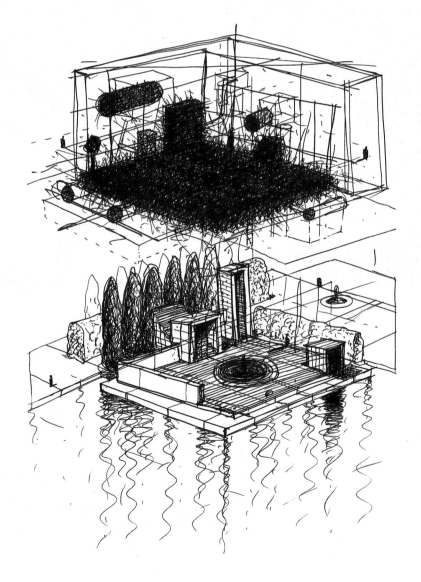

Gartenbilder der Resignierten und Verzweifelten. Ein stürzender Platz für Beckett und ein vereister Laubengang für Cioran.

Garden images for the resigned and the desperate. A plunging place for Beckett and an icy arbour for Cioran.

Gärten der langsamen Umnachtung. Eingebaut in Hölderlins Turm.

Gardens slowly becoming surrounded by night. Built into Hölderlin's tower.

»Ein Moment am hiesigen Ort, ein Moment des Beginns der eigenen Ortsveränderung, ein zutiefst aufgewühlter Moment, beim Entdecken eines schwarzen Moments.« (Henri Michaux)

»A moment in this place, a moment of beginning one's own change of place, a moment of profound disturbance at the discovery of a black moment.« (Henri Michaux)

»Groß sind die Wüsten, und alles ist Wüste.
Ein paar Tonnen Steine und Ziegel darüber
können doch nicht den Boden verdecken,
den Boden, der alles ist.
Groß sind die Wüsten und die Seelen verlassen
und groß –
verlassen, weil nichts sie durchzieht als sie
selber,
groß, weil man alles von ihnen aus sieht, und
alles ist tot.

Groß sind die Wüsten, meine Seele!
Groß sind die Wüsten.«

(Fernando Pessoa)

»The deserts are large, and everything is desert.
A few tons of stone and bricks on top of them
cannot in fact cover the ground, the ground that
is everything.
The deserts are large and the souls deserted and
large – because nothing passes through them
but themselves,
large, because everything can be seen from
them, and everything is dead.

The deserts are large, my soul!
The deserts are large.«

(Fernando Pessoa)

Neue Landschafts- und Gartenarchitektur
Zusammenfassung

New landscape and garden architecture
Summary

Im folgenden wird der Versuch unternommen, alle beschriebenen Elemente und Eingriffe in Gesamtkompositionen zusammenzufassen. Nochmals die beiden Blickbewegungen: nach innen, in die Natur-Innenwelt (Nahblick) und nach außen, in die Weite der Landschaft (Fernblick). Für den Nahblick steht der klassische ummauerte Gartenort, für den Fernblick der Park und die offene Landschaft.

Der zu Beginn des Buches beschriebene Riß zwischen Natur und Ich soll wieder ins Blickfeld rücken. Alle Entwürfe sollen Prozesse anregen, den Riß zu überbrücken. Alle Entwürfe sollen Dialoge herstellen zwischen dem »Kraftwerk Natur« und dem Vorstellungsraum des Menschen.

In what follows an attempt is made to summarize all the elements and interventions that have been described in overall compositions.
Again the two movements in the way we look: inside, into the inner world of nature (close-up) and outwards, into the expanse of the landscape (long distance). For the close-up we have the classical walled garden area, for long distance the park and the open landscape.
The rift between nature and the ego described at the beginning of the book should be brought back into the field of view. All designs should stimulate processes intended to bridge this rift. All designs should produce dialogue between ›power station nature‹ and human powers of imagination.

Blicke und Wege nach innen: Der Gartenort

Looks and ways inside: the garden area.

Grenze, Zaun, Mauer: Dieser gerahmte Natur- und Landschaftsausschnitt stellt den klassischen Gartenbereich dar mit Wohnhaus, Wiese, Beeten, Blumen, Büschen, Bäumen, Wegen und Wasserstellen.

Boundary, fence, wall: this framed section of landscape and nature represents the classical garden area, with house, lawn, flower-beds, flowers, bushes, trees, paths and water places.

Dieser Bereich hat die Tendenz zum Versteck, ist eine Privatangelegenheit zwischen Bewohner und Natur.
Hausgarten, Wohngarten, Nutzgarten, Blumengarten, Gemüsegarten, Bauerngarten, Rosengarten, Steingarten, Vogelgarten, Wassergarten, Ziergarten und eßbarer Garten.

This area has a tendency to be a hiding-place, is a private matter between residents and nature. House and garden, domestic garden, kitchen garden, flower garden, vegetable garden, country garden, rose garden, rock garden, bird garden, water garden ... decorative garden and edible garden.

Gartenort zwischen Stille und Expression. Meditationsort und Raum der Inszenierung. Sehnsuchtsraum für Naturerotik: den Baum umarmen, die Blume küssen.

A garden area between stillness and expression. A place of meditation and space for staging things. A longing space for nature's eroticism: embrace the tree and kiss the flowers.

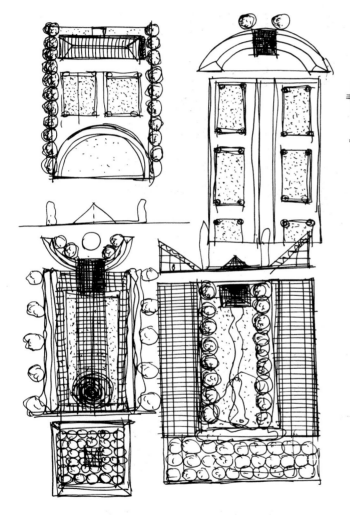

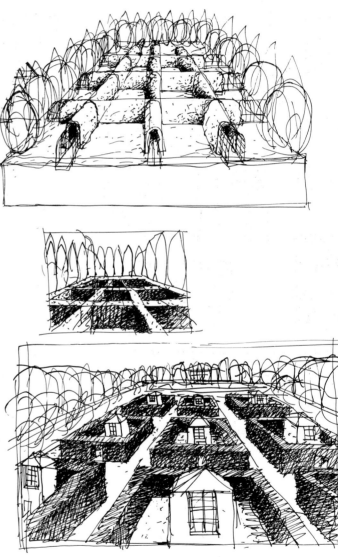

325

Wie zu Beginn beschrieben: geometrische Anlagen, organische Anlagen. Innenhofgärten mit Tempeln, mit Drehtüren, mit Beetsplittern. Religiöser Garten. Philosophischer Garten. Garten mit gepflanzten Bildern aus der Kunstgeschichte (z. B. Bilder von Picasso, Klee, Miró, Mondrian, Kandinsky usw.).

As described at the beginning: geometrical layouts, organic layouts. Courtyard gardens with temples, with revolving doors, with splinters of flower-beds. Religious garden. Philosophical garden. Garden with planted images from the history of art (e. g. pictures by Picasso, Klee, Miró, Mondrian, Kandinsky etc.).

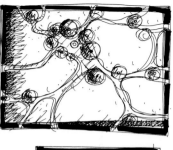

Die Fantasie des Bewohners verwebt sich mit der Fantasie der Natur.

The occupant's imagination interwaves with nature's imagination.

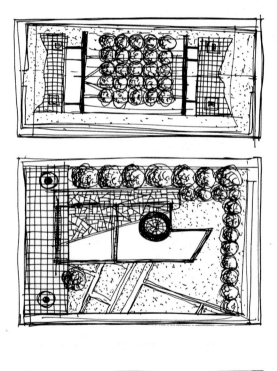
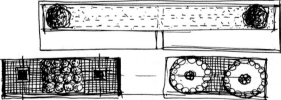

Die Architektur des Wohnhauses ist ein strenges Gehäuse, ein klar gefaßter Kubus oder eine sich im Gartenbereich auflösende Struktur.

Domestic architecture is an austere casing, a clearly defined cube or a structure that dissolves in the garden area.

Grundrisse möglicher Garten-Häuser.
Grundrißgarten.

Ground plans for possible garden-houses.
Ground plan garden.

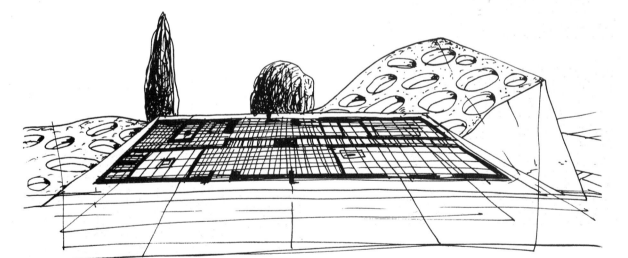

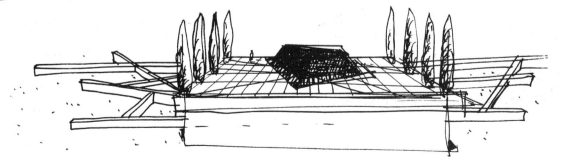

Vorstellung: Man betritt die Mitte des Gartens nie mehr. Eine am Anfang installierte Videokamera überträgt aus der Mitte des Gartens das Entstehen des Dickichts.

Imagine: you never go into the middle of the garden any more. A video camera installed at the edge broadcasts daily from the middle of the thicket, from nature's power centre.

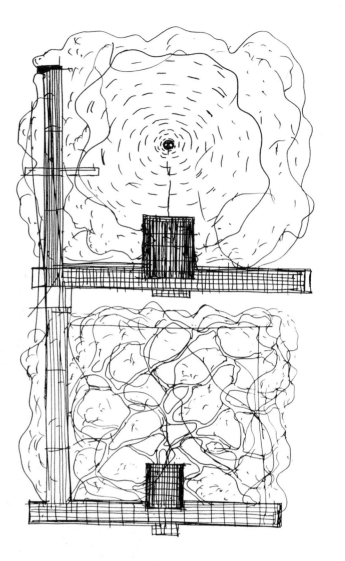

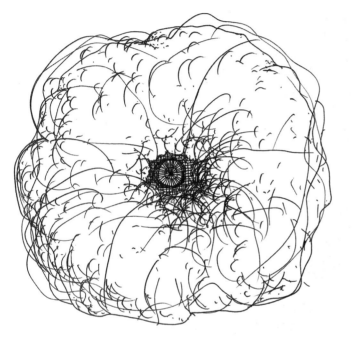

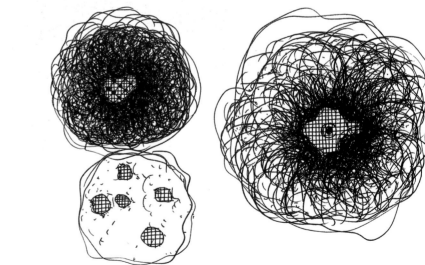

Wohngärten mit Wasserbecken und Arkaden-
gängen, mit Laubengittern, Alleen, Wiesenstücken, Wasserfällen, mit Brücken, Ruinen ...

*Residential gardens with pools and arcades, with
arbour lattices, avenues, lawns, waterfalls, with
bridges, ruins ...*

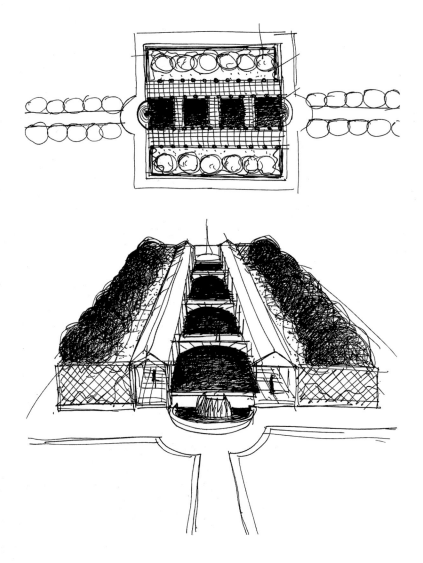

Erweiterung: Der Innenhofgarten erhält Öffnungen und wird nicht mehr bewohnt. Die Arkadenreihen, die Einbauten, die Baumreihen, die Wiesenstücke werden zu einem öffentlichen Garten. Denkbar mitten in den Städten als Ruhezonen und Kirchenersatz (weltliche Klostergärten).

Extension: the courtyard garden is provided with openings and is no longer lived in. The arcades, the buildings, the rows of trees, the patches of lawn become a public garden. Conceivable in the city centre as areas of quiet and as a substitute for church (secular monastery gardens).

Oder: Der ummauerte Bereich wird zur Siedlung erweitert. Viele Familien wohnen hier. Es gibt ein zentrales Wasserbecken, Treppen, Torbogenreihungen, Laubengänge, Haine, Alleen, Blumenfelder und Wohnungen.

Or: the walled area is extended to form a settlement. A number of families live here. There are a central pool, steps, series of gateway-arches, arbours, groves, avenues, fields of flowers and accommodation.

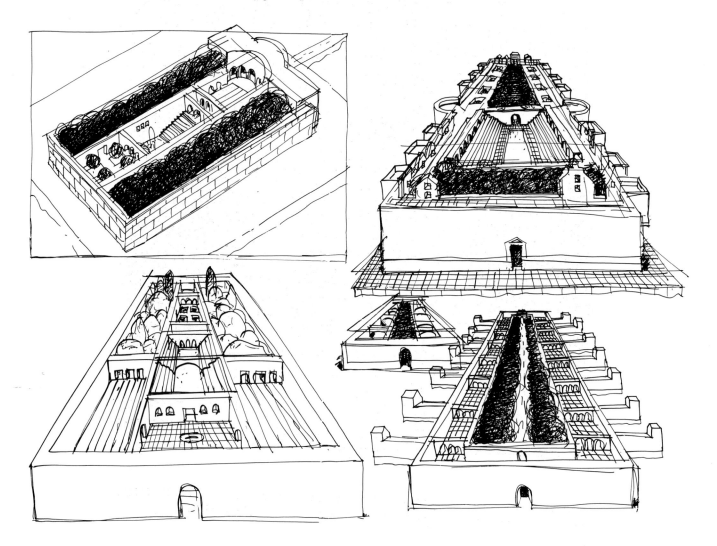

Auch dieser Verflechtungsbereich öffnet sich, die Mauern sind nicht mehr ringsum geschlossen, die Plätze greifen in das Stadtkontinuum oder in die Landschaft hinein.

This area of interconnection opens up as well, the walls are no longer closed all round, the squares impinge on the city continuum or the landscape.

Fernblick: Wege nach außen.
Der öffentliche Gartenort, der neue Stadtpark,
Gartenprogramme, Gartenstationen, Gartenthe-
men

Distant view: ways outward
The public garden, the new municipal park, gar-
den programmes, garden stations, garden
theme.

Geöffnete Bilder. Durchgehbar.
Öffentliche Natur.

Opened pictures. Possible to walk through.
Public nature.

Die Umgrenzungen der Gärten, die Mauern und Zäune verlieren sich in der freien Landschaft. Die großen Bewegungen nehmen zu.

The gardens' borders, the walls and fences get lost and wander away in the open landscape. Large-scale movements increase.

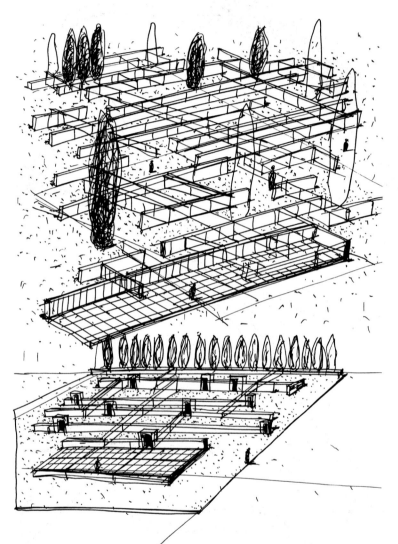

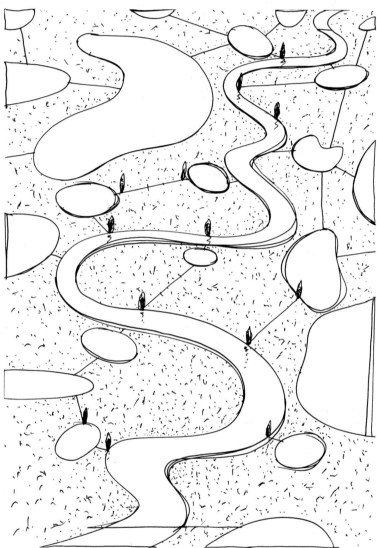

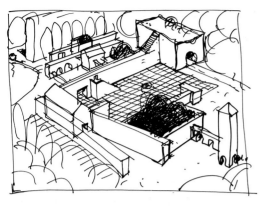

Wege mit begleitenden Pflanzungen, Rhythmen.

Paths with accompanying planting. Rhythms.

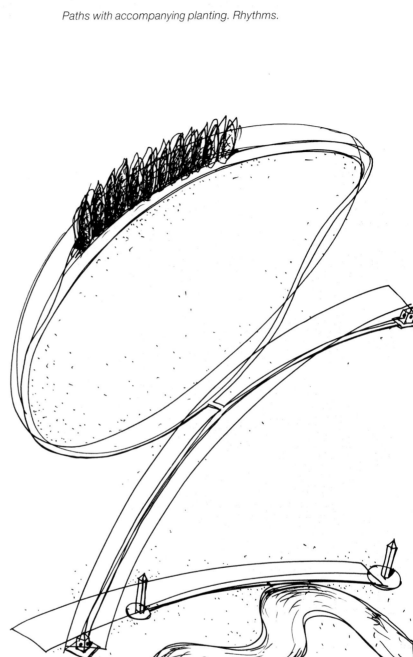

Alle Eingriffe sollen Spuren und Inseln bleiben im Gesamtkontinuum »Landschaft«.

All interventions should remain traces and islands in the total ›landscape‹ continuum.

Weg-Melodien. Fließen. Verengungen, Erweiterungen. Waldränder mit Anbauten. Einsame Türme. Sackgassen.

Path tunes. Flowing. Restrictions, extensions. Edges of woods with buildings. Isolated towers. Culs-de-sac.

333

Alle am Anfang beschriebenen Strukturen tauchen hier wieder auf: der Punkt, die Linie, das Feld, der Bogen, die Ordnung, das Zufalls-Chaos, die Geometrie, das künstliche Raster.

All the structures described at the beginning crop up again here: dots, lines, fields, arches, order, random chaos, geometry, artificial grids.

Organische Wegverläufe in Form von Blättern, Adern und Geweben: öffentliche Gärten als Wege in die Natur-Innenwelt.

Organic runs of paths in the form of leaves, veins and webs: public gardens as paths into the inner world of nature.

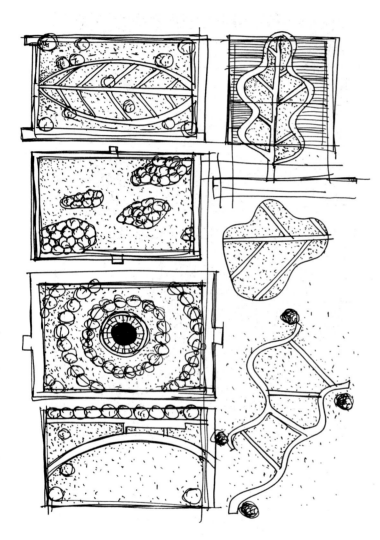

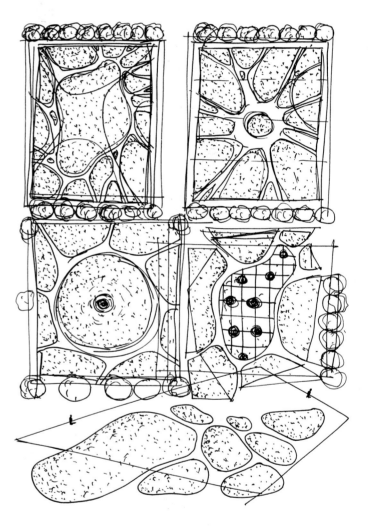

Wegstücke mit Hainen, Alleen und Wiesenkreis-segmenten.

Fragments of path with groves, avenues and circular lawn segments.

Weit geschwungener Weg durch die Landschaft mit Einzelstationen wie Punkten, Plätzen, kleinen Gartensplittern.

Path sweeping in curves through the landscape with individual stops like points, squares, small splinters of garden.

Grundrißkompositionen mit Wiesenstücken, Alleen, Baumkreisen, Wegen, Brücken, Schwimmbadfragmenten, Platzflächen, Brunnenbecken, Bibliotheksräumen, Museumspavillons, Zooeinbauten usw.

Ground plan compositions with sections of lawn, avenues, circles of trees, paths, bridges, swimming-pool fragments, squares, fountains with pools, library spaces, museum pavilions, zoo buildings etc.

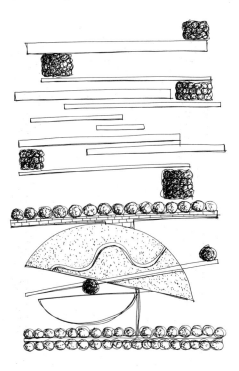

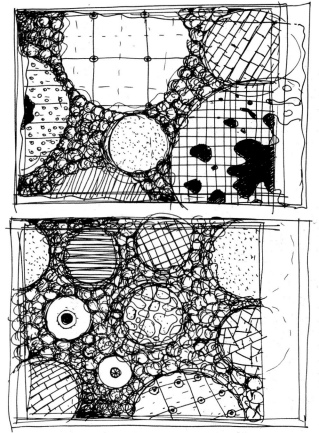

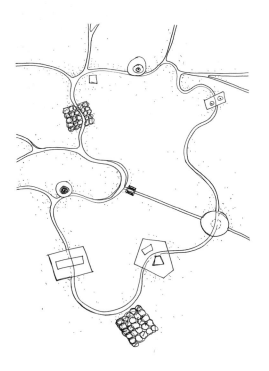

Positive und negative Formen: Kreisplätze und Kreisgärten in Wälder und Wiesen geschnitten. Lichtungen. Kreisflächen aus Erde und Gras, aus Steinplatten und Metallbahnen, aus Wasserfeldern und Denkmalsplantagen.

Positive and negative shapes: circular spaces and circular gardens cut into the woods and lawns. Clearings. Circular areas of earth and grass, stone slabs and metal tracks, areas of water and memorial plantations.
Between meditation and entertainment.

335

Das Umkreisen einer Mitte: Suche nach Anfang und Ursprung, nach Zellkern und Energiezentrum.

Circling around a centre: looking for a beginning and an origin, nucleus and centre of energy.

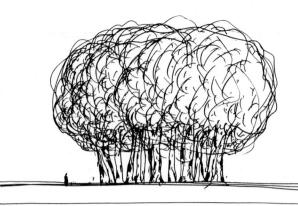

Zwischen Meditation und Unterhaltung.

Between meditation and entertainment.

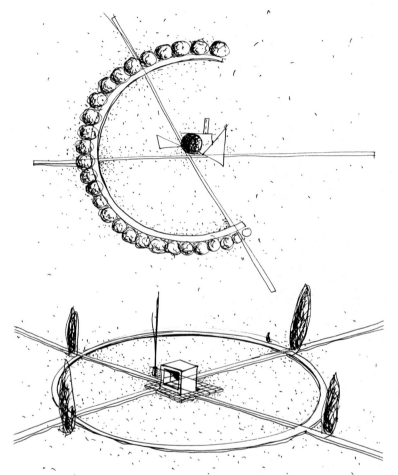

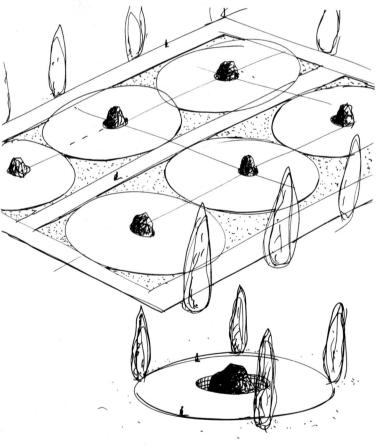

Verflechtungen. Inszenierungen. Collagen. Architektur und Landschaft ineinandergebaut. Vertauschungen der gewohnten Sachverhalte und Situationen: Landschaftsteile in der Stadt, Stadtteile in der Landschaft, Plätze auf Bergen, Brunnen in Lichtungen, Wohnungen in Höhlen, Sessel in der Brandung, Wolken im Keller, Gewölbe unter Schreibtischen, Sprungtürme in Wäldern, Büros in Wasserfällen, Terrassen in Baumkronen, Hochsitze auf Kreuzungen, Bibliotheken in Felsschluchten, Felsgärten auf Schiffen.

Interconnections. Stagings. Collages. Architecture and landscape built into each other. Transposition of the customary states of affairs and situations: areas of landscape in the city, areas of city in the landscape, squares on mountains, fountains in clearings, dwellings in caves, armchairs in the surf, clouds in the cellar, vaults under desks, diving platforms in woods, offices in waterfalls, terraces in the crowns of trees, raised hides at junctions, libraries in rocky gorges, rock gardens on ships.

Korridore durch Wälder. Rolltreppen in Felsen. Laufbänder durch Äcker. Balkone in Wasserfällen.

Corridors through woods. Escalators in rocks. Conveyor belts through ploughed fields. Balconies in waterfalls.

Die Wirklichkeit der Natur. Die Wirklichkeit der Stadt. Das Sichtbare und das Unsichtbare.

The reality of nature. The reality of the city. The visible and the invisible.

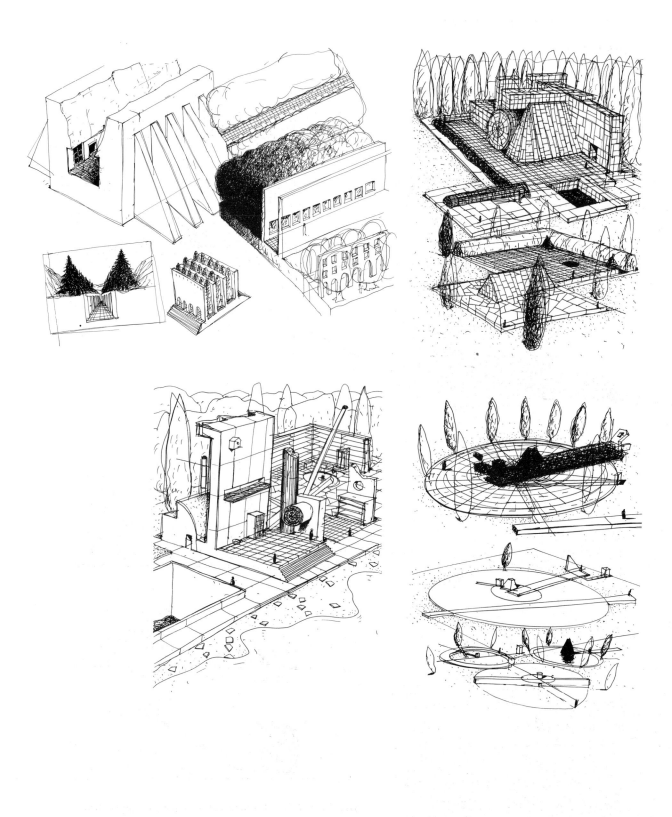

Geometrie des Alltags. Geometrie der Natur.
Geometrie der Zeit.

Geometry of the everyday. Geometry of nature.
Geometry of time.

Architektur-Garten. Garten-Architektur.

Architecture garden. Garden architecture.

Verflechtungen.

Interconnections.

Riesige Vogelhäuser. Aus den Löchern hört man
Urwald-Geräusche.

Giant bird houses. Jungle noises emerge from
the holes.

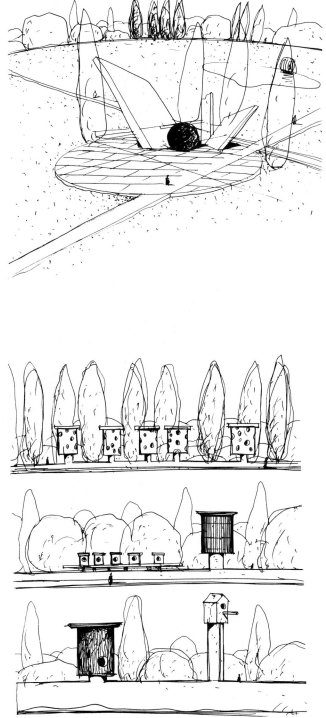

Fließbänder durch Wiesen und Wälder, vorbei an Ruinen, durch Laubengänge und Alleen. Fließbänder aus Metall oder aus Erde, aus Wasser oder aus Blumen.

Conveyor belts through meadows and woods, past ruins, through arbours and avenues. Conveyor belts made of metal or earth, water or flowers.

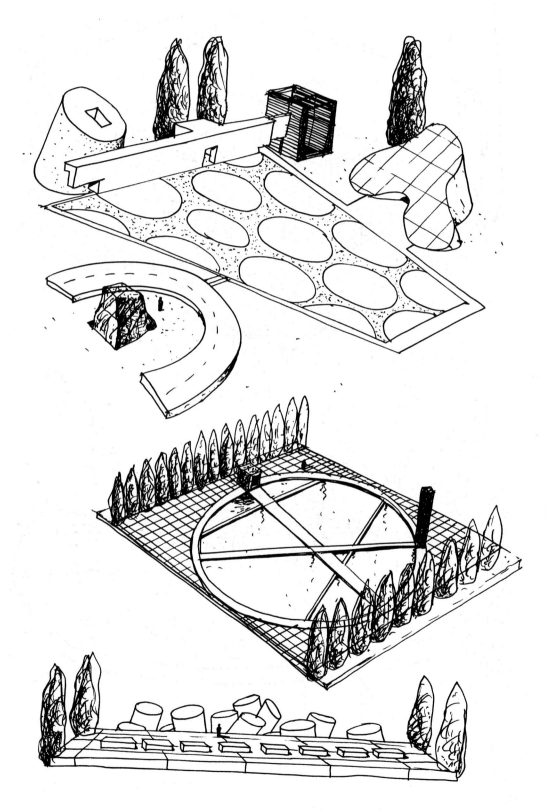

Rätselhafte Baustelle. Im Inneren ein Tonstudio, das alle Natur-Geräusche auffängt und verstärkt wiedergibt. Vogelsang an der Lärmgrenze, Blätterrauschen wie ein Sturm, Plätschern des Bachs wie ein Wasserfall.

Mysterious building site. Inside is a sound studio that records all the sounds of nature and plays them back amplified. Birdsong at the boundaries of sound, leaves rustling like a storm, a stream rippling like a waterfall.

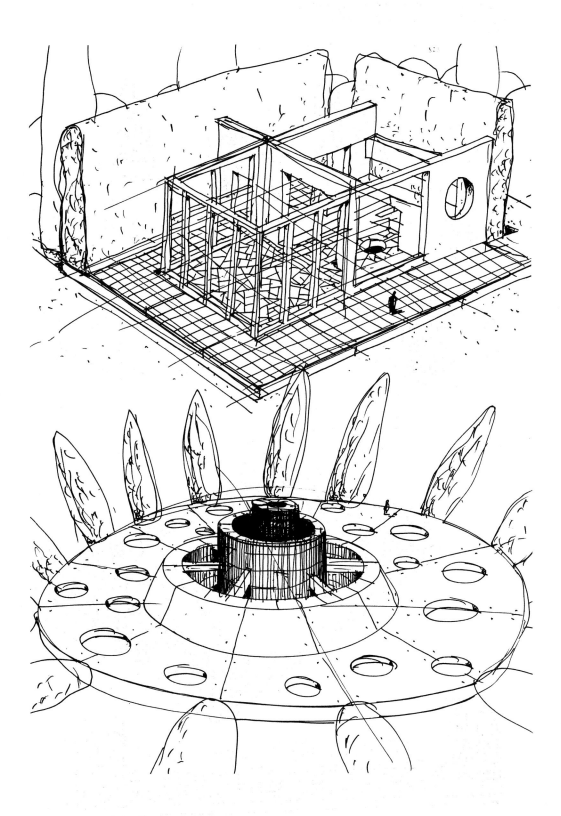

Plätze und Gärten gemischt.

Squares and gardens mixed.

Die Dorflinde, isoliert auf einem Platzfragment, das langsam durch die Landschaft fährt.

The village lime tree, isolated on a fragment of square travelling slowly through the landscape.

Elemente aus Film und Tourismus. Die schönen Stellen erinnern an Capri vielleicht und ein Schiffsdeck. Geräusche von Brandung. Wärme.

Elements from film and tourism. Beautiful places reminiscent of Capri perhaps, and the deck of a ship. Surf noises. Warmth.

Gartenprogramme: Einwachsen der Realität, Metamorphosen, Zerstörung der Romantik. Natürlich und künstlich, farbig und farblos, laut und leise, nüchtern und betrunken, schlafend und wach, offen und geschlossen, banal und übertrieben, sachlich und pathetisch.

Garten als Experimentalort.

Garden programmes. Ingrowing reality, metamorphoses, destruction of romanticism. Natural and artificial, colourful and colourless, loud and soft, sober and drunk, asleep and awake, open and closed, banal and exaggerated, down-to-earth and dramatic.

Garden as a place for experiment.

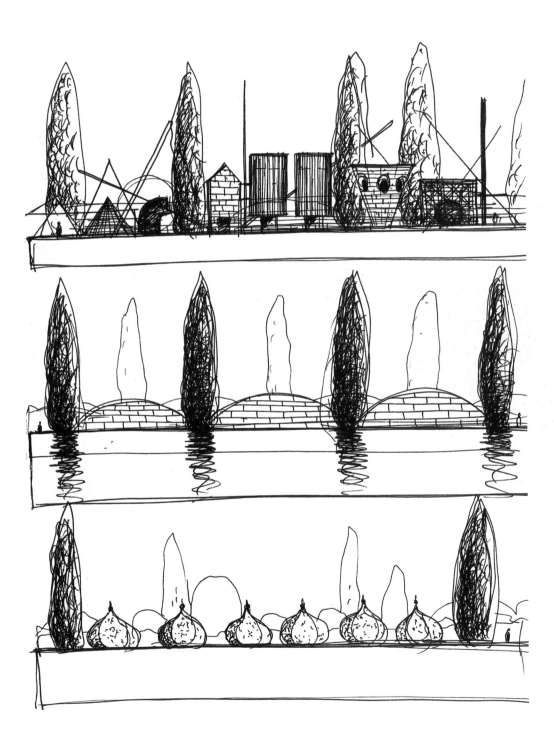

Garten-Architektur mit Wasserbecken: gefangene Wolken, gespiegelte Blätter und Vögel. Mauerstücke, Wege, Wiesen, Plätze, Tore und Bänke.

Garden architecture with pools: captured clouds, reflected leaves and birds. Sections of walls, paths, lawns, squares, gates, benches.

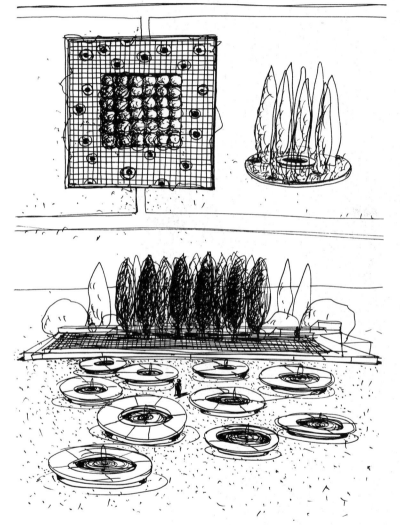

Kulissengarten, Brunnengarten, Wetterkartengarten, getarnter Garten, Landkartengarten, Blickgarten, psychologischer Garten. Pathologischer Garten. Garten unter Wasser, Garten des Fernwehs, Garten der Lüste, Garten der Jungbrunnen, Tourismusgarten, Garten der Fruchtbarkeit, Schrebergarten, Garten der Lüge, Garten der Wahrheit, Garten der Verdrängung, Garten der gefährlichen Idyllen.

Geheimgarten. Rätselgarten.

Stage-set garden, fountain garden, weather-map garden, disguised garden, map garden, view garden, psychological garden. Pathological garden. Garden under water, wanderlust garden, garden of pleasures, garden of the fountain of youth, touristic garden, garden of fertility, allotment garden, garden of lies, garden of the truth, garden of suppression, garden of dangerous idylls.

Secret garden. Mystery garden.

Möbel-Garten.
Garten mit leuchtenden Wald-Vitrinen.

Furniture garden.
Garden with glowing woodland showcases.

Holzstapelgarten, Treppengarten, Kinderspiel-garten, Lichtgarten, Nachtgarten, Betrunkener Garten, Negativgarten, Kostümgarten, Bücher-garten. Wegegarten. Bewegungsgarten. Tisch-tennisgarten. Bocciagarten. Kegelgarten. Feder-ballgarten. Fußballgarten. Schachgarten. Garten voller Gartenzwerge. Garten voller Postkarten und Photoalben.

Woodpile garden, stair garden, children's play garden, light garden, night garden, drunken gar-den, negative garden, costume garden, book garden. Path garden. Movement garden. Table tennis garden. Bowls garden. Skittle garden. Badminton garden. Football garden. Chess gar-den. Garden full of garden gnomes. Garden full of postcards and photograph albums.

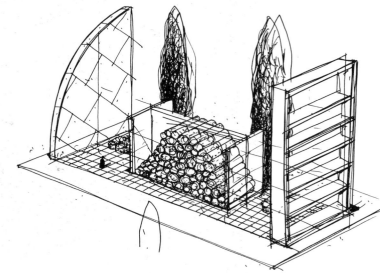

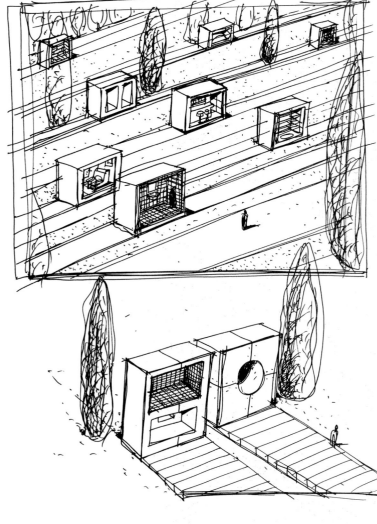

Archäologischer Garten.

Archaeological garden.

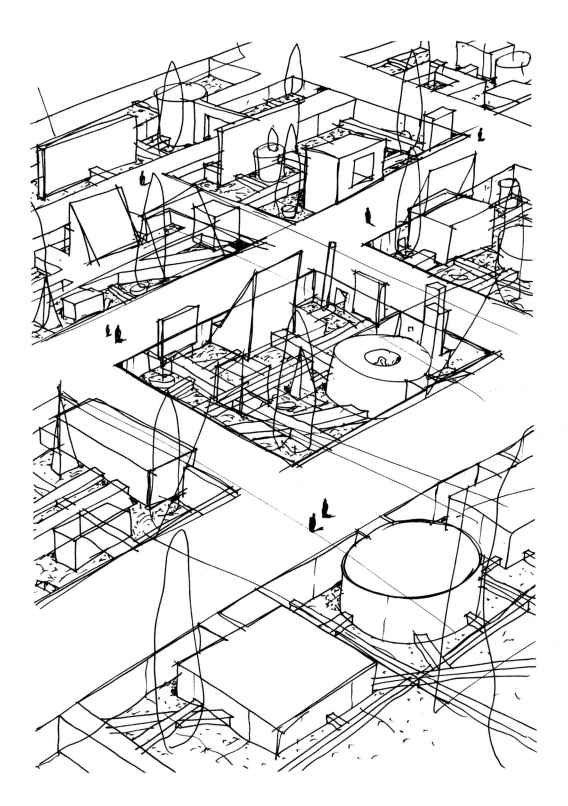

Garten-Labyrinthe.
Garten wie ein Körper, mit Kopf, Armen, Beinen,
Geschlecht, Lungen, Herz, Adern. Garten wie ein
Gehirn.

Garden labyrinths.
Garden like a body, with head, arms, legs, sexual
organs, lungs, heart, veins etc.
Garden like a brain.

Wurzelgarten unter der Erde, Grundwassergar-
ten, Richtung Erdmitte. Lavagarten, Aderngarten,
Innenwelten der Bäume und Büsche, der Blüten
und Stengel. Röntgen-Garten (Felsen, Stämme).
Unterirdischer Garten (neonbeleuchtete Seen,
gläserne Schiffe).

Underground garden, ground-water garden,
heading for the centre of the earth. Lava garden,
vein garden, inner worlds of trees and bushes,
blossoms and stems. X-ray garden (rocks,
trunks). Underground garden (neon-lit lakes,
glass ships).

Romantische Zitate wieder einmal. Ruinen und Wasserfälle beispielsweise.

Romantic quotations again: ruins and waterfalls for example.

Das Inselmotiv taucht wieder auf. Tellerartige Plätze, tellerartige Seestücke, tellerartige Parkstücke. Alle Entwürfe umkreisen das Paradies des Anfangs.

The island motif crops up again. Plate-like squares, plate-like areas of lake, plate-like sections of park. All designs encircle the paradise of the beginning.

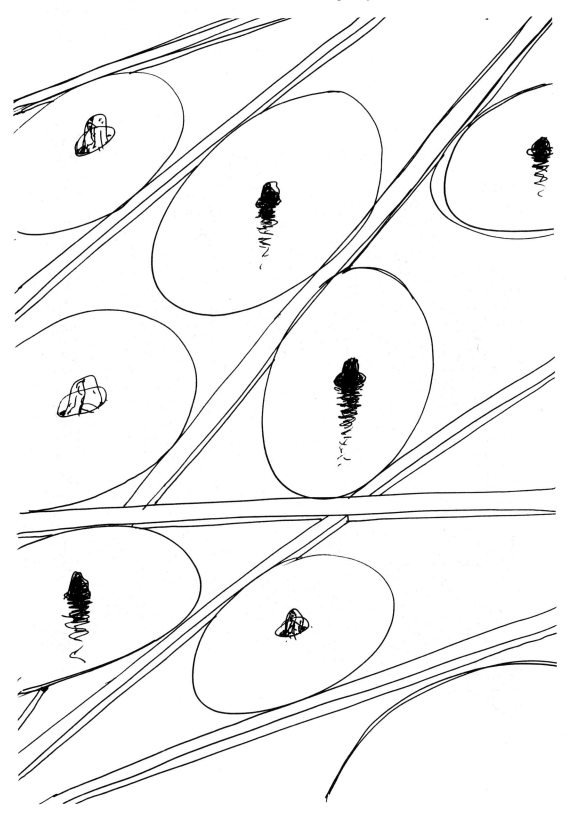

Der gebaute Riß. Die gepflanzte Tangente.
Fragmente von Handlungen.

The built crack. The planted tangent.
Fragments of actions.

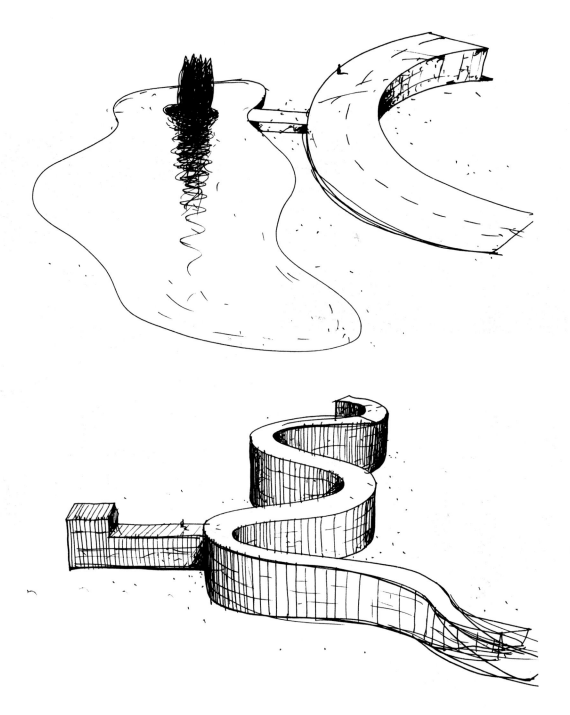

Erinnerungen ...

Memories ...

Garten mit Hafenmotiv.

Garden with harbour motif.

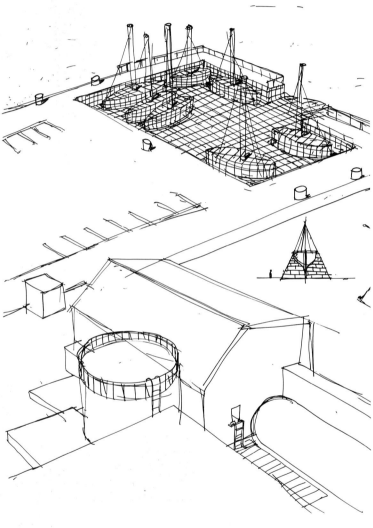

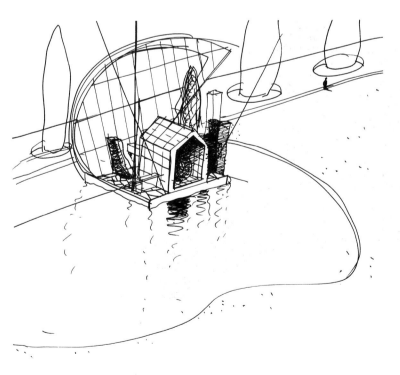

351

Wieder einmal Laubengänge. Container für blaue Blumen. Die Steine des Anfangs. Die ersten Sackgassen. Irrtumsfelder. Trümmer. Dazwischen Pappeln als Trost.

Arbours again. Containers for blue flowers. The stones of the beginning. The first culs-de-sac. Fields of error. Ruins. In between are poplars, for consolation.

Bilder der Unruhe, Bilder des Suchens und Fragens.

Images of unrest, images of seeking and asking.

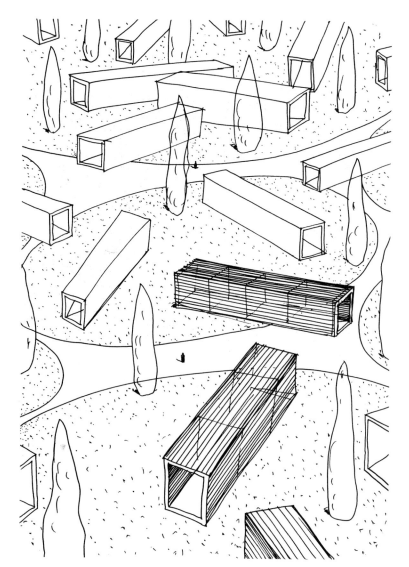

Garten-Plätze mit bedeutungsvollen Einbauten. Hinweise auf die Schwerkraft, auf kosmische Strahlung. Hinweise auf das Magnetfeld und auf die Erdkugel. Bilder der Zusammenballung. Bilder des Wirbelns.

Garden squares with meaningful structures. Indications of gravity, of cosmic rays. Indications of the magnetic field and the terrestrial globe. Images of agglomeration.
Images of vortex.

Gesamtkompositionen wie Musikstücke, wie Symphonien, wie Opern. Im Spannungsraum zwischen Steinzeit und science-fiction, zwischen Mittelalter und Zukunft. Natur-Choreographie. Baum-Ballett.

Overall compositions like pieces of music, like symphonies, like opera. In the field of tension between the Stone Age and Science Fiction, between the Middle Ages and the future. Nature choreography. Tree ballet.

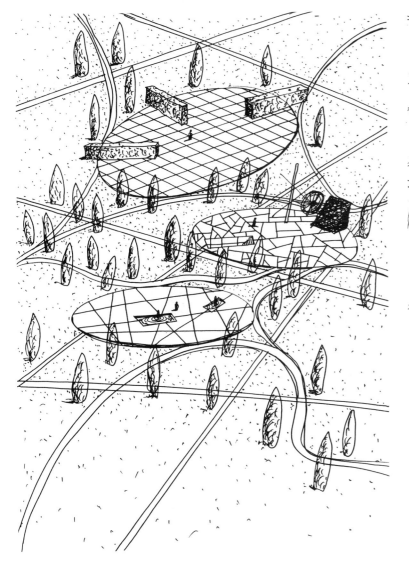

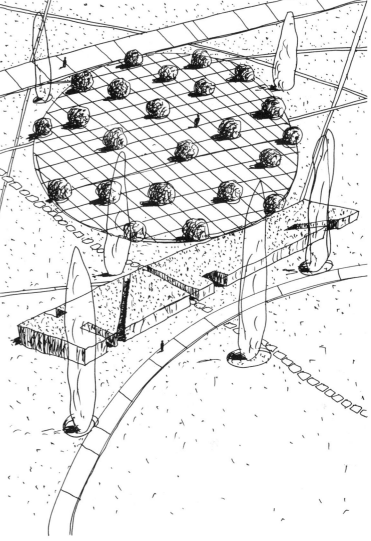

Bild der Verflechtung: eingebettet in die Natur-Landschaft, in ihr unberührtes Leben, ihr sanftes Verströmen, liegen die Splitter der neuen Gärten, Parks und Plätze wie Teile einer großen Bild-Komposition.

Image of interconnection: bedded into the nature-landscape, into its untouched life, its gentle flow are splinters of new gardens, parks and squares like parts of a great pictorial composition.

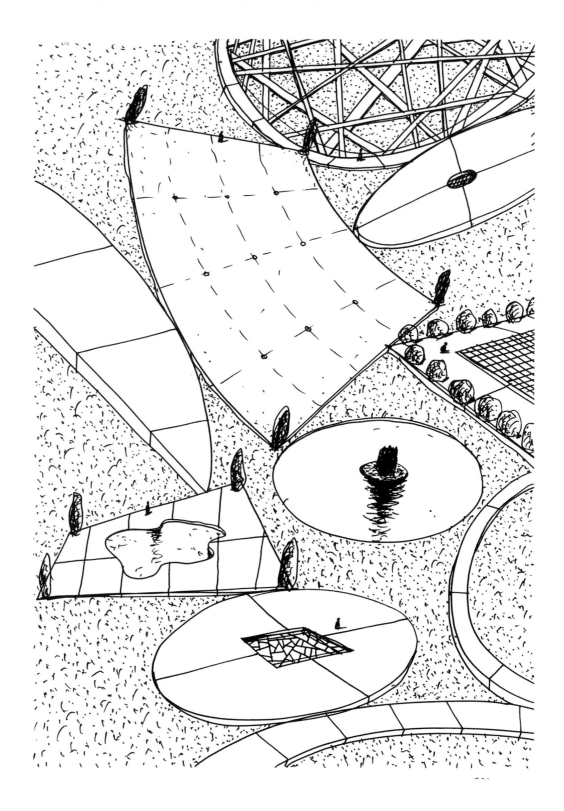

Neue Landschafts- und Gartenarchitektur
Konkrete Projekte: ausgeführte und geplante Beispiele

New landscape and garden architecture
Concrete projects: realized and planned examples

In den letzten Jahren wurden zahlreiche Garten-
und Platz-Projekte bis zum Modell-Stadium entwickelt. Hier eine kurze Fotodokumentation.

*In the past few years numerous garden and
square projects have been developed to the
model stage. A short photographic documenta-
tion follows.*

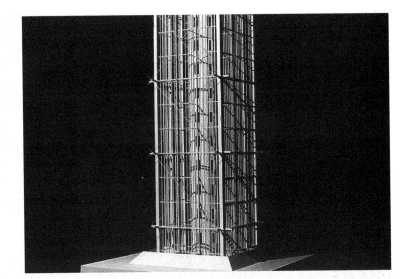

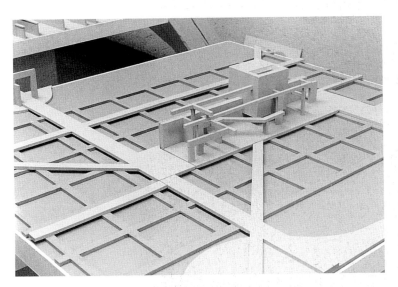

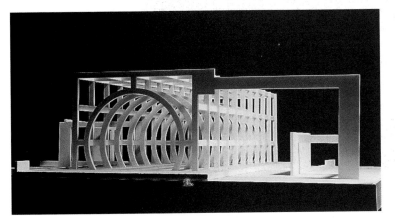

Realisierte Projekte:
reine Landschaftsarchitekturen mit Erdverfor-
mungen, mit Wegen und Pflanzungen konnten
bisher nicht verwirklicht werden. Dagegen gibt es
einige realisierte Projekte, die als Architektur in
die Landschaft und die Architektur verflochten
sind. Am Anfang steht ein hölzernes Laubenhaus
in Stuttgart aus dem Jahr 1979.

Realized projects
It has nor yet been possible to realizc pure lands-
cape architecture with earth distortions, with
paths and planting. But there are some realized
projects that are interwoven with landscape and
architecture, as architecture. At the beginning is
a wooden summer-house in Stuttgart dating from
1979.

Der Haupteingang zur Landesgartenschau in
Freiburg, gebaut 1986, ist ebenfalls aus Holz.

The main entrance to the Landesgartenschau in
Freiburg in 1986 was also built of wood.

Die Urnenanlage im Waldfriedhof von Singen am Hohentwiel (1983–86) steht als Beispiel für eine Architektur, die sich zur Landschaft und zur Natur öffnet. Der Besucher nähert sich der Anlage durch eine ehrwürdige Eichenallee, den steinernen Totenbezirk betritt er durch einen talartigen Mauerspalt. Die Urnenfächer sind in die Wände eingelassen.

The columbarium in the forest cemetery in Singen am Hohentwiel (1983–6) is an example of a kind of architecture that opens up to the landscape and to nature. The visitor approaches the cemetery through an avenue of venerable oaks and enters the stone precinet of the dead through a vallcy-like wall fissure. The compartments for the ums are let into the walls.

Friedhof in Singen: Blick vom höhergelegenen
Brunnenbecken in die Mittelachse der Anlage.

*Cemerety in Singen: view from the higher foun-
tain basin in to the centrel axis of the grounds.*

Auf dem verwilderten Gelände einer im Krieg zer-
störten Gründerzeitvilla konnte zur Internationalen Gartenbauausstellung in Stuttgart 1993 eine
Architektur realisiert werden, die als Beispiel für
die Verflechtung von Natur und Architektur steht.
Die Ruinenreste und die Vegetation wurden kaum
berührt und in ihrem verwunschenen Zustand
belassen. Darüber »schwebt« die Architektur aus
Tor, Terrasse, Treppe, Steg, Belvedere und Bal-
kon. Es entsteht ein Weg durch Verfall und Verwesung, durch das Innere der Zeit, der Natur und
der Romantik.

At the Internationale Gartenbauausstellung in
Stuttgart in 1993 it was possible to realize, on the
overgrown site of a late 19th century villa that had
been destroyed in the war, a piece of architecture
that stands as an example of interwoven nature
an architecture.
The ruined fragments and the vegetation were
scarcely touched and left in their enchanted con-
dition. Above this 'hovers' an architecture of
gate, terrace, stairs, bridge, belvedere and bal-
cony. A path is created through decay and
decomposition, through the inside of time, nature
and romanticism.

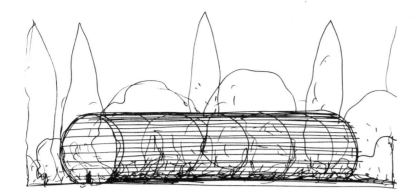

Das Eingangstor im Bereich des ehemaligen Villenhaupteingangs. Eine Sackgasse vor einer wild wucherenden Blätterwand. Vögel sind die neuen Bewohner des Geländes.

The gate near the former main entrance to the villa. A cul-de-sac that ends today in front of a wildly proliferating wall of leaves. Birds are the new occupants of the grounds.

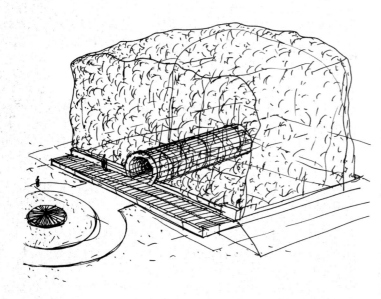

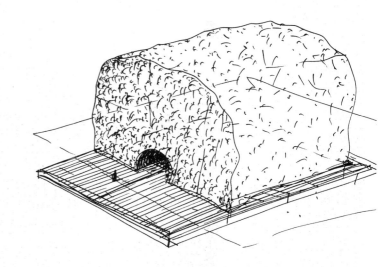

Die Anlage »Villa Moser-Leibfried« in Stuttgart:
Blicke auf das Treppenhaus, die Stege und das
Belvedere.

*The grounds of the 'Villa Moser-Leibfried' in
Stuttgart: view of the staircase, bridges and the
belvedere.*

Ebenfalls zur Internationalen Gartenbauausstellung 1993 in Stuttgart konnte dieser Platz verwirklicht werden. Er steht als Beispiel für den Themenbereich »Künstlich-natürlich«.
Ein regelmäßig gebauter Wald aus weißen Betonstützen mit darübergelegter Stahl-Pergola lädt die Besucher ein, über das Gewachsene und das Gebaute, über Natur und Kunst, über Raum und Zeit zu reflektieren. Ein transparentes Raumgitter, ein Lichtrechen, eine Schattenuhr.

*This square was also realized for the Internationale Gartenbauausstellung in Stuttgart in 1993. It is an example of the 'artificial-natural' theme.
A regularly structured forest of white concrete posts with a steel pergola above them invites the visitor to reflect about what is grown and what has been built, about nature and art, about space and time. A transparent spatial grid, a light grid, a shadow clock.*

Blick auf eine Ecke des Stangenwald-Platzes in Stuttgart.

View of a corner of the post-forest square in Stuttgart.

Große landschaftsarchitektonische Gesamtkompositionen wurden in den vergangenen zwanzig Jahren im Rahmen zahlreicher Wettbewerbe erarbeitet. Der abgebildete Entwurf aus dem Jahr 1977 für die Bundesgartenschau in Berlin 1985 wurde als erster Preis eine Zeitlang ernsthaft diskutiert, schließlich aber nicht realisiert.

Large landscape-architectural general compositions were developed and proposed for numerous competitions. The illustrated design dates from 1977, and was submitted for the Bundesgartenschau in Berlin in 1985. It won first prize and was seriously considered for a while, but finally not realized.

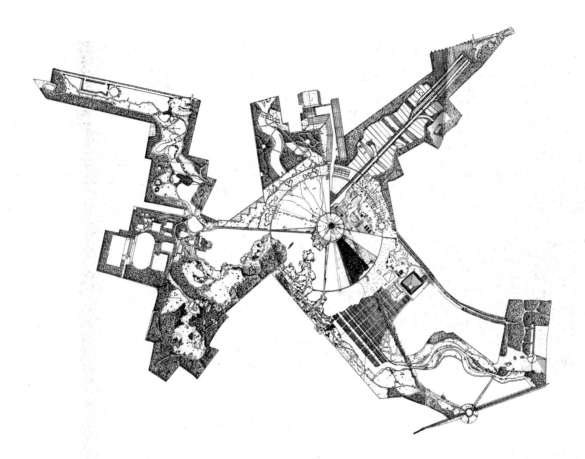

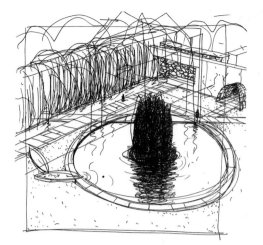

Für die Stadt Biberach an der Riß entseht zur Zeit ein neuer Bürgerpark nach den Planungen des Autors. In der Mitte der Anlage liegt ein runder See mit der bekannten Pappelinsel. Zwischen den Pappeln befindet sich eine Nachbildung des Mondes (3 Meter Durchmesser), als Zellkern der neuen und alten Romantik.

The town of Biberach an der Riss is at present acquiring a new municipal park designed by the author. In the middle of this park is a circular lake with the familiar island with poplars. Between the poplars is a replica of the moon (3 m in diameter), as a cell nucleus of the new and the old romanticism.

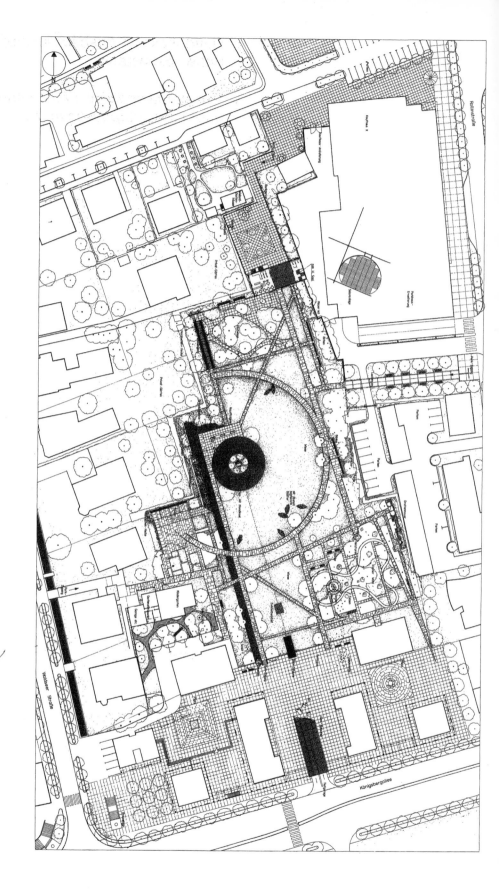

Rundblick und Ausblick im utopischen
Schwebezustand

*Panorama and view of the future in a
codition of utopian hovering*

Das Fenster hat seine Unschuld verloren. Wer innen sitzt, ist nicht mehr in Sicherheit. Die Strahlen und Wellen dringen durch jede Wand, durch jedes Fensterglas. Draußen wölbt sich der Horizont und kreisen die Gestirne mit unermüdlicher Gleichmäßigkeit durch die schwarze Unendlichkeit des Alls.

The window has lost its innocence. Anyone sitting inside is no longer safe. Rays and waves penetrate every wall, every window pane. Outside the horizon arches and the stars circle with tireless regularity through the black infinity of the universe.

Die Wurzeln streben dem Erdmittelpunkt zu und die Blüten der Sonne, wie zu allen Zeiten. Gärten, Parks und Plätze werden geplant und gebaut. Die Perspektiven zielen durch Alleen dem Himmel entgegen. Die letzten Steingötter stützen Tempelruinen und halb zerbrochene Dächer. Kopfunter, stürzend durchs Weltall, im Strömen der Zeit. Gehen, bleiben, gehen, bleiben ...

Roots strive towards the centre of the earth, and flowers towards the sun, as at all times. Gardens, parks and squares are planned and built. Perspectives aim at the sky through avenues. The last stone gods support temple ruins and half broken roofs.
Head down, falling through outer space, in the rivers of time. Going, staying, going, staying ...

Wer Gärten anlegt und Architekturen baut, glaubt
an die Schwerkraft, an das Leben und an das
Fortbestehen der Zeit. Was aber, wenn der Wirbel im Kopf zunimmt, wenn die Zentrifugalkraft
die Oberhand gewinnt, wenn die Flugzeuge nicht
mehr zurückkehren und die Steine und Bäume
den Boden verlassen?

*Anyone who lays out gardens and builds archi-
tecture believes in gravity, in life and in the per-
sistence of time. But what if the swirling in our
heads increases, if centrifugal force gets the
upper hand, if aeroplanes do not come home any
more and stones and trees leave the earth?*

»Geometrie, jenseits der Geometrien,
Linien, verlangsamten Strahlungen gleich:
beharrlich, voll Klarsicht
geheimnisbeladen –
Zeichnung zur Rückkehr in Unbedingtes.
Schicksals-Entwurf«
(Henri Michaux)

*»Geometry, beyond geometries,
lines, like slowed-down radiations:
laden with mystery –
drawing to return into the unconditional.
Fate-design«
(Henri Michaux)*

Weltraum-Gärten? Gärten auf anderen Planeten,
auf Meteoren?
Gärten auf dem Mond?

*Space gardens? Gardens on other planets, on
meteors?*
Gardens on the moon?
*And again the view of the horizon's vault, of the
calming flight of the clouds.*

375

Die Überlegungen, Texte, Fotos, Zeichnungen, Skizzen, Planungen und Fotocollagen entstanden zwischen 1975 und 1993. Die Skizzen-Originale sind meistens auf DIN A4 Blätter gezeichnet. Nur die Fotos auf den Seiten 346, 347, 351, 352, 353, 354, 355, 356, 357 und 358 stammen nicht vom Autor, sondern von dem Architekturfotografen Peter Horn aus Stuttgart.

Hans Dieter Schaal

1943 in Ulm/Donau geboren
Architekturstudium in Hannover und Stuttgart. 1970 Diplom, seitdem arbeitet Schaal als freier Künstler, Architekt, Ausstellungsgestalter, Bühnenbildner und Landschaftsarchitekt in Attenweiler bei Ulm.
Buchveröffentlichungen:
Wege und Wegräume (1. Auflage, weitere Auflagen, Berlin 1985 und 1993), Architektonische Situationen (1. Auflage 1980, 2. Auflage Berlin 1986), Denkgebäude (Wiesbaden, 1983). Architekturen, 1970–90, Stuttgart 1990).

The observations, texts, photographs, drawings, sketches, plans and photographic collages stem from the period between 1975 and 1993. The originals of the sketches were mostly drawn on DIN-A-4 sheets.
Only the photographs shown on pages 346, 347, 351, 352, 353, 354, 355, 356, 357 and 358 are not from the author, but rather from the architectural photographer Peter Horn (Stuttgart).

Hans Dieter Schaal

Born 1943 in Ulm an der Donau, studien architecture in Hamburg and Stuttgart, diploma 1970. Since then he has worked as a frec-lance artist, as an architect, exhibition designer, stage designer and landscape architect, lives in Attenweiler near Ulm.
Published books:
Wege und Wegräume (first published 1978, reprinted Berlin 1985 and 1993), Architektonische Situationen (first published 1980, reprinted Berlin 1986), Denkgebäude (Wiesbaden 1983), Architekturen, 1970–90 (Stuttgart 1990).

Literatur/Literature:

Ilse Aichinger, Kleist, Moos, Fasane, Fischer Taschenbuch, S. Fischer Verlag, Frankfurt a. M. 1991.

Ilse Aichinger, Schlechte Wörter, Fischer Taschenbuch, S. Fischer Verlag, Frankfurt a. M. 1991.

Louis Aragon, Pariser Landleben, Rogner & Bernhard from Zweitausendeins, München and Frankfurt 1969.

Norbert Bolz, Die Welt als Chaos und Simulation, Wilhelm Fink Verlag, München 1992.

Norbert Bolz, Theorie der neuen Medien, Raben Verlag von Wittern KG, München 1990.

Jorge Luis Borges, Die letzte Reise des Odysseus, Fischer Taschenbuch Verlag, Frankfurt a. M. 1992.

Roger Caillois, Steine, Edition Akzente, Carl Hanser Verlag, München 1983.

Carl Gustav Carus, Briefe und Aufsätze über Landschaftsmalerei, Gustav Keipenhauer Bücherei, Leipzig/Weimar 1982.

E. M. Cioran, Gevierteilt, Suhrkamp Verlag, Frankfurt a. M. 1991.

Martin Dean, Die verborgenen Gärten, Carl Hanser Verlag, München, Wien 1982.

Renato Dulbecco in Lust am Denken, edited by Heidi Bonet and Klaus Piper, Piper Verlag, München 1992.

Gustave Flaubert, Bouvard und Pècuchet, Karl Rauch Verlag, Düsseldorf 1957.

Vilèm Flusser, Ins Universum der technischen Bilder, European Photography, Göttingen 1985.

Ronald Fraser, Die Erde, Suhrkamp Wissen, Suhrkamp Verlag, Frankfurt a. M. 1969.

Ludwig Ganghofer, Bergheimat, Droemer-Knaur Verlagsanstalt, München/Zürich 1976.

Peter Handke, Die Geschichte des Bleistifts, Residenz-Verlag, Salzburg 1982.

Edmond Jabès, Das Buch der Fragen, Suhrkamp Verlag, Frankfurt a. M. 1989.

Geoffrey and Susan Jellicoe, Die Geschichte der Landschaft, Campus Verlag, Frankfurt/New York 1988.

Franz Kafka, Tagebücher 1910–1923, Moderner Buchclub, Darmstadt 1962.

Kevin W. Kelly, Der Heimat-Planet, Zweitausendeins, Frankfurt a. M. 1989.

Henri Michaux, Momente, Edition Akzente, Carl Hanser Verlag, München 1983

Jules Michelet, Das Meer, Edition Qumran, Campus Verlag, Frankfurt/New York 1987.

Novalis, Das dichterische Werk, Carl Hanser Verlag, München/Wien 1978
Peter Omm, Nützliches Lesebuch für Gartenfreunde, Wilhelm Heyne Verlag, München 1984.

Cesare Pavese, Das Handwerk des Lebens. Tagebuch 1935–1950, Suhrkamp Verlag, Frankfurt a. M. 1974.

Fernando Pessoa, Algebra der Geheimnisse, Ammann Verlag, Zürich 1986.

Fernando Pessoa, Das Buch der Unruhe, Ammann Verlag, Zürich 1985.

Sylvia Plath, Die Bibel der Träume, Fischer Taschenbuch Verlag, Frankfurt a. M. 1990.

Francis Ponge, Einführing in den Kieselstein, S. Fischer Verlag, Frankfurt a. M. 1986.

Francis Ponge, Das Notizbuch vom Kiefernwald, Bibliothek Suhrkamp, Suhrkamp Verlag , Frankfurt a. M. 1982.

Hermann Fürst von Pückler-Muskau, Andeutungen über Landschaftsgärtnerei, Deutsche Verlags-Anstalt, Stuttgart 1977.

Jules Renard, Ideen, in Tinte getaucht, Tagebuch-Aufzeichnungen, dtv-Klassik, Deutscher Taschenbuch Verlag, München 1990.

Herbert Reeves, Schmetterlinge und Galaxien, kosmologische Streifzüge, Carl Hanser Verlag, München/Wien 1992.

Joachim Ritter, Subjektivität, Bibliothek Suhrkamp, Suhrkamp Verlag, Frankfurt a. M. 1989.

Heinrich Rombach, Leben des Geistes, Verlag Herder, Freiburg im Breisgau 1977.

Raymond Roussel, Locus Solus, Suhrkamp Verlag, Frankfurt a. M. 1977.

Schlipf, Praktisches Handbuch der Landwirtschaft, revised by Martin Zimmermann, Verlagsbuchhandlung Paul Parey, Hamburg/Berlin 1969.

Georg Simmel, Philosophische Kultur, Verlag Klaus Wagenbach, Berlin 1983.

Paul Virilio, Rasender Stillstand, Edition Akzente, Carl Hanser Verlag, München/Wien 1992.

712 SCH

12

6